# THE MYTH OF THE FRENCH BOURGEOISIE

# THE MYTH
## OF THE
# FRENCH
# BOURGEOISIE

An Essay on the Social Imaginary
1750–1850

SARAH MAZA

HARVARD UNIVERSITY PRESS
Cambridge, Massachusetts, and London, England
2003

*Library of Congress Cataloging-in-Publication Data*

Maza, Sarah C., 1953–
The myth of the French bourgeoisie : an essay on the
social imaginary, 1750–1850 / Sarah Maza.
p. cm.
Includes bibliographical references and index.
ISBN 0-674-01046-9 (alk. paper)
1. Middle class—France—History—18th century.
2. Middle class—France—History—19th century.
I. Title.

HT690.F8 M39 2003
305.5′5′0944—dc21        2002031809

For Sean Shesgreen and Deirdre Shesgreen,
francophiles and great writers

# CONTENTS

# ACKNOWLEDGMENTS

Writing this book was made possible by abundant institutional, intellectual, and personal support at every stage. I began reading and thinking about the bourgeoisie while a fellow at the Woodrow Wilson Center in Washington, D.C., and I am grateful to the Center's director, the late Charles Blitzer, his staff, and the other fellows for making that year so productive. I continued to work on the book thanks to fellowships from the John Simon Guggenheim Foundation and Northwestern University's Alice Berline Kaplan Center for the Humanities. I thank the Kaplan Center's director, Helmut Muller-Sievers, and associate director, Elzbieta Foeller-Pituch, for seeing me through the home stretch. I am indebted to the staffs of the Library of Congress, Regenstein Library, and Northwestern University Library, and very grateful for the expert assistance I got from three skilled research assistants, Molly Laird, Sean Field, and William Slauter. Joyce Seltzer of Harvard University Press took an interest in this project from the beginning, and I thank her for her confidence and astute advice throughout the process. Anita Safran edited the manuscript with great care and consummate skill.

Because this book's subject is so broad-ranging, and because I was fortunate to present my ideas to many groups, I received countless suggestions, ranging from comments by long-time friends and colleagues in my field to those by unknown audience members at talks. Since my thesis is counterintuitive and somewhat controversial, reactions to my presentations ran the gamut from enthusiastic agreement to complete disbelief. In all cases I benefited from these responses, which forced me to recast some arguments, clarify others, and think through the overall purpose of the work. I am accordingly grateful to those who heard me out and challenged me at the Woodrow Wilson Center, the University of Virginia, the University of Pennsylvania, Cornell University, Boston University, Purdue University, Northern Illinois University, the University of Warwick, Notre Dame University, the Massachusetts Institute of Technology, Harvard University, the University of Michigan, the University of Chicago, Yale University, Vassar College, and Northwestern University on three occasions. Especially helpful were the presentations I made to French history groups in the New York City, Washington D.C., and North Carolina Triangle areas.

Some of the arguments and evidence in this book have appeared in Richard Rand, ed., *Intimate Encounters: Love and Domesticity in Eighteenth Century France* (Princeton University Press, 1997), Colin Jones and Dror Wahrman, eds., *The Age of Cultural Revolutions: Britain and France, 1750–1820* (University of California Press, 2002), and in the journals *French Politics, Culture and Society* and *Journal of Modern History* (© 1997 by the University of Chicago. All rights reserved). I am grateful to the publishers of these books and journals for permission to re-use this material.

I cannot begin to name here all those who have helped and influenced me intellectually, but I do want to salute again my first mentor in the field, Michel Vovelle, who was thinking and writing so creatively about the bourgeoisie several decades ago. He will no doubt disagree with this book, but I hope it will at least amuse him. On a more personal level I am indebted to the women in my book group for being an anchor in my world as well as a source of unending gossip and debate. My extended family—Monica, Jonathan, Brigitte, Suzy, Sam, Deirdre and Jim—graciously assumed I was engaged in something worthwhile despite my repeated failures to explain the project coherently. Most of all, I am grateful to Juliette Maza Shesgreen for making the present and future more interesting than the past, and to Sean Shesgreen for his help with all aspects of this venture and for being the sanest person I know.

# THE MYTH OF THE FRENCH BOURGEOISIE

# Is There a Class in This Text?

This book is about what the social order looked like to the French between 1750 and 1850, and in particular about the vexed question of the French bourgeoisie. I was driven to write it because of frustration with several aspects of this question as I perceived them a few years ago. The first problem was that none of the general histories of "the bourgeoisie" in this period of French history made much sense to me. While there were, and continue to appear every year, excellent social histories of local elites, whenever a historian set out to write a synthetic history of the French bourgeoisie, the result looked like a laundry list. The bourgeois was defined, in these studies, as what he or she was not (neither a noble nor a person who did manual labor), and the result was an inevitable lumping together of everyone from the richest banker through intellectuals and professionals to the struggling neighborhood grocer.[1]

The project in these books became inevitably one of sorting all these disparate people into different categories, a task carried out with special enthusiasm in France, where classification has long been a national predilection. Adeline Daumard, the most distinguished historian of the nineteenth-century French bourgeoisie, lined up her people into "Financial Aristocracy," "High Bourgeoisie," "Good Bourgeoisie," "Middle Bourgeoisie," and "Popular Bourgeoisie." She went on to explain, slicing into her own categories, that if you were looking for "the middle class" you would find it in the lower end of category three (Good), all of category four (Middle), and the top of category five

(Popular).[2] Given the diversity of all these people, it inevitably became difficult to say much about the bourgeoisie except for general statements: that, for instance, the richest groups were getting richer, or that gaps between groups were getting larger, or that the lower end was sinking lower. What use could a historian make of such generalities?

Paradoxically, the sociological fuzziness of the bourgeoisie has been accompanied by an extraordinary specificity in assumptions about its culture and mentality, my second source of frustration. The word "bourgeois" as a noun, but even more as an adjective, has a remarkable magnet-like ability to attract clichés: the usually unstated assumption is that we all understand that bourgeois means individualistic, profit-oriented, competitive, conventional, moralistic, domestic, patriarchal, repressed—the list could go on a lot longer. Many historians, as well as scholars in other disciplines, use the word "bourgeois" in a cavalier, you-know-what-I-mean way, in such phrases as "bourgeois norms," "bourgeois mentality," "bourgeois culture," or the obscure but ever-popular "bourgeois sexuality."[3] Worse still, a hint of smug condescension often creeps into such usages: you and I know what the bourgeois are because we are not like *them*.

Finally, I was perplexed by an aspect of French culture which, though frequently noted, had never been adequately explained. Anyone who studies French culture or has lived in France for a significant amount of time knows that while it is widely assumed that France's dominant class is the bourgeoisie, nobody admits to being bourgeois. Even French people who explicitly embrace conservatism, espouse religious or moral norms, or celebrate family and property values never say "I am bourgeois" except in the most facetious, self-mocking manner.

The expression "middle class" does not come easily to the French either, less because of negative connotations than because it sounds strained and technical—*la classe moyenne* is not a natural idiom in the French language, and the adjective "middle-class" simply does not exist.

The French resistance to bourgeois identity contrasts sharply with the popularity of middle-class identity in the Anglo-American world, especially in the United States, where this status is claimed by just about everyone outside of criminals and the wretchedly poor.[4] The absence of claims to bourgeois identity represents a central feature of

French culture, yet it is usually explained, even by the French themselves, through recourse to glib psychocultural commentary—that everyone in France is bourgeois and nobody admits it, that the French
wear "their heart on the left and their wallet on the right," or that the
bourgeois are insecure self-haters who, by definition, will never acknowledge their own nature. I embarked on this project to demonstrate that the elision of bourgeois identity in French history was not
the reflection of widespread hypocrisy or self-hatred, but was driven by
a profound and specific historical and cultural logic. The French rejection of what the term "bourgeois" connotes is not a trivial quirk, but a
central element in the construction of a national cultural identity.

A few decades ago, the question of the bourgeoisie was a lot less
problematic than it has now become. Until the 1970s, most people still
believed in some version of a Marxian narrative whereby the bourgeoisie had been rising to prominence in the eighteenth century, seized
political power in 1789, and ruled supreme for most of the nineteenth
century, all because of the unstoppable tide of capitalist development.
(Even historians politically hostile to the left generally accepted some
version of this narrative.) For over three decades now, however, social
and economic thinkers have punched large holes in this tidy script.
The basic problem amounts to this: capitalism, inasmuch as it did
exist, was in this period marginal to the French economy, which remained dominated by agriculture and small-scale manufacturing
until, at the very earliest, the 1850s.[5] Well over thirty years ago, the
iconoclastic British historian Alfred Cobban had already pointed out
that landed proprietors were clearly the dominant group in French society and politics up to 1850, and that to call society in this period predominantly bourgeois or middle-class was disastrously misleading.[6]

But a majority of historians of France, even as they accept that the
rise-of-the-capitalist-bourgeoisie scenario is not applicable before
the later nineteenth century, cling doggedly to the word "bourgeois."
They do so in part because this term was historically applied to certain
groups (usually not capitalists) by the French themselves in the eighteenth and nineteenth centuries. But mostly they do so because they
are reluctant to let go of the security blanket of Marxian terminology;
because even if they accept that the bourgeoisie had little to do with
capitalism in this period, they reflexively assume that questioning the
existence of some form of bourgeoisie would amount to denying the

reality and importance of things like inequality, penury, power, or exploitation. Once you uncouple the bourgeoisie from the rise of capitalism, however, there is no real reason to use the word at all, except as a shorthand for middle and upper-middle class. To state that the elite of postrevolutionary France was the bourgeoisie means very little beyond saying that they were not noble, and it is problematic because of the assumptions and associations that the term always drags along in its wake. The question of the bourgeoisie is a puzzle badly in need of a solution. The elements of the puzzle are the near-total absence of industrial capitalism in France before 1850; the overabundance of meanings of the term "bourgeois" both for the French historically and for us today; the resistance of French people both in the past and today to calling themselves bourgeois; and the attachment of contemporary scholars to a term that is imprecise and unhelpful.

The problem is compounded by a subsidiary matter, that of the relationship between the overlapping, although far from identical, concepts of bourgeoisie and middle class. The term "bourgeoisie" in both its French and its English usages usually refers to a social elite. In France, the word's meaning evolved in the period covered here from referring to a civic elite to designating a capitalist ruling class, while it retained throughout connotations of debased, second-rate aristocracy. While the word *bourgeois* goes back to the early Middle Ages, *classe moyenne* was only used systematically starting in the 1820s, and derives its meaning from social science rather than history. "Middle class" is an expression which can designate an upper rather than a truly middling class, as it long did in Britain and still does in some developing nations, but its social range is usually greater than that of "bourgeoisie." The appearance of the term "middle class" in Western culture is linked to views of society as an abstract and quantifiable entity (rather than something which could be concretely figured as a body or a ladder). I argue in this book that the French embraced neither term as a social ideal, for roughly the same reasons: a strong resistance to singling out any group within an ideally homogeneous nation, and a rejection of material factors—whether based on commerce or on quantification—as a basis for social distinction. The emphasis here, however, is on bourgeoisie rather than middle class, because in France the former term was far more frequently used, and much more laden with historical and cultural significance.

I started this project by reading as broadly as possible in primary sources for the whole period 1750–1850 that described society and identified groups and social problems. The result was striking. Before the Revolution of 1789, there was a huge amount of commentary, much of it deploring social and economic change, but none of it identified a bourgeoisie or middle class as either the source of the problem or its solution; in the years after 1789, none of the people involved in the supposedly "bourgeois revolution" claimed to be acting on behalf of a middle class or bourgeoisie. Only after 1815 was a category called "the bourgeoisie" identified as prominent in society, but almost invariably in negative terms: it was mostly described with hostility or contempt, and after 1830 was often assumed to be in decline. There were only two exceptions to this general pattern of absence (before 1815) and aversion (after 1815): the existence of a limited and precisely defined legal category of *bourgeois* before 1789; and the attempt by a group of prominent liberal politicians during the Bourbon Restoration of 1815–1830 to make a bourgeois class central to the history and politics of France.

The central thesis of this book is that the French bourgeoisie did not exist. Initially, no such group was identified by contemporaries, and when it eventually appeared in description and commentary, it did so as a myth which served (and possibly still does) to define negatively France's deepest social, cultural, and political ideals. By saying that the bourgeoisie did not exist, I am not disputing that throughout this period hundreds of thousands of French men and women led prosperous and respectable lives in the middle ground of society between rich and poor. I am not denying either that people often used the word *bourgeois* in the eighteenth and nineteenth centuries in its multiple and often contradictory quotidian meanings: a town resident, a person with some money, a worker's boss, or someone lacking in taste and social flair. What the statement means to convey is that, with the exceptions noted above, no group calling itself bourgeois ever emerged in France to make claims to cultural or political centrality and power: bourgeois was almost invariably what *someone else* was.

To argue that the French bourgeoisie did not exist is something of an exaggeration, but I offer it deliberately as such, in the spirit of a comment by Richard Klein: "The validity of hyperbole, the truth that exaggeration may often convey, depends on a principle well recognized by marksmen: there are times when aiming to overshoot the mark is the condition of hitting it."[7] As far as the bourgeoisie is concerned, the "did not exist" statement could be qualified in an array of manners. But the problem is that this whole question has long suffered from a surfeit of careful shading: the social contours of the bourgeoisie are so elastic and the term itself so pregnant with different and contradictory meanings that most attempts to generalize about it tend to get qualified into a state of chaos. If we take the radical position of assuming the group's nonexistence, we will be in a better position to evaluate and explain the mythic nature and function of the idea of bourgeoisie.

This thesis of bourgeois nonexistence derives from my belief that classes only exist if they are aware of their own existence, a knowledge which is inseparable from the ability to articulate an identity.[8] I posit here that the existence of social groups, while rooted in the material world, is shaped by language and more specifically by narrative: in order for a group to claim a role as actor in society and polity, it must have a story or stories about itself, it must take direction from a tale that links memories of the past to desires for the future. The French bourgeoisie was briefly offered an inspiring story of this sort, the one written mostly in the 1820s by liberal politicians and historians such as Augustin Thierry, François Guizot, and Adolphe Thiers. That narrative, however, did not prove compelling for very long.

To the argument that the bourgeoisie did not exist because it did not in any conspicuous or compelling way identify itself and tell its own story, some historians will respond that bourgeois consciousness did indeed exist in the eighteenth and early nineteenth centuries, but its nature was concealed under other appearances. This is the classic argument about so-called "bourgeois universalism."[9] When eighteenth-century upper-class liberals spoke of *humanité,* or revolutionaries about *égalité,* or nineteenth-century politicians about "the nation," while restricting, sometimes severely, access to education and political rights, they were promoting their own class interests under cover of something broader and nobler-sounding.

This view presumes an objective, material reality of social existence that is passively reflected in, and sometimes concealed by, language. I believe, however, that language is not passive but performative; people's identities are constructed by the cultural elements they absorb and then articulate as individual and collective stories.[10] Why should the bourgeoisie, if it existed, refuse to name itself, why should it feel compelled to conceal its own existence and purpose? It is true that political leaders tend to couch their claims in a language that assures them the broadest support; but the examples of England and the United States show that the middle class can be extended infinitely for political purposes—and yet the French chose not to do so. And why should the bourgeoisie be the only class to deny its own existence, when aristocrats and especially workers were not shy, in this period, about making claims based on group identities? Bourgeois self-interest has often been treated in a manner reminiscent of popular understandings of Freud's concept of denial: the more people claim that it isn't there, the more they prove that it is. One is led to suspect that the argument about bourgeois universalism reflects the distaste of intellectuals for the bourgeoisie, their assumption that bourgeois identity is a shameful secret, something people would naturally want to conceal if they could.

In the following chapters I endeavor to take language seriously on its own terms, to read the words of eighteenth- and nineteenth-century commentators without attempting to translate them into the categories of later social science. I seek here to establish patterns of meaning in recurrent images and themes (such as "luxury," "aristocracy," "the nation," and indeed "bourgeoisie") without any a priori assumptions about the social realities they refer to, though with the ultimate goal of connecting them back to broad social and political dynamics.[11] In short, I am applying to the realm of the social the cultural approach that historians have, for many years now, been bringing to the study of politics, gender, race, and nation.

The turn toward cultural history which began in the 1970s led historians to approach identities in the past as culturally constructed. The impulse came first from feminist historians intent on demonstrating that female and male were not fixed, transhistorical categories, but concepts whose meaning and relationship to one another differed among cultures and had changed dramatically over time. The tradition, now close to two decades old, which one could awkwardly term "cultural constructionism," has focused, not surprisingly, on different objects in different national contexts. Historians working in the United States have been interested in the construction of identities that were the object of twentieth-century struggles for pride or liberation: gender, race, sexual orientation, and ethnicity; the upshot has been a vast and sophisticated literature on what it has meant from the distant past to the present to be female, black, gay, Irish, Jewish, and so on.[12] Historians in France, but also historians of France, gravitated initially toward the big questions in that national history, which traditionally concerned nationhood and political ideologies: back in the 1980s, French historians were already at work on a prestigious multivolume collection about the construction of national identity through historical memories, and the study of politics as culture first took shape on the scholarly battleground of French revolutionary history.[13]

When historians and other social scientists rattle off a standard list of identities, class is usually included in the mix along with race and gender. It is intriguing therefore that comparatively little work by historians has addressed the question of how class is constructed through language and culture along the same lines as gender or race.[14] There are isolated exceptions to this proposition, as, for instance, the innovative work of William H. Sewell, Jacques Rancière, and Donald Reid on nineteenth-century French workers, but the most sustained and self-conscious writing has come in recent years from British historians.[15] Britain is the Western nation where class is the most conspicuous marker of identity, and arguably the one where the trauma of class division has caused the deepest wounds. As a result, reflection about class has been more sustained and creative in British historical practice than in France and the United States.

Britain boasts a long tradition of social history focused on class, stretching back at least to the early twentieth century and culminating some four decades ago with Edward Thompson's 1963 historical masterpiece, *The Making of the English Working Class*. Thompson himself always took a cultural approach to social identities, insisting that class was not a matter of arbitrarily drawn economic categories but was instead defined by the interactions between people of unequal power as these were expressed in words, symbols, and actions: historians could only uncover class by looking at words and behavior which, in many cases, bore little relation to formal economic or political relationships.[16] Later British historians have built upon Thompson's sensitivity to questions of language and culture in class analysis, while abandoning his ultimate commitment to a base-superstructure model.

Already in the early 1980s Gareth Stedman-Jones argued that the language of Chartism—the radical movement which in the 1830s and 1840s pressed for the vote for working men—did not "reflect" the social experiences of the working classes, but actually created that experience, and in doing so, a political tradition. Patrick Joyce, in case studies of the construction of middle-class and working-class identity, posits that class "is an imagined form, not something given in a 'real' world beyond this form"; he highlights the instability of class identity and the way in which narrative creates a social "subject" which can then act upon the world through politics. Dror Wahrman has studied the creation of class in the political arena, examining how Liberal politicians in England from the 1790s to the 1830s invoked their relationship to the "middle class" to counter radicalism and stake out a central position in the political sphere. And David Cannadine has drawn a broader panorama of the ways in which the centrality of class in Britain has been alternately asserted and denied for political purposes, from the eighteenth century to the era of Margaret Thatcher.[17]

Much of this recent work on Britain has centered on the role of political language in the creation of social identities. None of the historians mentioned above argues that class is a political fiction, or that words have no relation to lived experience. Dror Wahrman, for instance, is at pains to point out that material factors and social experience do limit the range of ways in which the world can be described; but they do not determine such descriptions. Given certain inescapable developments such as the growth of towns and commerce or the decline of small rural property, what is of interest to a historian is whether, and why, a politician might choose to frame such processes as the advent of a middle class. Wahrman acutely describes the object of his study, as I would mine in this book, as "the space of possibilities between social reality and its representation."[18]

This study of the bourgeoisie in the French sociocultural landscape adopts a similar approach, although, unlike the historians mentioned above, I do not focus so heavily on political language as the generator of social definitions. As the following chapters suggest, I would agree that politics is probably the most important source of social imagery in public life. Politicians ranging from absolute monarchs to leaders of revolutionary crowds usually assert their own legitimacy by invoking the social groups they claim to embody, represent, or fight for, from "the aristocracy" or "the undivided people" to "angry white men" or "soccer moms." In doing so they sometimes create those categories, but more frequently they draw upon powerful concepts and images already at large in the culture. More than other creators of social mythologies—except perhaps for marketing professionals in some present-day societies—political speakers and writers have an interest in broadcasting their claims as widely as possible.

If the purpose of this book is to say something new about the difficult question of the bourgeoisie in French history, its aim as a contribution to methodological conversations is to help define as an object of historical investigation what I call "the social imaginary." To my knowledge there exists no standard definition or account of "the social imaginary," an expression more common among French scholars than their counterparts elsewhere.[19] While historians have produced countless studies of representations—in different cultures, of distinct groups, especially those which are a focus of intense reactions and polemics (women, racial others, criminals, prostitutes)—only very recently have we begun to think more systematically about how we construct our views of society. I would define the social imaginary simply as "the cultural elements from which we construct our understanding of the social world." The most obvious sources of social imagery are political discourse (written, spoken, or embodied in visual artifacts), academic (in the widest sense) and other social commentary, and fictional works such as novels, plays, and films: these are the sorts of documents which speak directly to what is considered wrong or right with any given social world, and the type of source I have used most heavily in the discussion that follows. (A full list would also include police records, which sometimes contain direct commentary on social status and expectations, and legal sources such as trial records and briefs, which often generate striking social imagery.)[20]

Our experience of the social world is made up of three components which can be distinguished for analytical purposes, even if they are inseparable in people's actual lives: the raw elements of social position such as wealth, status, or power; social practices such as tilling a field, playing the piano, or joining the army; and what I call the social imaginary. Most of what falls into the "social history" category addresses the first two questions (including, within social practices, such cultural matters as religious beliefs, schooling, and recreation), but ne-

glects the third element, understandings of, and polemics and fanta-
sies about, the social world. If we give the latter more room and take it
seriously on its own terms (rather than taking the approach: "What
they really meant was . . ."), we can arrive at conclusions that shed new
and unexpected light on how people in the past experienced the social world.

Indeed, the most interesting areas of investigation are those many
instances when the discourse about society does not seem to reflect
what we historians see as the reality of a social landscape: when hundreds of eighteenth-century writers, contemplating the growth of
trade, cities, and consumerism, all understood these developments as
a terrifyingly palpable social disease called "luxury"; when so many actors in the French Revolution, in the face of tension and outright violence between revolutionaries of different social classes, stubbornly insisted that the French people were one nation united; or when writers
around 1850 confidently asserted that the bourgeoisie had enjoyed its
heyday and was now in decline. Such language cannot be dismissed as
ideology, propaganda, or denial, for it is precisely the disjuncture between what they saw and what we think we know that is most illuminating. The cultural aspects of social life have not been neglected by
historians: in French history, which includes the twentieth-century tradition of social and cultural history known as the Annales school, that
is patently not the case. But much social history has failed to take into
account and integrate the ways in which contemporaries themselves
viewed the social world, and I hope to suggest in this book how paying
attention to such matters might change our view of a historical period.

This is a short book on a very large subject, and I am painfully aware
of all that it does not include. A completely systematic attempt to con-
nect discourses about society to social and political developments in
the most intensely scrutinized century of France's history would take a
lifetime of study, and what follows, the result of a few years of reading
and thinking, is necessarily partial and selective. In the interests of
concision I have neglected some fine monographs that I know of, and
surely others of which I am unaware, and skipped over many important eighteenth- and nineteenth-century writers. Since this book is an
overview based on printed sources, it inevitably over-represents the
perspective of the literate male population. Another kind of study
drawing on archival material would have a lot more to say about the so-

cial imaginary among the nonliterate poor,[21] and might begin to address the important question: do women experience the social world differently than do men? While I am not comfortable referring in a general way to "the French," as I do often in this book, I also believe that generalization is a necessary evil at certain points in grappling with a complicated question. I hope that readers will approach the book taking note of the word "essay" in its title: what follows is emphatically meant to be suggestive rather than definitive, intended to move the question of the bourgeoisie forward by provoking in the best of cases some disagreement, more research, and further debate.

Another word central to the book's title, "myth," points to both the critical and the constructive aspects of the argument. Webster's Dictionary offers two different meanings of the word myth: "a usually traditional story of ostensibly historical events that serves to unfold part of the world view of a people," and "an ill-founded belief held uncritically."

The myth of the bourgeoisie discussed in this essay is, in the second sense mentioned above, the myth constructed by modern historians of a hegemonic, self-conscious, and more or less unified bourgeoisie. This is the myth which I challenge from a post-Marxian—though emphatically not anti-Marxian—perspective. But this book is also—and more importantly—about the ways in which the myth of the bourgeoisie functioned for the French in the eighteenth and early nineteenth centuries: why such a group came to be perceived as central to society and systematically vilified, and how rejection of the category "bourgeoisie" became such an important element in the construction of French national identity. I adopt here the definition of myth of the semiologist Roland Barthes, who insists that what we call myth is not a lie or a negation, but a message or a means of communication: it is the way in which societies make sense of themselves by turning history into nature. Those who produce myth—historians, journalists, advertisers—neither conceal their object nor reveal it as ideology; they make it appear natural. Myth in this sense is neither a falsehood nor an overt statement of ideology, but an inflection of language which makes the invented seem natural.[22] "Luxury" was such a myth in the eighteenth century, "bourgeoisie" in the nineteenth and beyond.

Although the central theme of this book concerns the nonexistence of the bourgeoisie, its ultimate argument aims to be positive rather than negative. If the French did not believe in bourgeois or middle-class norms and ideals, what did they believe in? I make the case that an imaginary and much reviled bourgeoisie loomed large in French culture because its purpose was to define by contrast the nation's real, if often implicit, social ideals: antimaterialism, civic service, a transcendent state, and an undivided people. Historians have proceeded on the assumption that in spite of all the criticism directed at it, the bourgeoisie was, and has remained, the normative group in French society. This book aims to show that a much clearer picture of the birth of modern French culture emerges when the bourgeois is displaced from the center to the periphery, and understood as an imaginary other against whom the nation's values and destiny were forged.

# The Social Imaginary in
# Prerevolutionary France

## 1

Have "middle classes" existed throughout history, in most times and places? Most complex societies contain a range of social groups from rich to poor, and most include people located between the conspicuous extremes. Certainly the existence of one or several significant middling groups correlates with objective factors such as the importance of towns, trade, and services. But the crucial historical question is whether a middle class is seen: whether the existence of a unified and pivotal middling or upper-middling group is, first, acknowledged, and second, invested with historical, moral, and/or political importance.[1] In any given historical instance, do middling groups, whatever they are called, represent the imagined essence of society, its most cherished ideal, its significant past, its feared or desired future?

The wide variety of answers to these questions suggests how elastic, and at the same time symbolically fraught, the idea of a middle class really is. It is commonplace to remark that in the United States in our time, because of longstanding suspicions of working classes and aristocrats, all those who live above the direst poverty, including the very rich, identify themselves as middle class. Something close to the opposite prevailed in Old Regime France. Significant middling groups certainly existed in that society, including a legally defined urban bourgeoisie, but they drew very little comment, either negative or positive. While the bourgeoisie was often ridiculed, it was perceived neither as a source of serious problems nor as a solution to society's ills. Most of the time, those who described society or argued about it did not see the middle classes at all. Social commentators in the Old Regime obsessed about the nobility—where it came from, what its role should be, whether to reform it or possibly abolish it. But the alternatives to aristocracy, when they were imagined, were located either in the state or in the soil: they had nothing to do with the middle class.

## GOD-GIVEN ORDER

Society is not a physical object but a concept, and therefore people who describe or discuss it must usually have recourse to metaphors. We commonly speak of the social order, imagined as a kind of ladder, or of a social structure, which might look like a building, or of that flatter but pleasantly pastoral space, the social field. In Old Regime France, as in most of preindustrial Europe, metaphors of order prevailed. By ancient tradition, French society was divided into three orders, Clergy, Nobility, and Third Estate. This division makes no sense to the modern mind: the Clergy was a small, socially mixed group, the Nobility a tiny elite, the Third Estate the huge mass of "everyone else." We are so far removed from the archaic origins of this scheme that it is almost impossible for us really to understand a vision of society based not on numbers of people or levels of income, but on spiritual functions. Indeed, the ancient division made no sense to a majority of the French by the eighteenth century. The Revolution of 1789 was triggered by the rebellion of Third Estate deputies to the Estates General; they saw no reason to grant precedence and political dominance to the representatives of two tiny elites, and proclaimed their own sovereignty on numerical and functional grounds.

Yet the division into three orders had made sense for centuries: the number three expressed the divine origins and nature of society, while the concept of order established the intimate link between monarchy and society. The classification in three groups (most often of clerics, warriors, and agriculturalists) derives from an ancient and widespread Indo-European pattern which can be traced from India to Scandinavia.[2] In Christian Europe, the medievalist Georges Duby explains, such triune social schemes made the human world analogous to the Trinitarian heaven and to the broader tripartite nature of creation (divine, animal, and inanimate). Society was figured as a triangle, a pyramidal shape long associated with divinity and which expresses unitary power, hierarchy, and stability, three functions folded into one entity.[3]

As for order, it was a natural property, inherent in a society which mirrored on a smaller scale the Great Chain of divinely ordained creation.[4] The linguist Marie-France Piguet has noted a very telling difference between the terms *ordre* and *classe,* both of which were applied to social groups in the eighteenth century. *Classe* was used with active verbs, in the context of human agency: a ruler or administrator would divide the population into classes in order to levy taxes, just as, for analytical purposes, a natural scientist would make up classes of animals or a philosopher classes of ideas. But when scholars like the abbé Dubos or Montesquieu described the society of some historical or foreign nation, they used the word *ordre* within a passive construction, noting for instance that the population of Saxony *was divided* into several orders. "An order," Piguet concludes, "is a set of persons (and infrequently of things) whose existence appears independent of human intelligence or will."[5]

Divine in origin and natural in essence, the orders of society were also an expression of the sovereign's authority. To be ordered is not just to be organized, but also to receive command. The social world was arranged as a ladder of ranked conditions so that each could have power over the ones below, thus ensuring the ultimate authority of the monarch. Society was ordered like an army and for the same purpose: to ensure discipline, stability, and the effective use of ultimate power.[6] Only in the seventeenth century did natural law theorists begin to imagine social organization as existing prior to, and independent from, sovereign power (in other words, to view the social as something essentially different from the political), and it took well over a century for those theories to spread and have concrete effects. Prior to that, the organic, most often bodily images through which people understood the human world meant that what mattered was function, not numbers or averages: a body has a heart, limbs, lungs, and bowels, not a mathematical median.

This is why observers in the Old Regime typically described society by listing its elements from top to bottom, in a sort of rolling film with commentary, rather than by calculating statistics. What mattered was the quality of persons rather than their numbers—where they stood in the pecking order, and whether they actually lived up to their status. Take, for instance, a police report about the population of Paris addressed in 1709 to Father Letellier, who had just taken office as Louis XIV's new confessor.[7] The document first goes over the official *ligne directe* of groups making up the city population, and then deals with what might be described as the liminal, and therefore more dangerously volatile categories. (The court and the clergy are the objects of separate sections.) The report describes a multiplicity of strictly ordered groups and offers opinions on them along the way. First comes the highest nobility, then the "urban nobility" of magistrates and city officials, followed in third place by the capital's "ancient and wealthy bourgeoisie"—merchants, financiers, tax farmers. Professionals such as doctors and lawyers hover around the lower end of the latter group, often managing, the author commented, to marry their daughters up. Lower down are skilled and wholesale merchants such as goldsmiths, jewelers, drapers, "big" pharmacists, and grocers. [8]

By the time the author gets to the next group down, the retailers, his contained irritation about snobbery among the upper orders gives way to outright indignation at lesser merchants, "big-mouthed talkers, quarrelsome speechifiers, always ready to hang up a chain on a street corner to make a barricade."[9] In their wake come the guild workers, followed by the unskilled workers like water carriers and day laborers from Auvergne and Savoy. These are the last of the *ligne directe,* the author continued, but then there were those who lived in the city and did not fit into the official grid—or not yet. Yes, the clerks and other students were bandits who deserved to be hanged *en masse,* but they usually grew up to be honest family men. Male servants such as lackeys and pages, however, usually came to a bad end because they mimicked their masters' debauchery. The very bottom of society is occupied by an underclass of crooks, gypsies, and con artists, which included some surprising elements like astrologers, academicians, and the English.[10]

The list does contain a bourgeoisie, but that group does not include all of those we would call bourgeois (wholesale merchants are excluded, for instance), much less those we would term "middle class." In fact, it is remarkably hard to figure out where the middle of this society might be located, so fragmented is the description. In this portrait of an urban world, groups are pegged less in reference to the whole than in relation to those who come right before and right after them. The police report gives us something that looks much less like an archeological excavation of social layers than like a procession.

Indeed, ceremonial procession was the most common way of representing urban society under the Old Regime. Within the public culture of prerevolutionary France, monarchy and society were analogous in that both had to be concretely embodied, made present. Just as the bread and wine of communion made divinity visible and palpable, the monarch literally embodied the state: his body, from ceremonial rising through lavish court spectacles to his very public extramarital sex life, stood at the symbolic dead center of the realm. In the same way, social distinctions were represented, or made present, by means of visible sartorial signs. Canonical discussions of the social order, like Charles Loyseau's 1610 *Traité des ordres,* have a lot to say about the colors and lengths of robes, the right to flaunt accessories like croziers, spurs, and swords, the nature and decoration of headgear.[11] The status of a group was also made manifest through its rights of precedence, equally concrete matters of who got to walk or sit before whom.[12]

Two decades before the Revolution, in 1768, an anonymous provincial writer described the southern city of Montpellier in terms quite similar to Loyseau's, stressing order, rank, and precedence. In a close reading of this remarkable text, Robert Darnton argues that even though the author does not actually describe a procession in Montpellier, his description is the textual equivalent of such an event. "[T]he procession served as a traditional idiom for urban society," Darnton writes. "It was a statement unfurled in the streets through which the city represented itself to itself."[13] The figure of a procession does indeed seem implicit in the author's opening presentation of the city's religious and administrative elites in strictly ranked succession and with great emphasis on the minutiae of costume. The bishop with his purple vestments, the cathedral and church chapter members in white or gray surplices, some wearing enameled crosses on crimson ribbons, the White Penitents and Blue Penitents wearing hoods and sackcloth in their emblematic hues. The secular authorities were also presented in a burst of color and texture, from the black silk and ermine hoods of the officials of the *Cour des aydes,* to the red robes of the lawyers and the short robe, cloak, and sword of the chief justice's lieutenant. No less impressive were the top city officials, the Consuls, with their scarlet satin purple-hooded costumes and their retinue of *escudiers* dressed in half-red, half-blue outfits emblazoned with the city's coat of arms. And so it goes through the university, the chamber of commerce, and the one hundred and nine officially recognized trades.[14]

Traditional depictions of society as a procession of "dignities"—or indeed "indignities" such as unruly clerks, servants, or criminals—were anchored in the concrete. The place of a person in the social order derived either from a tangible object of labor (soil, leather, bread, meat) or, in the case of more abstract occupations, was made manifest through the details of costume. A way of imagining society so closely connected to the tangible or visual would make it hard, even impossible, to dream up categories based on abstraction—a bourgeoisie including all the owners of different means of production, for instance, or a middle class defined statistically. How could one figure the means of production in a parade? Where is the middle of a procession?

And yet the author of the Montpellier text was not content with his opening presentation of the city's official, ceremonial ordering. Recognizing that it did not represent the real picture of social life in this busy and prosperous provincial center, he offered, about halfway through the manuscript, his own view of what the real social order was. Significantly, having dealt with the town's God-given order, he now offered his own division into *classes* in a short overview entitled: "*Noblesse. Classes des habitants.*" In this section he identified, first, an ancient feudal nobility though it was so small as to be invisible, and in second place an extensive robe nobility of magistrates and other royal administrators. Next came the *état bourgeois* or Second Estate (located, confusingly, in third place), made up of professionals and merchants, followed by artisans and other workers in fourth place, and domestic servants in fifth.[15]

Although this scheme does locate a middling bourgeoisie in the third of five categories, the overall description is quirky and personal. It dismisses the high nobility as nonexistent, devotes a whole category to servants as an excuse to rant against them, and omits the clergy altogether. As Darnton observes, the Montpellier author had a hard time settling on an idiom to describe the city's social makeup.[16] The traditional figure of the procession of dignities did not account for the realities of a changing city, so the author came up with something that looked like the old tripartite division, although he chose to revise the scheme drastically. While the classification he devised looks at first glance rather modern, with a commercial-professional bourgeoisie at its center, this group is in fact framed by two sets of nobles above, and a distinctly premodern group, personal servants, on the bottom.

The Montpellier chronicler's difficulty in settling on a social idiom that made sense was in fact quite typical of eighteenth-century authors, many of whom struggled to find a way of describing society that both preserved and updated the three traditional orders. A frequent solution was to subdivide the three orders into six. The chevalier d'Arcq, for instance, writing in defense of the traditional nobility, noted that the first estate comprised the "first and second order of the clergy," the noble estate a similar higher/lower division, and the third a bourgeois and a popular category.[17] The six-group model took slightly better account of real social diversity, but it still had four elite groups lording it over two classes of commoners, and the bourgeoisie relegated to the penultimate position. Other writers proposed a fourfold division which still heavily privileged the elites but reflected the growing importance, or at least the growing claims, of France's courts of high justice, the *parlements*. Writing at mid-century, the prominent economist marquis Victor de Mirabeau listed the estates as clergy, nobility, magistrates and the "municipal order," and the pamphleteer Berenger in 1789 concurred in the number four, though his were slightly different: clergy, nobles, magistrates, and people.[18] The term Fourth Estate was used in France from the sixteenth century on, but what it designated varied a good deal, from magistrates to lawyers to urban workers.[19]

Still other writers came up with even more idiosyncratic enumerations. Around the same time as the Montpellier observer, another progressive writer also saw five main social groups: royal family and *grands,* lesser nobility and high magistracy, the "bourgeoisie of first rank," a lesser group of minor officers, retailers, and artisans, and finally the inhabitants of the countryside.[20] A decade later, the count du Buat-Nançay broke tradition by enumerating upwards: indigents, cultivators, merchants, "the rich," and nobles.[21] And a few years before the Revolution, the social critic Antoine Polier de Saint-Germain also identified five "different estates and conditions of man in the places assigned to him by [public] opinion": the great, the lesser nobles, the wealthy non-nobles, the artisanal class, and all those who worked for others.[22]

All of these examples date from the second half of the eighteenth century, and what is striking about them is their diversity. The lists were top-heavy with elites, a fact which reflects both the generally high status of the writers (this was *their* social world) and the force of a tradition willing to grant the royal family and their kin a whole social group of their own. Some, like Mirabeau, barely saw the working poor who made up over three quarters of the population. Beyond this basic orientation, however, there was no consensus on either the number or the nature of social groups: nobles were granted either one or two estates, the mostly noble magistrates sometimes got their own niche but more often did not, the clergy was usually but not always absent, and the nonelite majority was variously stowed in one or two groups.

But while most eighteenth-century writers had jettisoned the traditional three-estate model, they continued to adhere to the assumptions behind it: that social groups had different functions, that these needed to remain distinct, and that the maintenance of a strict ranking of groups was the core principle of their monarchical society and government. This delicate balance of conditions was crucial to the monarchy, wrote the chevalier d'Arcq; if too many people shifted upwards you would have a republic, if they were leveled downwards despotism would ensue.[23] As a result, what mattered most was the structure of the whole, not the exact identity of any given part. It was because rank and specificity of function mattered so much that the bourgeoisie (and a fortiori a middle class) was so elusive in discourses about society in the eighteenth century. Authors sometimes included a specific group we would call bourgeois with reference to its precise function: magistrates, merchants, Mirabeau's "municipal order." But it was almost impossible within such a framework to imagine a broader bourgeoisie or middle class. Such a group could be located in practice, but not really in theory, as the Montpellier example suggests. For the most part it was not natural for eighteenth-century French thinkers to contemplate a group whose functions were multiple and whose social location was ambiguous. To conjure up such a labile, ill-defined, and capacious group would threaten the very essence of monarchical society. If the choice of seeing a middle class or not is at bottom a political matter, then it makes sense that from the point of view of an ordered monarchical system the bourgeoisie was essentially invisible.

## BOURGEOIS GENTLEMEN

Readers familiar with French history may be inclined to protest that the bourgeoisie was not at all invisible in the Old Regime, that it was explicitly named in most of the social enumerations cited above, and that indeed it existed as an official category of prerevolutionary urban society. While all of this is unquestionably true, both the official status of the group called *bourgeoisie* and the political-cultural connotations of what was more loosely deemed *bourgeois* were deeply problematic. In the short and longer terms alike, the legacy of the *bourgeoisie d'ancien régime* was one of the elements that made it impossible for bourgeois identity to emerge later in France as a central norm or ideal.

As every textbook on Old Regime society explains, *bourgeois* was the title given to a legally distinct, privileged, non-noble upper class; it was an appellation first granted in the eleventh and twelfth centuries by the Capetian kings to the free men dwelling in new towns.[24] Over time, the status of bourgeois evolved into a variable set of obligations and privileges. In earlier times, when the category was more socially mixed and bourgeois were still masters of their towns, it meant heavy fiscal and military obligations, such as helping with the upkeep of the town walls and serving in the local militia.[25] With the consolidation of the royal state and the growing divide-and-rule impulses of French kings, the status of bourgeois became more clearly a matter of privilege with respect to royal taxes.

By the eighteenth century, while the precise rights and responsibilities of legally defined bourgeois varied significantly from place to place, the status had become strongly associated with *de jure* or *de facto* idleness. In Paris, different statutes regulating the title of *bourgeois de Paris* forbade persons of that status to work with their hands, sell anything but the fruit of their properties, and do anything that legally jeopardized their status—strictures that were very similar to those imposed on nobles. In return the *bourgeois de Paris* enjoyed an array of fiscal and honorific privileges—not as many as nobles, but similar in kind.[26] In short, the legally defined bourgeoisie of Paris looked very much like a lesser version of the nobility. In Paris, the legal title of *bourgeois* was hereditary. In a provincial town like Chartres it was not, but it usually sanctioned the sort of financial success that meant that one could live off one's income without working and become, to use the confusing terminology of the tax rolls, a *bourgeois vivant noblement*—a bourgeois living nobly.[27] Thus, although the legally defined *bourgeoisie* was an intermediate group between nobles and the poorer commoners, it hardly corresponds to our idea of a hard-working, meritocratic middle class, since its juridical status was usually based on some combination of fiscal privilege, hereditary rights, and enforced idleness. All of this is a problem to historians in search of the origins of the French middle class, who feel the need to include this group because of its label, but then tend to hide it carefully among the more familiar purposeful types like merchants, doctors, and lawyers. The fact is—a fact laden with historical consequences—that, strictly speaking, the Old Regime bourgeoisie was a shadow aristocracy.

Further confusing the matter is the fact that *bourgeoisie* was a political term roughly synonymous with "urban citizenship." In fact, one could argue that the social vagueness of the term was the corollary of its political specificity. The articles on *bourgeois* and *bourgeoisie* in the standard Old Regime dictionaries usually opened with the traditional definition of the urban bourgeoisie as analogous to classical citizenship: an elite which stood metonymically for the city and held the right to political agency. The 1694 edition of the hallowed Académie Française dictionary, for instance, begins its entry for *bourgeois* and *bourgeoisie:* "Citizen, inhabitant of a town. 'Bourgeois of Paris', 'solid bourgeois'. In the definite mode one says 'the Bourgeois' in reference to the whole body of a town's inhabitants. 'The Bourgeois rose up', 'The Bourgeois took up arms.'"[28] The Jesuit *Dictionnaire universel* in 1704 used the Latin term for citizen as a synonym, and was more pointed about the danger of urban unrest in its example. "*Bourgeois.* Collective noun. The assemblage of persons [*peuple*] residing in a town. *Cives.* 'One must not put weapons in the hands of the *bourgeois.*' . . . *Bourgeois* is also said of each inhabitant of the town. *Civis.* 'This merchant, this lawyer, is a good *bourgeois.*'"[29] These same dictionaries noted, of course, that bourgeoisie was synonymous with privilege, that it included in particular exemption from the standard commoners' tax, the *taille.*

The Revolution was quick to repudiate this unholy association of privilege with citizenship. A 1791 dictionary of political and constitutional terms had this to say in its article on *Citoyen:* "[T]he French were not citizens before the Revolution returned to them their natural rights . . . *Citoyen* and *bourgeois* were synonymous for them; the latter title, like that of *noble,* referred only to the privileges enjoyed by the inhabitants of a few towns."[30] While grounded in legal and historical fact, the concept of the bourgeois as citizen was problematic. It was too dangerously democratic for the Old Regime (hence all those cautionary examples of the bourgeoisie taking up arms), too heinously exclusive, indeed aristocratic, for the Revolution. In later generations—at various points in the Restoration, July Monarchy, and Third Republic— the image of the Old Regime bourgeois as proud citizens and city fathers would be seized upon by groups eager for political reasons to promote their claims in the name of the bourgeoisie. Under the Old Regime and the First Republic, however, bourgeoisie as urban citizenship was a threatening concept for roughly similar reasons in both cases: it raised the possibility of defection from *universal* subjecthood or citizenship.

If the bourgeois was politically problematic, he was also socially ambiguous and culturally reviled. It will come as no surprise that the sociocultural definition of the bourgeois in Old Regime dictionaries was almost entirely negative. Always apprehended from below or from above, the bourgeois was who you were *not*. To workers the term *le bourgeois* meant the master or the boss. (The word kept this meaning well into the twentieth century.) From the 1690s to the 1790s, the Académie Française dictionary explained that it was the word used by workers or servants to designate employers: "One must serve the *bourgeois,* one must not cheat the *bourgeois,*" "The mason and the artisan always try to cheat the *bourgeois,*" ran the examples written by and for people who were no doubt all *bourgeois* in this sense.[31] But conversely, the adjective was identified in every dictionary as a way of characterizing a person lacking in the breeding and polish of high society. It means, explained the French Academy dictionary of 1694, "a man who is not of the court; 'It reeks of the bourgeois' [ *'Cela sent bien son bourgeois'*]. In this meaning, [the word] is usually in the adjective form: 'A bourgeois manner, bourgeois conversation, he has a bourgeois look.'" Other dictionaries chimed in: "not polite enough, too familiar, not respectful enough"; "in contrast to a man of the court, a man with little gallantry or wit."[32] Several decades and a revolution later, the definition was still there, but with a trace of disapproval at the usage: "It is also said out of contempt to put down a man who is not a gentleman or has no experience of high society."[33]

The contempt laced with disgust expressed in these definitions ("It reeks of the bourgeois") begs questions, especially as it is aimed at a group one would assume to be prosperous and law-abiding. The double negative through which the bourgeois was apprehended—not a worker, not a gentleman—is telling in that it suggests a repulsive liminality or mongrelization rather than a complacently positive middlingness. And indeed, comments by contemporaries do suggest that it was the bourgeois's Janus-like social position that triggered the revulsion of contemporaries. The writer Marivaux explained in 1717: "The bourgeois of Paris, Madame, is a mixed animal, who takes after the great lord and the people. When he has grandeur in his manners he is always an ape, when he is petty he is natural: thus he is noble by imitation, and plebeian by disposition."[34]

Since the Middle Ages, an abundant satirical literature in France had used the bourgeois as a target, branding him crude in manners, vain, avaricious, and ambitious. The best known instance of this type is of course Molière's Monsieur Jourdain, the oxymoronic *bourgeois gentilhomme* who takes crash courses in minuet dancing and epigram writing. Jourdain is but the best-known of many stage and page bourgeois denounced for their lowly origins, their greed (financiers were a favorite target), their desire to pass as nobles. The themes of this extensive antibourgeois literature are worth noting: excessive focus on money, drastic social mobility, the exercise of professions that mediated between producer and consumer—commerce, the law, finance.[35]

The ambiguity of bourgeois status was a constant threat to the very principle of an ordered society.[36] Like domestic servants, the bourgeois could move too quickly in the interstices of a highly structured system, and indeed the bourgeois is often depicted—as in Lesage's play *Turcaret*—as a successful, upwardly mobile former domestic.[37] In French culture the bourgeois has had much in common with another socially ambiguous and much reviled type, the Jew. Like the bourgeois, the Jew was a cultural outsider trying to pass, a creature overly invested in the material world, and a person who made a living by mediating between groups. As the analogy between bourgeois and Jew suggests, perceptions of the bourgeois in the Old Regime defy our assumption that middle-class types are usually seen as stable, reassuring, and praiseworthy. The Old Regime bourgeois was, on the contrary, perceived as both despicable and dangerous—he was too ill defined, too mobile, the vehicle of too many different and contradictory meanings.

Thus far I have been using the masculine pronoun because the bourgeois defined in dictionaries and portrayed in fictions was over-whelmingly male, his wife mostly ignored. Yet matters of gender are not absent from definitions and images of the bourgeois in the Old Regime. In dictionary definitions, one usage of the word *bourgeois* was invariably positive: that which attached it to domestic and private life. The later editions of the dictionary of the French Academy point out that the adjective "bourgeois" is applied *en bien* to the following: a meal, a soup, a good wine from one's cellar as opposed to the sour wine you get in taverns.[38] Darnton finds a similar clustering of posi-tive meanings in the Montpellier chronicler's text around the idea of *cuisine bourgeoise*—the simple, satisfying four-course meal.[39] While Darnton interprets the positive emphasis on food, wine, and domestic comforts in his author's text as the reassuring core of bourgeois iden-tity, I would suggest a different, less sanguine emphasis. The bourgeois was dangerous and despised when he laid claim to the public world— when he threatened to take up arms as a citizen, when he aspired to noble status, when he tried to perform, and invariably disgraced him-self, on the public stage of high society. The quality of bourgeois-ness was praised only when it pertained to the private world, when it was at-tached to the rituals of domestic intimacy: soups, meals, wines. The bourgeois, in short, was implicitly gendered female, or at least subject to the same restrictions as women: praised when he confined his activ-ity to the home, denounced and satirized when he dared step outside his designated realm.

The bourgeoisie did therefore certainly exist in Old Regime France, both as a legal category and as a distinct, if problematic, element of the social imaginary. The so-called *bourgeois d'ancien régime* had long flourished as a privileged local elite, although both the similarity of their status to that of nobles and the particular nature of urban citizen-ship would ensure their rapid disappearance after 1789. The bour-geois defined in broader social and cultural terms was the object of scorn and even fear, a creature whose existence challenged the very principles of a society based on the stability and distinctness of social categories. For anyone attempting to diagnose or remedy social ills in the eighteenth century, offer suggestions for social reforms, dream up a more peaceful and moral vision of what the nation should be, the materialistic, unstable, and uncouth bourgeoisie would have been a most unlikely place to look for a solution.

## RETHINKING NOBILITY

It is only in retrospect, from the vantage point of the two centuries following the Revolution, that the question of the bourgeoisie—who they were and how they were viewed—seems important. To denizens of the eighteenth century, such a question was nonexistent. Until the eve of the Revolution, when the Third Estate became an intense focus of debate, nobody much cared about the identities, rights, and responsibilities of rich or middling commoners. If anyone did, that concern was drowned out by the much louder and more intense debates about the nobility. What people argued about in the Age of Enlightenment was not the possible emergence of a new elite, but the origins, nature, role, and future of France's ancient aristocracy. To anyone even slightly acquainted with the literary works of the period, the characters that stand out most sharply are aristocrats, usually dissolute libertines like the vicomte de Valmont and the marquise de Merteuil. While we may be unsure of the valet Figaro's exact social location (middle or working class?), there is no mistaking the social identity of his master, count Almaviva, the brutal rake who wants to revive his feudal right to Suzanne's virginity. The loudest social theme of the Revolution, the crusade against aristocracy, had its roots deep in a century of debate over whether nobles embodied the nation's honor or threatened its health and integrity.

It is telling, for instance, that the most celebrated mid-century debate about the social implications of economic change concerned not the bourgeoisie but the nobility. In 1756 a relatively obscure author and former Jesuit, abbé Gabriel Coyer, published a short treatise entitled *La Noblesse commerçante* (The Trading Nobility).[40] Drawing on the arguments of the economist Jean-François Melon that trade had become more important to a nation's international power than warfare, Coyer proposed that nobles be allowed to engage in it without incurring the traditional penalty, loss of their noble status. (He tagged the law against noble commerce "a relic of the Gothic spirit.") France had been at peace for twenty years, Coyer pointed out, and many noblemen were not only impoverished but idle as well. Why should they not devote themselves to trade, that inexhaustible source of wealth both for themselves and for their nation? Besides, he reasoned, warfare had shifted from land to sea, and the nation needed cash for the new power struggles.[41] It was no coincidence that the publication of Coyer's piece coincided with the outbreak of the Seven Years' War.

Whether or not he intended to provoke it, Coyer's seemingly practical proposal touched off a blizzard of debate. His pamphlet was reprinted several times, as was the most famous response to it by the chevalier d'Arcq, and dozens of other writers joined the fray. The controversy was covered extensively in both national and international periodicals.[42] Most of the response to Coyer was negative, often stridently so. For many people in the 1750s, *noblesse commerçante* was as much of an oxymoron as *bourgeois gentilhomme*—for much the same reasons. What Coyer presented as the pragmatic jettisoning of an outdated law was, his antagonists responded, an attack on the nation's deepest social and political identity. Individual mobility was, and long had been, perfectly acceptable; not so the reshuffling or confusion of fundamental categories. A female contributor to the debate, Octavie Guichard, made this clear. If a particular nobleman wants to pursue riches like a commoner, let him do so, she wrote, "but once satisfied with this gain let him not imitate those amphibious creatures which lay claim to both elements." If a commoner does well enough in the law courts or on the battlefield to become noble, that is equally acceptable: "At least there will be only individuals displaced, whole classes will keep their integrity."[43]

The chevalier d'Arcq and many others following him held that Coyer's proposal was dangerous to the very essence of French government and society. Since the publication of Montesquieu's *Spirit of the Laws* in 1748, every educated person knew that different types of government depended on different principles, and that honor was the core value in an ancient and moderate monarchy such as France. Replace that honor, which can be won only on the battlefield, with mercantile pursuits, d'Arcq argued, and either the resulting wealth would corrupt ruler and subjects into "luxurious" despotism, or else the whole country would veer into the soulless materialism of a republic.[44] Behind the harshness of the response to Coyer lay the fear of two related threats at mid-century: the combined menace to the nation of commercialism and English power. As a partisan of d'Arcq put it explicitly: "Material interest governs [the English] nobility, while honor alone guides our own. Let us not seek to debase it by replacing the love of glory with greed for profit."[45]

But the essence of the French monarchy, beyond the honor defended and preserved by its martial nobility, was the monarch's relationship to society. Within the context of an ordered society, Coyer
was proposing, according to his opponents, to shift the designated
function of one group onto another. Inequality of ranks, d'Arcq intoned, is the very essence of a monarchical state, and that state will
sway and topple "the moment those ranks cease being distinct from
one another, when they mingle and merge, when they begin to absorb
each other."[46] Arguments along these lines also derived from
Montesquieu, in this instance from his doctrine of the centrality of intermediate ranks to a moderate monarchy. Within the context of this
debate, the metaphors used were either structural (remove one card
and the whole lot will topple) or connective. One of the more striking
illustrations of the latter came from the pen of Octavie Guichard, who
wrote that Coyer's suggestion would "remove all middling estate between the Artisan and the Gentleman." As a result, with the mediating
position of the merchant class gone, the slope up to the throne will be
too abrupt, and the steep incline between subjects and their king will
make the latter seem "a Colossus, to whom they will scarcely dare direct their eyes."[47] Tamper with the nobility, she warned, and the relationship of all subjects to their sovereign will be jeopardized.

The assumption behind the whole debate was that it was the nobility
who defined the identity of the French nation. From our own vantage
point, it is remarkable that nobody conspicuously argued for a different answer to the quandary: that is, let the nobility get on with their
heroics or their idleness, and let the state promote the social and political standing of the merchant class. Writing about the latter, d'Arcq
could barely manage a few haughtily patronizing remarks: "Let us favor among the third estate all those who attain distinction through
commerce. Let there be rewards for them, even honors, as long as
those honors are not the same as those granted to noblemen . . . I am
far from eager to plunge tradesmen into an obscurity from which they
deserve to escape."[48] If the proposal to let a few noblemen engage in
trade aroused such passionate opposition, one can imagine how unthinkable was the notion of putting merchants anywhere near the
helm of the nation.

The Coyer-d'Arcq debate should not, however, be reduced to an archetypal collision between a progressive commoner and a reactionary

nobleman. The abbé drew fire not because he was suggesting that the nobility needed to question some of the traditional justifications for its existence, but because of the specific nature of his proposals. The nobility's *raison d'être* was (ideally, of course), the performance of transcendent, selfless functions: they were raised and trained to risk their lives on the battlefield to uphold the honor of their family and their king. Coyer's proposal was shocking because, behind the arguments about commerce being the new form of warfare, he seemed to be telling the nobility to exchange their spiritual function as guardians of the nation's honor for the self-serving pursuit of material gain. The argument that commerce was a public service held little sway for people who thought that nobles were being asked to sell their souls to Mammon. But that does not amount to saying that eighteenth-century noblemen were resistant to any attempt to redefine the function of their class.

The eighteenth-century French nobility was by no means a uniformly reactionary and traditionalist body. If anything, nobles were the most conspicuously progressive group in the nation. Noblemen, for instance, were at the forefront of the struggle against the perceived abuses of absolutism. It was a magistrate of impeccably aristocratic lineage, the baron de Montesquieu, who wrote the script for the decades-long resistance, based in the courts of high justice, against royal and ministerial despotism. Many of the most radical among the philosophes (d'Alembert, d'Holbach, Helvétius, de Sade) were blue bloods, and the Enlightenment as a whole, from the *Encyclopédie* to the salons to the provincial academies, was subsidized and patronized far more by the nobility than by any other group. Aristocrats, finally, were conspicuous ideologues and leaders of the early Revolution, many defecting from the ranks of their order to join the rebellion of the Third Estate.[49] It is not surprising, therefore, to find that noblemen themselves were involved throughout much of the century in redefining the bases of their collective existence. In his classic revisionist study of the eighteenth-century French nobility, Guy Chaussinand-Nogaret shows that noblemen widened the list of qualities upon which their claim to leadership rested. To the traditional *honneur* and *valeur,* the qualities of courage and moral distinction traditionally separating them from their inferiors, nobles after the 1760s began adding qualities such as *mérite* and *capacité,* which ostensibly pertained to individual achievement rather than superior bloodlines.[50]

From there Chaussinand-Nogaret jumps rather quickly to the conclusion that this expansion of the nobility's ideals should be seen as their absorption of bourgeois individualistic and meritocratic values. But why should respect for individual talent be considered especially bourgeois? And is there necessarily a contradiction between the importance of lineage and the value of personal achievement? These are the questions posed in an important recent book by Jay Smith on the culture of royal service in the seventeenth and eighteenth centuries.[51] Smith takes on the hackneyed opposition between merit and birth, arguing that ideals of merit and meritocracy were not inventions of the Enlightenment but valued components of a traditional culture of aristocratic service to the king. Long before the eighteenth century, the French kings had sought their highest administrators among the members of old and prominent families, but also selected those who stood out for their personal talents. Lineage ensured both loyalty to the king and the need to uphold a noble family's reputation for courageous and faithful service to the sovereign.

As for merit, it was established, Smith argues, through a personal relationship with the king. The verb *mériter* in French means to deserve or earn something, but is and was also used with the preposition *de* (*mériter de*) in the sense of having merit in the eyes of a person or group. The king's gaze, and in particular the gaze of Louis XIV, was of central importance to the construction of what Smith calls "the culture of merit." By keeping a close watch on those who worked for him, Louis "hyperpersonalized the established culture of service," creating a desire to compete and excel in the king's eyes.[52] With the extension of the royal bureaucracy in the eighteenth century, the transitory nature of the individual king's gaze gave way to a more permanent, less personal authority, that of the state: the king's presence was now implicit rather than actual.[53]

The competitive and meritocratic culture of high civil service prominent in France even today was therefore not constructed against the monarchy and aristocracy, but by them and in their midst. The idea of a "career open to talents" was attractive to nobles long before it came to be thought of as quintessentially bourgeois. The central social ideal in France of skilled and dedicated state service, an ideal which bridges and transcends regimes (monarchy, republic, empire), carried related notions of honor and selflessness. It was this ideal, this notion of honor, that d'Arcq and his allies were promoting, rather than some benighted cult of ancestors and privilege. And it is the enduring power of this ideal which explains the resistance, in the Coyer debate, to the nation's elite engaging in dishonorable, self-serving mercantile pursuits. Competition was admirable when directed to the administration or the battlefield, but despicable in the pursuit of material self-interest.

Eighteenth-century aristocrats were eager to reassert the honor and utility of their estate, because the existence of a titled and privileged elite certainly did come under fire in the eighteenth century. Literary and philosophical denunciations of nobles were a mainstay of the Enlightenment, of course, from the pointed satires of Montesquieu and Voltaire, to Rousseau's wholesale condemnation of the corruption of high society, to Figaro's bitter remark to his master, in the century's most successful play: "What did you do to deserve such advantages? Gave yourself the trouble of being born, nothing more."[54] *The Marriage of Figaro,* with its shocking plot about the lord's right to deflower a servant's bride, is only the best-known of a whole genre of writing which, from the 1760s to the 1780s, invented and sensationalized something called feudalism. The later decades of the eighteenth century witnessed an explosion of writings on the subject of real or imaginary seigniorial rights. Feudal rights were the object of loud disputes between rural communities and seigneurs, with jurists on either side burrowing into the archives to establish claims and counterclaims.[55] Physiocrats and other economists wrote of feudal dues as a major obstacle to agrarian improvement.[56] Most strikingly, a generation of humanitarian writers, Voltaire in their lead, denounced feudal abuses, many of them perfectly imaginary. Among the more ghoulish inventions were allegations about the origins of the term *mainmorte,* the right which limited a tenant's free disposal of his goods after death: writers claimed that in the past lords had demanded to see the severed hand *(main morte)* of their deceased serfs. The most famous legend, the one so successfully put to use by Beaumarchais, was the *droit du seigneur* or *prélibation,* the lord's "first drink" of his tenant's bride. Although it is not clear that any such right ever existed at all, the *Encyclopédie* took it seriously enough to devote an article to it, and Voltaire gleefully asserted that even clerical seigneurs had made full use of this privilege.[57]

The really substantive controversies around the nobility, those which defined most powerfully the meaning of feudalism, took place in the area of historical writing. By the eighteenth century no educated person believed that the three orders were eternal or God-given, and from the early decades of the century historians quarreled bitterly over the origins of the realm's competing powers. Centrally at stake in these debates, at least initially, were the respective powers of nobility and monarchy: which of these came first, which was invested with most power, what were the relations of each to the French nation?

The opening salvo in this early historians' war was fired in 1727 by the count of Boulainvilliers in his *Lettres historiques sur les parlemens,* a manifesto of noble supremacy. In Boulainvilliers's version of the traditional Germanist thesis, the French nobility descended from the Frankish (Germanic) tribes who had invaded France and subdued the Gauls in the fifth century.[58] That claim was less original and tendentious than Boulainvilliers's further argument that Clovis, founder of the Merovingian dynasty, was nothing but a military commander elected by his Frankish fellow officers, a first among equals rather than a divinely ordained being. Writing at a time of aristocratic unrest during the minority of Louis XV, Boulainvilliers brazenly set forth the claim that the nobility had historical—and therefore political—precedence over the monarchy. Nor did he shy away from the aspects of his narrative that would later prove most damaging to the nobility: that the French aristocracy were racially distinct from the common man, and that they owed their preeminence to the brutal fact of conquest. "Certainly," he wrote, "all men are equal in common law. It was violence that introduced the difference between *Freedom* and *Slavery, Nobles* and *Commoners;* but though they might be heinous in origin, [these distinctions] are in such common use throughout the world that they have acquired the authority of a law of nature" [italics in original].[59]

It did not take long for the monarchy to fire back at Boulainvilliers, through the pen of the abbé Dubos, who laid out his Romanist thesis in his 1734 *Histoire critique de l'établissement de la monarchie françoise dans les Gaules.* Dubos did not deny the Frankish origins of the nobility, but for him they were not victorious conquerors but a group which governed Gaul in alliance with, and subordination to, the Roman Empire. Clovis was not an elected military commander but an administrator named by Rome and allowed, with the backing of the Roman Empire, to pass his power on to his descendants. Yes, aristocratic power was indeed born of violence, Dubos argued, but their conquest took place later and was internal to the kingdom. Once the loyal servants of the crown, dukes and counts overstepped their mandate starting in the tenth century and began, at the expense of both prince and people, to assert dominion over lands that originally were only theirs to administer. Far from giving birth to kingship from within their midst, the aristocracy established its claims in rebellion against an already well established monarchy.

Antiaristocratic writings, political as well as historical, often were penned by authors who were supporters of the monarchy. The most important French historian of the second half of the eighteenth century, abbé Gabriel Bonnot de Mably, began his writing career in the 1740s as a firm monarchist before evolving into the most influential exponent, along with Rousseau, of classical republicanism.[60] In his historical works and especially his highly influential *Observations sur l'histoire de France* first published in 1765, Mably offered his contemporaries a narrative critical of both monarchy *and* aristocracy, a text whose power made it a favorite among liberals and radicals under the Revolution and well into the nineteenth century. In the beginning, Mably argued, there was no aristocracy and no monarchy either. The Franks were a brutal and proud warrior society, with leaders but no kings. They never enslaved the Gauls, who remained free men. The nation in these earliest centuries was governed by princes like Clovis, who were merely "first magistrates" presiding over a quasi-democracy of warriors. As this rough democracy of roving bands settled down and acquired riches, the most unscrupulous and greedy among them grabbed land and property for themselves, "public good was sacrificed to private interest," and the French aristocracy was born.[61]

The French kings bore much of the responsibility for this development, for it was they who gave away tracts of land as fiefdoms to ensure the loyalty of their most predatory followers. While originally the only distinctions in this society were awarded on the basis of personal merit, soon the grandees with money and land insisted on making their advantages hereditary, thus creating a separate caste: "As soon as there appeared within the nation citizens in possession of particular privileges, which they held only by virtue of their birth, these men came to despise those who were no longer their equals and to form a corporate body *whose interests were distinct from both those of the Prince and those of the*

*People"* [italics mine].[62] With only the brief exception of the reign of Charlemagne, the country degenerated under the first Capetian kings (10th–11th centuries) into "feudal anarchy," the unstable rule of feudal grandees in a vacuum of public power.

To later generations, and especially in the 1820s, Mably was to become important as the prophet of bourgeois history, since he located the seeds of redemption in the free towns founded in the eleventh and twelfth centuries by the French kings as counterweights to the overmighty feudal lords. But what struck contemporaries most in the writings of Mably, and of the later historians he inspired like Linguet and Le Trosne, was his vivid portrayal of the evils of aristocratic government, the ways in which feudal anarchy, the rule of greed and self-interest, tore the nation apart.[63]

From all of these historical narratives emerged an image of the nobility as racially distinct, violent, and self-interested. For Boulainvilliers, an apologist for the nobility, racial difference was a given (Franks over Gauls), whereas for Mably the nobility created its own obsession with bloodlines, but in the end the result was the same: the formation of a group that was biologically different and therefore essentially foreign—the "impure blood" which in *La Marseillaise* waters the furrows of the French soil. In the royalist and republican versions of French history, the defining characteristic of this group was self-interest, material greed, and the effect of its presence in the national landscape was profoundly disjunctive. The feudal aristocracy created anarchy, which in the eighteenth-century lexicon was the opposite of freedom.

The image of nobility had been turned inside out by the eve of the Revolution. The traditional rationale for nobility had been the unselfish devotion to king and nation, but the creation of a lore of feudalism in various genres, especially in historical writing, cast the noble as something close to a bourgeois type: a profoundly self-interested creature, heedless and destructive of the broader interests of the national community.[64] If privilege made the Old Regime bourgeois seem like a lesser nobleman, the combination of wealth and self-interest could make the nobleman look like an anomalously powerful bourgeois. Foreign and self-serving, the nobleman would emerge as the Revolution's defining enemy, while his bourgeois double waited in the wings to become the scapegoat of later regimes. If in the second half of the eighteenth century the nobleman was perceived as a problem, the bourgeois could hardly appear to be the answer.

## THE GOOD EARTH

By the later eighteenth century, the idiom of orders and estates was proving unsatisfactory to describe real social experience. Many among the nobility, under attack for its traditional prerogatives, were casting about for new or updated definitions of their social role. Did the Enlightenment devise no coherent new language for talking about the social order, identify no social group as the carrier of the nation's hopes? In fact an influential segment of the intellectual elite of pre-revolutionary France, the group known as the Physiocrats (or more commonly in their day, as the Economists) did provide a new way of understanding society. But although these early proponents of political economy believed in the free circulation of goods (one of their number coined the phrase *laissez faire),* they were no more inclined than any other contemporaries to identify a modern middle class or assign to it a leading social role.[65]

The Physiocrats believed in the centrality of agriculture to the social order, positing that of all economic pursuits only the cultivation of land produced a net surplus. Their analytical descriptions of society reflected this postulate. The first instance of what was to become a standard formula for describing society appeared in 1766 in the writings of one of the movement's founders, the doctor and economist François Quesnay. The nation, wrote Quesnay, could be "reduced" to three "classes of citizens": the "productive class" which renews the nation's wealth annually through the cultivation of the soil; the "class of proprietors," including the sovereign and the clergy, which owns the land; and the "sterile class" made up of everyone else, those who provide services or work other than agrarian.[66] Quesnay's classification was rapidly adopted by his fellow-travelers in the movement, and while there might have been some disagreement over specific labels, Baudeau, Mirabeau, Dupont de Nemours, Mercier de la Rivière, Le Trosne, and Turgot all fell in line behind the canonical triad. The land-working class was sometimes called "productive," sometimes "cultivating," sometimes "class of land workers" *(laboureurs);* the land-owning class was called "proprietary," or "available" *(disponible),* or even

"noble"; the last class was "sterile," "industrious," "mercenary," "manufacturing," or "class of artisans and salaried workers." Although they
were always cited in the order above, the land-owning class was called
"first," the land-working class "second," and the final class "third" or
"last."[67] This contradiction acknowledged the point that a group's usefulness to society did not necessarily coincide with its social status.

The physiocratic scheme is remarkable both for its fidelity to tradition and for its conceptual novelty. Most obvious is the Physiocrats'
dogged attachment to the triune model, as if the division of society in
anything but three would be heretical. The emphasis on land and
landed classes also seems traditional, but it would be more accurate to
say that it was tradition stood on its head: the last group in the ancient
tripartite division, the *laboratores,* now came first. More generally, the
physiocratic model is an inversion, in some ways a mirror image, of the
traditional estates: instead of two spiritual categories followed by a vast,
mostly land-working one, Quesnay and his followers had two groups attached to the land followed by a catch-all "unproductive" category.
Their reversal provides one more illustration of the broader intellectual process typical of the early Enlightenment, the replacement of
Spirit by Nature as a universal organizing category.[68] Where the Physiocrats were most modern, however, was in their approach to social
groups as "classes"—a term which, as mentioned above, suggested human classificatory activity. Theirs was a classification based not on the
tangible and observable, but on a scientific abstraction, a purely conceptual operation.[69] It would be a short step from defining classes according to their production of wealth to defining them in terms of
their relationship to the means of production.

Obviously, though, the modern-sounding analyses of the Physiocrats
did no more than traditional schemes to identify a middling group or
to promote respect for commercial or financial endeavors. If anything,
the urban middle classes came off worse in the physiocratic scheme,
lumped among the "sterile" population alongside lackeys and latrine
cleaners. It is true that the label "sterile" provoked controversy among
the Physiocrats themselves. Quesnay was at pains to explain that his
three designations applied not to persons but to expenditures, establishing purely analytical distinctions between those who spend their
labor productively and those whose work produces no measurable surplus. He could not, however, arrest the inevitable metonymical slip-

page from work to worker; this led his friend Turgot to protest that it was a scandal to insult all the *honnêtes gens* involved in industry and commerce by calling them, at best, useless.[70] But even when they were upgraded from "sterile" to "industrious" or "manufacturing," it was clear that the commercial and industrial groups were as subordinate in this new worldview as the Third Estate had been in the older scheme.

Scientific analyses are never value-free or judgment-free, and the equation between "agrarian" and "productive" had deep cultural and emotional resonances in the mid-eighteenth century. Rhapsodizing about agrarian pursuits sounds anything but analytical in, to take but one example, the marquis de Mirabeau's early and influential *L'Ami des hommes* (1756). Agriculture, wrote the marquis, cannot be compared to any other art since it is "divine in institution; it is as crucial to our existence as is breathing . . . agriculture is in a word the universal art, the art of innocence and virtue, the art of all men and all ranks."[71] It would be difficult to say whether the Physiocrats were echoing, in their economic views, the cultural assumptions of their contemporaries, or whether they played a major role in defining certain elements of the social imaginary—it would be safe to guess that both were true.

No doubt the Physiocrats gave a scientific framework and therefore greater legitimacy to what was already the cultural obsession of their age where social issues were concerned: the ubiquitous fixation on "fertility" linked to both population and agriculture. From the second third of the eighteenth century, the French were convinced that their country was threatened with both economic anemia and depopulation, and a wide range of writers and artists sought answers and reassurance in images of bountiful agriculture, happy village life, and healthy infants gorging on milk from their mothers' breasts. Conversely, danger crystallized around those who were celibate or practiced unproductive sex—monks and nuns, domestic servants, libertine aristocrats—hence the extreme stigma of the adjective "sterile" applied to merchants and artisans. Rousseau and Beaumarchais were but the most famous devotees of the maternal breast, and long before Marie-Antoinette played milkmaid in the rococo village she built for herself and her friends at Trianon, the French upper classes were consuming idealized images and experiences of what they thought of as country life. The Physiocrats harnessed powerful themes from their culture to an economic analysis which glorified landowners and peasants while disparaging merchants and artisans—the very groups that might form the core of a middle class.

Cultural analysis suggests why the question of the bourgeoisie in pre-revolutionary France has always been so vexed and inconclusive. Although a large number of people we would call middle class lived and prospered in this society, none of the dominant ways of talking about society could easily identify anything like a broad middle class or argue for the merits of such a group. The oldest idioms either bypassed the middle class completely (the Three Estates) or broke it up into so many different groups that it dissolved in the very process of being described. The specific category known as *bourgeoisie* was a compound of different meanings, all of them problematic: privilege, social ambiguity, cultural deficiency.

The distinctive feature of prerevolutionary writings about society was their conflicting commitment to ideals of both nobility and equality, and their insistent need to define society as a form of moral community. The abbé Coyer, for instance, never argued for the utilitarian merits of commercial self-interest, far from it: he defined commerce as a patriotic and selfless pursuit, and argued that if nobles engaged in trade, they would merge more easily into the productive, hence *virtuous*, mainstream of the nation. All parties in the Coyer dispute argued for the need to redefine the relationship between society and the polity, and all agreed that society should rest on some combination of virtue, citizenship, and honor—they merely disagreed on how best to achieve these ideals.[72] Many writers still looked to the nobility to carry the nation's honor onto the battlefield, while prominent economists believed that France's future depended on its peasantry and landed gentry. Nobody made a case for the intrinsic value of commercial activity: at best it was defended as a means to higher ends, such as the glory of the state or the pursuit of honor in war.

From the cacophony of voices diagnosing social ills emerged a need to find for society a higher, quasi-sacred meaning. In traditional absolutist theory it was royal will that balanced the interests of different members of the body politic so that, as Keith Baker has put it, "Frenchmen related to one another indirectly, as subjects of the crown."[73] The highest forms of social status were traditionally located in groups which directly served either the deity (clergy) or the state (nobility). The Physiocrats simply inverted traditional orderings, rhapsodizing about the spiritual, regenerative virtues of those who worked the land. In all of this the urban middling groups of professionals, merchants, and artisans found few conspicuous champions and no major ideologies touting their merits. Ironically, this was the case at a time when France was experiencing a remarkable surge of commercial wealth, urban growth, and material comfort.

# Commerce, Luxury, and Family Love

## 2

The anonymous chronicler of Montpellier in 1768 was proud of his ancient and busy town, but he kept harping on two related anxieties. One was that there was too much mixing and reshuffling of categories at different levels of society. He was resigned to the merging of nobles and bourgeois; because of the bourgeoisie's wealth and luxurious expenditures, it was, he wrote, "a sort of necessity."[1] But lower down there was confusion too, and "the meanest of artisans now ranks with the most elevated of artists."[2] Worse still, these lowly folks were sending their sons to the Jesuit schools, where the lads along with literacy picked up contempt for their fathers' trades, and where their bad example contaminated the *fils de famille*.[3] Worst of all were domestic servants, especially the valets and chambermaids who had access to their masters' cast-offs and could impersonate their betters. Wearing embroidered and brocaded clothes, sporting swords, these social mutants passed as gentlefolk in the town's public walks. "This is revolting," spat the author; their sort should be forced to wear a visible mark of their servile status. The only people who remained blessedly fixed in place, he concluded, were the land-working peasants.[4]

The social order, which had once been a bedrock, now seemed more like an expanse of shifting sand on which people struggled, sank, or tumbled into each other. The cause of this alarming development, the author's second major concern, was the desire for what eighteenth-century writers called "luxury." Ambition and social confusion ran rampant in the provincial city, he said, because people had access to all manner of beautiful things unknown to their parents and grandparents. Luxury was most visible in the display of clothing. Upper-class women went in different clothes each season, mostly of silk, with lace mantillas and white damask slippers. The men wore velvet and silk, with gold or silver waistcoats. Their baubles and accessories were something to behold: "plumes, earrings, rings, glittering buckles, gold watches on clasps with dangling charms, gold snuff-boxes and gold-encased perfume bottles, muffs and fans."[5] All manner of people changed their cuffs and linen every day now, and even working girls wore white silk stockings. The same riot of elegant novelty had appeared in domestic furnishings, which were "luxurious and crammed into the houses."[6] With the new fashion for colonial delicacies, the rich flaunted precious breakfast sets straight out of a Boucher painting, little matching chocolate and coffee pots, water jugs, spoons, and the like, all of solid silver. Even modest households had new assorted sets of dishes down to olive-spoons, oil caddies, salt-shakers, and candlesticks, and "a great many simple artisans own silver plate."[7]

On the subject of luxury the author of this text had very mixed feelings, and indeed sometimes appeared to be engaged in a running debate with himself. Montpellier had been a modest but thriving industrial and commercial center since the Middle Ages, producing cotton and wool fabric and miscellaneous products ranging from verdigris to playing cards.[8] Who could object to the kind of industry which, the writer admitted, gave work to a multitude of people of all ages and both sexes? But what if the production of superfluous objects lured people away from the soil, and left it untended? What harm, others might ask, if no work on the land was available in some seasons or years? In the end, though, his verdict on the luxury bred of manufacturing was negative; just look, he said, at its effects on morals. Young seamstresses earned four or five *sous* a day, but they spent ten on those silk stockings, on snuff and coffee and other delicacies. It did not take much imagination to figure out where the extra money came from.[9] In the end, for all of its benefits, luxury was a threat to both morality and the social order.

Here we have, then, a proud citizen of a commercial city, an author who was probably an upper-middle-class bourgeois, denouncing as luxury the pursuits that we take to be typically bourgeois—industry, commerce, consumption. His attitude was representative of the majority of writers who addressed social concerns at the time. What this writer described in Montpellier was in fact happening in French towns of all sizes in the middle decades of the eighteenth century: increasing wealth, more people, more commerce, and most visibly, big changes in people's access to consumer goods. The period from the 1720s to the eve of the Revolution was indeed one of definite economic expansion, especially in the urban and commercial centers of the realm, and this was made most dramatically manifest in new access to and attitudes toward housing, clothing, and furnishings.

The new evidence emerging about wealth and material culture in this society might suggest that the old Marxian argument about an eighteenth-century rise of the bourgeoisie is valid after all. The problem with this view, however, is that contemporaries perceived no such rise. They duly noted the growth of commerce and consumerism, but what they called luxury was not associated with any discrete social group. Most commonly it was viewed as a disease affecting all of society and whose main symptom was the alarming confusion of social conditions. And the remedies they advocated for growing materialism and self-interest were aimed not at a single group but at the whole social fabric. The sentimental cult of family and morality which flourished so conspicuously in the later decades of the eighteenth century had little to do with middle-class or bourgeois morality: it was a universal response to the disruption of an entire social world.

## WEALTH, CIRCULATION, AND THE NEW WORLD OF OBJECTS

The canonical rise-of-the-bourgeoisie interpretation of the eighteenth century was based on the view that some sectors of the economy were thriving—most visibly the Atlantic trade—and creating the kinds of fortunes that gave the bourgeoisie the wherewithal for its bid for political power in 1789.[10] In the 1960s and 1970s, the revisionist school forcefully countered that such sectors were marginal to an economy which remained for the most part traditional and a culture that was generally resistant to sustained capitalist undertaking. So strong were aristocratic social ideals, these historians argued, that the profits from entrepreneurial venture, whether in business or finance, were more likely to be spent on buying a chateau and the title to go with it, or keeping an expensive mistress, than ploughed back into one's capital assets.[11] Depending where one looks—at the huge, sluggish agrarian sector, or at the dynamism of commercial cities like Bordeaux or Lyon—the glass can be described as either half full or half empty. Since the late 1970s, however, economic historians have formulated a synthesis of both views. The dominant paradigm now holds that in the eighteenth century, from 1715–1720 right into the 1790s, the French economy did experience remarkable and sustained growth, albeit in the absence of classic (read: English) patterns of industrialization.[12] It is now well established that France's foreign commerce, spearheaded by the Atlantic trade, quintupled in the eighteenth century, and that its share of European, if not American, markets grew faster than England's. Economists have calculated that France saw a sevenfold increase in its industrial output over the course of the century, so that by the eve of the Revolution its per capita output was on par with England's. Whether France experienced an agricultural revolution in this period is still subject to debate, but there is no question that substantial enough improvement took place to support a population increase of over 25 percent.[13]

French economic growth in the Age of Enlightenment occurred, however, in the absence of many of the traditional markers of industrialization—industrial concentration, the existence of a large urban workforce, the development of heavy industry. France industrialized in a different way from England, producing mainly light consumer goods and with a workforce mostly scattered in small workshops and rural cottages—this model is now known as "protoindustrialization."[14] But France's pattern of industrialization was no less successful than England's, and arguably less traumatic for the workers who lived through the process than for their counterparts across the Channel. As William H. Sewell has argued: "The French pattern of economic growth, which combined substantial industrialization with the continued expansion of handicrafts and of peasant agriculture, should therefore not be seen as a failed effort to imitate British achievements, but as an entirely appropriate response to the French situation."[15]

Although France did not go through the drastic changes that accompanied the beginnings of British industrialization, there is no question that significant social shifts accompanied the expansive economy of the eighteenth century. In the most general terms, a nation of

rather sedentary country dwellers became, in the decades before
1789, significantly more urban, more mobile, and more commercially
oriented. The best recent estimates suggest that the number of French
men and women living in towns of over 2,000 inhabitants grew from
about four million in the first quarter of the century to five to six million around 1790—a growth of 15 to 20 percent. This increase affected
different areas differently, of course, with the larger urban centers
expanding most dramatically. While the older market towns of northern France—Rouen, Angers, Chartres—grew little, for instance, the
population of manufacturing towns like Saint-Étienne, Lyon, and
Strasbourg swelled considerably, as did most strikingly that of the
realm's northern and western port cities—Dunkirk, Le Havre, Nantes,
and Bordeaux. Paris grew more than any other city, by over a third,
from under half a million people in 1700 to possibly 700,000 in 1789.[16]
The growth of cities was the result mostly of immigration, as the century's dramatic population increase pushed peasants off the land and
into the nearest towns to work in manufacturing, construction, or domestic service.[17] While members of this immigrant underclass would
hardly be the ones to revel in luxury, they certainly helped to produce
it, and their presence was undoubtedly one of the reasons so many
writers felt that the social landscape around them was frighteningly
unfamiliar.

Not only were more people living in cities in the eighteenth century,
but the way they were living also changed gradually but profoundly in
the period between 1720 and the Revolution. In the last twenty years,
historians working on after-death inventories of town dwellers have
been able to reconstitute in vivid detail the material environment of
the broad middling segment of the population who left such documents at death—a group ranging from better-off workers to lesser nobles, but in which the following categories are most conspicuous: merchants, traditional bourgeois, master-artisans, and journeymen.[18] All of
these studies conclude that it was in the last two thirds of the eighteenth century when the living conditions and material possessions of
town dwellers—Parisians especially—changed most dramatically.

For middling categories of the population in particular, the family's
most immediate environment began to evolve decisively as the result
of a surge in building. New lodgings were built in France's expanding
towns, but older dwellings were also remodeled and enlarged in ways

that changed living conditions at home.[19] Prior to the eighteenth century, the typical dwelling for all but the very rich was made up of two to four rooms, each of which served several purposes: typically a modest residence included a kitchen plus one or two rooms ambiguously designated *chambre* or *salle*. The kitchen was for cooking, eating, sometimes entertaining, and one or more people often slept there as well. A 1660 dictionary defined the *chambre* as "The place where one sleeps and receives company." The *salle* was more specifically used for social purposes, and was typical of more affluent households.[20] Most of the time these rooms were located on at least two floors: a ground floor kitchen and maybe a *salle*, a couple of other rooms overhead. If the main rooms were public and unspecialized, these premodern dwellings also differed from ours because they often included tiny private closet-like rooms and many nonresidential "dependencies": shops, workshops, cellars, stables, outhouses, and attics.[21]

Sometime after 1730, and especially after mid-century, these traditional forms of housing began to evolve into structures that would be more familiar to us. One-story apartments became more common after the 1730s, their numbers increasing steadily until century's end. At a time when routine household tasks were back-breakingly arduous, living on a single level was considered a luxury, and to this day in French real estate parlance the expression *de plain-pied*—on a level—connotes status and comfort. In the newer apartments rooms tended to be more specialized, and wealthier households now boasted a *salle à manger* (dining room) and a room entirely devoted to socializing, a *salon* or *salle de compagnie*.[22] A good instance of the new specialization of rooms would be the property left by the widow of Pierre Foubert, a surgeon, in 1779 in Paris: its six rooms *de plain pied* were a salon, dining room, bedroom, kitchen, cook's room, and chambermaid's room.[23]

More striking even than the structural changes in housing and the functions of rooms were modifications in the way dwellings were equipped and decorated, and the advent of new norms of comfort and beauty. New technologies such as better heating systems were responsible for some of the transformations affecting living space. In older dwellings the heart of the space was the towering fireplace around which people gathered. Older hearths were vast affairs with high mantles and sloping hoods, so inefficient that on cold days people actually sat inside them to keep warm. By the eighteenth century fireplaces

were less conspicuous and more decorative—lower mantels, gracefully
curved flues—as well as more efficient, and stoves were more commonly used to heat some rooms in the house.[24]

At the same time, the furnishing and decoration of even modest
interiors went through enormous changes after 1730. In the seventeenth century the towering items in most homes were the family's
one or more massive, often lavishly appointed beds—great four-poster
affairs whose value often amounted to half of a family's fortune, and
whose drapes, galons, fringes, and slipcovers were carefully detailed in
after-death inventories.[25] (The main bed was to many families what a
car is today, a symbolically charged compound of necessity, luxury, and
claims to status.) With few such exceptions, however, traditional furniture was multipurpose, nondescript, and by later standards at least
awkward and uncomfortable to use. Richer people had chairs and
armchairs, of course, but rarely so many that guests and family members did not have to perch on folding stools. Ubiquitous in the seven-
teenth-century home was the *coffre*, the low storage chest that could
double as a small table. It was the eighteenth century that saw the displacement of the *coffre* by the chest of drawers, which allowed for
better storage without all the bending and stooping. By the end of the
century almost half of all workers had chests of drawers, and richer
folks owned elaborate variations on the object such as secretaries and
dressing tables. Finally, the reigns of Louis XV and Louis XVI saw the
"triumph of the armchair" and the spread of the sofa into homes beyond those of a small elite.[26]

These changes all worked toward affording city dwellers more ease,
comfort, and pleasure in their homes by changing the gestures of
everyday life and hence the physical experience of domesticity: less
trudging up and down stairs, less crouching and bending over trunks;
better light and heating, more comfortable seating, more usable
space. (It all makes one wonder how much the rise of the literary salon
and of the "public sphere of rational discourse" had to do with the possibility of sitting for a few hours without developing a backache.) But
the most visible change in the way city people lived was a revolution in
interior decoration and furnishing. In barely a couple of generations,
urban interiors traded the austere and dark-hued look of a Georges de
la Tour or a Chardin for the bright colors and airy pastels of the rococo. In the seventeenth century, the walls of houses and apartments

were usually covered in order to keep out the cold and humidity. Only the rich could afford tapestries, and for everyone else the typical wall-hanging was a cheerless dark green Bergamot cloth or a drab gray serge. The eighteenth century saw an explosion of color and form, with bright greens, reds and blues in an overall lightening of the palette, and patterned paper or fabric such as the archetypal Toile de Jouy even on the walls of people of modest standing.[27]

Finally, the look and experience of domestic life were transformed by the unprecedented availability of more and fancier goods for the home. Mirrors, clocks, prints and paintings, vases, statuettes, all once a mark of significant wealth, now became ubiquitous, often adorning the newly lowered mantelpiece.[28] In the new world of cheap and plentiful objects, cooking and eating became more elegant, as matching sets of earthenware dishes replaced the traditional pewter. Though only the wealthy used china dishes and silver cutlery (our man from Montpellier notwithstanding), their social subordinates had tin forks and spoons, and dining sets that included such refinements as terrines, serving platters, salad bowls, and salt-cellars.[29] Beyond the crucial kitchen- and tableware, households by the mid-eighteenth century possessed a whole range of new consumer objects aimed at convenience or pleasure: umbrellas, fans, snuffboxes, watches, books, cards, and games.[30]

The transformation of living spaces to provide more comfort and pleasure must have been central to what contemporaries denounced as the scourge of luxury. But despite their importance, such changes were not always visible and therefore drew less commentary than the more obvious realm of change, that of clothing. Clothing was the most important way of advertising the status and power of different social groups on such occasions as ceremonial processions, when the city offered its citizens a spectacle of the social order embodied. In a culture where power was conveyed visually, as it was in court in the ceremonies surrounding the monarchs, such occasions were more than just festive displays; they ordered the urban world, and costume was a central part of the process.

Even on a daily basis, clothes served to identify the wearer's status quite precisely. François Besnard, writing in the nineteenth century of his childhood in mid-eighteenth century provincial Anjou, reveals how specific was the semiology of clothing. *"Fontanges,* or brightly colored ribbons placed on head-dresses, and ruffles along the hem of gowns were adornments exclusively reserved for noble women or girls or to those who were clearly above other bourgeois families through the financial or professional distinction of their husbands." The wives of notaries, surgeons, and merchants, he continued, "allowed themselves only white ribbons," while the spouses of workers, peasants, and servants wore dark hooded coats. There was a hierarchy of footwear too, from the very high heels of aristocratic ladies, to the clogs and slippers of working women, and a similar system of signs governed men's clothing.[31]

As Besnard's memoir shows, clothing in the Old Regime starkly divided the sartorial world. For the rich and the prominent, bright colors and flashy ornaments advertised the wearer's place in the social order. For the poor, dressed in coarse, dark items or drab second-hand garb, clothes were mostly utilitarian, a protection against dirt and bad weather.[32] (Male domestics, who were not rich but wore elaborately decorated liveries, were a constant source of anxiety.)[33] All of this began to change in the decades after 1730, when the spectacular growth of the Atlantic trade with its shipments of cotton and dyes and the development of the domestic textile industry brought into the market new supplies of varied and plentiful clothing. Prior to the eighteenth century, commerce in clothing was limited, since the rich had their clothes made to measure, and the poor sewed their own or bought cast-offs from the ragpickers (called *fripiers).* In the eighteenth century, clothing became much more commercialized, in the hands especially of female retailers such as *marchandes de mode, mercières,* and *dentellières.*[34]

In the middle decades of the eighteenth century, the wardrobes of people in most social categories grew spectacularly in both size and worth. The value of wardrobes in the professional middle classes in Paris rose by over 300 percent, that of domestics by over 400 percent. This change affected even, or perhaps especially, the working poor, among whom the value of clothing doubled for men and increased sixfold for women. As Daniel Roche notes, working-class families had entered "the cycle of consumption."[35] Not only did the poor have more clothes than before, they also dressed in fashions closer to those of their superiors. The older costume of working women, for instance, was a collection of separate pieces: a skirt, several petticoats, bodice, apron, and mantle. The one-piece gown or dress *(robe)* was a rich woman's costume, the stuff of tales in which fairy godmothers gave kitchen maids gowns of gold or pink satin. By the end of the eighteenth century, however, working class women frequently owned one-piece dresses: 53 percent of the plebeian women who left inventories in Paris owned at least one.[36] At the other end of the social scale, the popularity of simpler, Rousseau-inspired fashions among elite women probably increased the perception of social confusion, though it would be wrong to conclude that the upper classes went in for restraint in clothing. Abundance and ever-changing fashion were the norms for rich women, and the middle decades of the century saw an explosion of sartorial creation. Gowns came in an array of new shapes (*levites, polonaises,* Turkish-style confections) and a range of new colors, some of them obscure ("queen's hair," "king's eyes"), others alarmingly evocative ("Paris mud," "goose shit").[37]

At all levels of society, abundance of clothing and more rapidly changing styles became the norm in the eighteenth century, and the gap between male and female wardrobes increased dramatically. Clothing and fashion were redefined decisively as a female concern which played both to women's fickleness and to their innate sense of taste. Taste, in turn, spoke to national concerns, as (French) commentators praised a specifically French ability, shared by women across a wide social spectrum, to exercise discernment in their choice of fashion.[38] It would be a great exaggeration to conclude that by the late eighteenth century clothing no longer revealed a person's social standing. But with the increased commercialization of fashion and its growing volatility, and with the access poorer groups now enjoyed to more numerous and more stylish attire, the use of clothing to signal rank and status was no longer reliable. It is the panic brought on by this change in meaning that lies behind the innumerable jeremiads against the lower classes for aping and upstaging their betters through their scandalous appropriation of upper-class dress.

Although the evidence we have about changes in clothing and housing comes mostly from Paris, there is plenty to suggest that commercialization and consumerism affected the provinces and even the countryside. Jean-Claude Perrot's classic study of Caen in Normandy, for instance, shows this provincial town transformed in the eighteenth century from a local textile center to a hub for national and international commerce, its population swelling after 1740 with an influx of rural immigrants.[39] Another historian, following the evolution over four centuries of the rural seigneury of Pont-Saint-Pierre, has documented the concentration of property, the monetarization of village economies, the expansion of rural markets, and the rise by the eighteenth century of what the author calls "rural capitalism."[40] And most recently, Colin Jones has highlighted the importance of local advertising in the provincial newspapers called *affiches*. The forty or so *affiches* (of towns like Rouen, Marseille, Toulouse, Auxerre, or of regions like Franche-Comté or Picardy) tendered information about local cultural and commercial events, but their staple offering, like that of free papers today, was advertising. The *affiches* advertised real estate as well every kind of consumer object, from mundane clothing and furniture to unexpected items such as horse manure to the unusual rarity such as pet monkeys. Anticipating France's modern obsession with health and pharmacology, they prominently hawked medical goods and services: public baths and private infirmaries, medical supplies such as anatomical dolls and glass eyes, endless and often dubious pills and elixirs, from *chocolat de santé* to *pilules raisonnables* for the deranged.[41] These local papers, Jones concludes, "open a window onto an increasingly materialistic, consumerist world inhabited by increasingly entrepreneurial and publicity-minded professional groupings too easily written off as traditionalist or deferential."[42]

Are we not back, then, to the rise of the bourgeoisie? Should we not read the evolution of housing, the new abundance of clothing and other commodities, the intense traffic in local goods and services, as symptoms of the advent of a middle class? Colin Jones has argued that it is indeed time to admit that alongside the rarefied intellectual public sphere of salons, coffeehouses, and masonic lodges, there was a commercial and consumerist public sphere presided over by the bourgeoisie, in which buyers transacted with each other in fraternal equality, and editors of the *affiches* encouraged "a commerce of friendship between citizens."[43] In more general terms, Jones believes that the accumulating evidence about the booming economy, population growth, commercialism, and consumerism all suggest that it is time to return, armed with new ammunition, to the classic paradigm of bourgeois ascendancy.[44]

The problem, once again, is that if a bourgeoisie was rising, it did not identify itself nor did others identify it. Jones himself cannot locate any explicit bourgeois ideology or consciousness, and has to resort on that score to reading such things into other forms of discourse: scrutinizing the language of professionals such as doctors, military officers, and lawyers, he identifies a new language of "civic professionalism." By the later eighteenth century, he argues, professionals were rejecting their traditional corporate outlook (intense identification with, for instance, the Order of Barristers) and resorting to a new language of devotion to the Nation, the Public; viewing themselves as citizens rather than just doctors or lawyers, they could more easily forge the bonds between occupations that would eventually lead to class formation during and after the Revolution.[45] But civic consciousness of the sort Jones describes is not class consciousness—it is universalistic, whereas class ideology means that class members identify themselves as a specific group; in the end Jones himself has to admit that what he purports to describe is, in his own terms, "a silent bourgeois revolution."[46] For all that it was rising, the bourgeoisie apparently remained the class that dare not speak its name.

The new evidence about commercialism and consumerism is overwhelming, and cannot be ignored by historians of the eighteenth century. But why should we use all of this fresh information to return, somewhat discouragingly, to an old-fashioned paradigm? We need instead to find new ways of understanding the link between material experience and consciousness in that society, and in order to do so we must abandon some of the associations we are trained to make automatically. For instance, we tend to assume that wherever you find commerce, consumerism, and mobility, there shall you also find a middle class or bourgeoisie with some degree of pride or self-consciousness. But can we not imagine a situation in which the second might not follow from the first? While the economy and material world in eighteenth-century France were indeed changing in the ways described above, the framework for understanding these changes was not the one that historians doggedly expect to find. While we need to pay heed to these concrete transformations, we need even more to listen carefully to the terms in which contemporaries described and understood them.

## LUXURY AND "LES MOEURS": DECAY AND REGENERATION

In the second half of the eighteenth century, literally hundreds of texts painted the same gloomy picture of what was happening to the French nation. The French countryside was in ruins because peasants had left it for the towns, drawn by a desire for material wealth and pleasure. Once there, they worked at sterile occupations such as domestic service. They failed to get married or else produced few children, and as a result the population was declining. In the cities the example was set by the profligate rich, who consumed immoderately, thought only of themselves, and taught debauchery to all those below them in society. Upper-class women led especially scandalous lives, throwing money away on clothes and other pleasures, wantonly taking lovers, sending their few babies to mercenary wet-nurses who often let the infants die. The elite had become so selfish and the poor so acquisitive, money and goods circulated so fast, that social distinctions had collapsed and it was often hard to tell who was who anymore. Both rich and poor had lost their moral and religious sense, and France, increasingly governed by material greed and social ambition, had come to resemble either a craven despotic state or a soulless "republic" like England or Holland.

A single, powerful term stood for this whole ominous vision: *le luxe*, luxury, and most commentary on social and economic change in prerevolutionary France, whether by conservatives or liberals, provides some version of the description sketched out above. "Luxury" was obviously the prism through which contemporaries took note of and reacted to the growth of commerce and consumerism in their society, and it is hard to overestimate the ubiquity and cultural importance of the concept. As Keith Baker has elegantly put it: "Few words had a deeper social resonance, or more widely spanned the spectrum of social and political problems facing eighteenth-century France than the term *luxury* . . . [A]t all points the debate over luxury merged with a larger and more fundamental debate over the nature and values of traditional society."[47]

Of course eighteenth-century France was not the first or the only country to produce a flurry of writings about luxury, far from it. Concerns about something called luxury can be traced back to the beginnings of Western history. From Genesis via Plato to Augustine and the Church Fathers right into the early nineteenth century, this "chameleon of a concept" adapted to many cultural environments while retaining its primary dual meaning: greed for the superfluous and social chaos.[48] The notion dominated social criticism in eighteenth-century England as well as France, to the extent that in Britain "luxury was probably the greatest single social issue and the greatest commonplace."[49] Anguished commentary about luxury cropped up especially when traditional societies experienced marked economic expansion— one could think of luxury as the flip side of Christian asceticism. If the latter is a way of controlling one's environment, the concept of luxury expresses the related fear that material abundance will lead to various forms of loss of control. "Luxury" was the code word for threatening social change, and it is telling that the concept as applied to entire societies disappeared in the early nineteenth century as historicist thinking became widespread.

What has been called the debate on luxury dominated writing about social and economic issues in eighteenth-century France, unfolding in several phases.[50] Around 1700 a few texts by Christian moralists like Fénelon warned against misplaced expenditure at court and in society. Lavish spending was proper when practiced by monarchs or traditional elites in order to maintain their rank—in that case it was called *faste;* in the wrong hands, however, those of parvenus or ambitious courtiers, ostentatious wealth was considered *luxe* and duly denounced. For a brief period between the 1700s and the 1740s luxury had some vocal defenders—French followers of Mandeville like the economist Jean François Melon, and a few writers like Voltaire and Montesquieu sang the praises of industry and commerce as promoting universal well-being.

But the tide turned decisively at mid-century, with the publication of Rousseau's *Discourse on the Sciences and the Arts* of 1749 and the subsequent growth of the physiocratic movement. Both Rousseau's attack on modern civilization and the Physiocrats' idealization of agrarian pursuits fueled a vast and repetitive literature—at least a hundred titles have been identified—about the corrupting effects of wealth, com-

merce, and urbanity. Critics of luxury vastly outnumbered and decisively out-argued defenders of the concept in the decades before the
Revolution.

The authors of this literature usually found it easier to describe
symptoms of *le luxe* than to figure out where this social malady came
from. The single most striking manifestation of luxury was the confusion of ranks through the anomalous promotion of most groups and
the desire of all to rise above their station. "What confusion in all conditions!" went a standard jeremiad: "*les grands* want to imitate the
magnificence of the sovereign; the citizens of moderate means want to
equal *les grands;* the poor want to equal the middling, and by this dangerous chain, the impulse for luxury is communicated from the highest rank down to the lowest classes of people."[51] This text suggests how
archaic was the concept of luxury, which mirrored exactly the classic
Great Chain of Being: if social order was configured as a ladder with
every rung in its assigned place, social dysfunction was imagined along
the same lines, as a hierarchy of disorder. If society, in other words,
could be envisioned only holistically, no single group could be imagined as the single agent or beneficiary of change.

The principal symptom of luxury was the confusion of social signs:
"Thus the exterior trappings which used to be permitted only to distinguish the separate conditions, no longer serve for anything but confusing them."[52] Or as the philosophe Paul-Henri d'Holbach put it, "Luxury is a sort of imposture whereby men have agreed to deceive one
another and manage even to deceive themselves."[53] These writings almost invariably express anxiety that social markers no longer functioned as such, or as a modern linguist might put it, that signifiers
were out of line with signifieds. Not infrequently, as in the case of the
Montpellier text, there are demands that certain groups or maybe all
social groups wear an identifying badge or sign. And while one does
find many a text denouncing the ambitions and pretensions of the
bourgeois and their wives,[54] the point of this literature is not to identify
or stigmatize a specific group: courtiers, nobles, merchants, workers,
servants, everyone except the allegedly virtuous and vanishing peasantry, was caught up in this cascade of social corruption.

The fear of luxury belongs to a worldview in which society really was
imagined as a body, and social corruption as something that could be
vividly described because it could be seen and felt. While its causes re-

mained obscure—writers typically confused the origins of the scourge with its symptoms—luxury's effects were made graphically clear in a series of riffs on themes of emasculation. One word, *mollesse,* conveniently summed up the physical effects of luxury on those who fell prey to it. *Mollesse,* which can be applied either to the physical or to the moral realm, means both slackness and softness. It is the antonym of tautness and hardness, and its sexual and gendered connotations need scarcely be pointed out.[55] In a literature that blames depopulation on *mollesse,* the sexual subtext lies awfully close to the surface: these authors are almost explicit about the effects of luxury on the male erection. Most remarkably, while the term *mollesse* obviously designates the feminine principle—it has connotations of weakness, softness, flaccidity—its effect on men was not a compensatory reinforcement of virility but the opposite, detumescence. According to René Girard's influential argument, social crises are often experienced not as the reinforcement of social barriers but as the opposite, the dissolution of boundaries between social and sexual groups.[56] In this instance, luxury did not just blur the line between upper and lower classes, it also transformed virile Frenchmen into effeminate freaks. Money, luxury goods, city life, and female power had provoked not just depopulation but also a national unmanning.[57]

What lay behind this tormented sense of weakness? The voluminous and anguished literature about luxury spoke to a crisis whose causes were deeper and more complex than just material change. While most obviously a response to the increase of commercial activity, the growth of towns, and the rise of consumerism, the obsession with luxury was also no doubt connected to the collapse of traditional forms of political authority. In principle, the force that guaranteed both hierarchy and cohesion in society was the monarch. According to absolutist theory, the king legitimated all official social groupings, from the order of nobility to the meanest artisanal corporation, and it was the royal will that balanced the interests of different members of the body politic. In the second half of the eighteenth century, under Louis XV and Louis XVI, the monarch's divinely appointed position at the center of society was undermined by a series of political crises, ranging from the personal misconduct of the debauched Louis XV to religious disputes between Jansenists and Jesuits and to violent clashes between the king and his courts of high justice, the *parlements.*[58] The crumbling of royal legitimacy in the second half of the eighteenth century was no doubt experienced as a social as well as political crisis, since the weakening of the monarch jeopardized the traditional source of social definition and cohesion. Many a French subject—of the literate, urban variety at least—may have agreed with the verdict of the philosophe and states-man Anne-Robert Turgot when he wrote in 1775, in the wake of the country's most severe prerevolutionary crisis: "This is a society com-posed of a variety of ill-connected orders, a people whose members have very few social bonds with one another; where as a result each man looks only to his particular and exclusive interest, and almost no-body is at pains to fulfill his duties or recognize his links to others."[59] Social commentators described a world in which many people felt adrift because of the crumbling of the monarchy as the sacred center of society.

The other likely source of the preoccupation with luxury was France's complex relationship with England, a political rival which was also perceived as a model for what France might become in the fu-ture. Writers of the early Enlightenment, most famously Voltaire and Montesquieu, had looked to England as a model, yet by the second half of the century anglophobia was more common than anglophilia among French intellectuals.[60] The causes of this shift are numerous, but certainly France's devastating defeat at the hands of the English during the Seven Years' War (1756–1763), and the consequent loss of most of her colonial empire, were of central importance. While the early philosophes had sung the praises of British social mobility and political liberalism, their successors saw English society as driven by greed and venality, and the English constitution, with its balancing of interests and parties, as a source of factionalism and violence: what kind of a system was it, they smugly asked, that could fall prey so easily to popular violence and commit the unthinkable, regicide?[61] The ex-ample of England was naturally invoked during the debate on nobility and commerce in the late 1750s, and usually dismissed. Albion was financially the prey of trading companies and mercenary soldiers, po-litically torn apart by factions and parties: such, one writer claimed, were the effects of commerce.[62] The use of England as a negative model was, moreover, not limited to the intellectual elites: in the pro-vincial town of Caen in the 1770s and 1780s schoolteachers had their students write essays deploring the corruption of "merchant nations" such as England and Holland and the moral decline of "anglicized" (that is, commercialized) French towns.[63]

Money, wrote d'Holbach in his pamphlet *Système social* (1773), was what corrupted the English political and social system. Arguing against Montesquieu's anglophilia, d'Holbach dismissed the idea that English representative government should be admired for balancing the interests of different segments of society. "Interest" was precisely the problem: the peers would always throw in their lot with the monarchy against the people, and the Commons were dependent on securing through bribes the votes of an indigent populace.[64] "What felicity, what security can there be," he bombastically asked, "for a people who can at any moment be thrust into useless wars by the scheming, the disorder, the sordid self-interest of a few rapacious merchants? Peoples of Albion . . . hear the true cause of your fears and afflictions: never did the love of gold make for good citizens."[65] England presented to many French writers the image of a country run on the principle of division and competition. At a time when French social commentators perceived their country as threatened by all manner of centrifugal forces, English freedom looked more like a threat than a promise.

What ailed France in the second half of the eighteenth century, as these commentators saw it, was the start of an evolution that would make the Gallic realm look more like its "greedy," "venal" neighbor across the Channel. They professed horror at the thought of what money was doing to social relationships: "Money will level all ranks, wash away all stains on birth, money will erase all crimes, money will stand in for talents, virtues, and services and everything, including love, will be for sale," was how Antoine Polier de Saint-Germain imagined France in the near future, with the rich more and more proud and hard-hearted, and the poor increasingly servile.[66]

The concept of luxury expressed, for French writers in the later eighteenth century, a deep sense of social crisis, one which could be illustrated by pointing to the obvious evils of the English social and political system. Increased wealth, circulation, commerce, and competing interests—all of which are usually counted as components of the rise of the middle class—were perceived as the core of the problem, and therefore could be no part of any solution. If the problem of luxury was viewed as engulfing most of society—the idealized rural world remained exempt—then the solution had to be imagined as similarly holistic, not as the redemption of, or by, any single social group.

In the last decades of the eighteenth century, writers ranging from luminaries to obscure scribblers promoted, in response to the dangers of luxury, venality, and social dissolution, ideals of ethically based social unity. Under the rubric of what they called *les moeurs,* they proposed a system of social morality that negated social differences and sought to bring the French together in a moral community called *patrie,* a sort of sentimental family writ large. Like *le luxe,* the concept of *les moeurs* (which I translate as "social morality")[67] is easier to describe than to explain. The theme of *les moeurs* was, if anything, even more ubiquitous than that of *le luxe,* and to anyone familiar with eighteenth-century French culture, it evokes the set of images which accompanied it with dreadful predictability: nursing mothers, venerable fathers, chaste peasant girls, agrarian utopias, and swooning families in the manner of Greuze.[68] *Moeurs* could be described as a virtuous predisposition which, in any given individual, would be manifest in three guises: as family love; as a more generalized *esprit social* or sense of human kinship expressed in spontaneous acts of kindness and compassion; and at the most abstract level, as the selfless community spirit known as *patriotisme.*

Clearly, this sense of social morality was intended as a substitute for traditional forms of religion. D'Holbach wrote that the problem began with the state's relinquishing morality to the Church; given the (implied) failure of the latter, this shift had resulted in an immoral society and polity. The cult of *les moeurs* was an attempt to promote new forms of spiritual fulfillment in one's sense of connectedness to a community of fellow human beings. The family occupied a towering place in this ideological system. As a natural unit and the embodiment of a feeling rooted in nature, it was both the origin of one's moral sensibility and a model for all other social connections. A passage in the historian and social critic Gabriel de Mably's much read *Entretiens de Phocion* (1763) is typical: "It is in the bosom of their families that loving and prudent fathers offered the first model for the laws of society . . . It is only through the practice of domestic virtues that a people prepares itself for the practice of public virtues . . . Domestic morality determines, in the end, public morality."[69] D'Holbach, like many others, explained why this should be the case: "Any political society is but an assemblage of particular societies; many families make up that larger one called the *nation*."[70]

A society in which *les moeurs* were heeded would be one in which each person would have for every other person the same feelings (presumed positive) that he or she naturally harbored toward family members. This was the assumption behind the vogue for "humanity" and sentimental benevolence characteristic of the period from the 1760s through the 1780s. In those decades, periodicals like the *Journal encyclopédique* began retailing anecdotes about acts of compassion and loyalty, prompting readers to send in money in aid of the virtuous and impoverished. Such stories were equally successful when gathered and sold in anthologies with titles like *Tableau de l'humanité* or *Annales de la bienfaisance*.[71] The ubiquitous celebration of country life in the last decades of the Old Regime sprang from the fanciful assumption that remote villages and farms were places where such natural feelings of human community survived.

Political considerations were deeply embedded in this promotion of social morality. D'Holbach expressed this pointedly in his *Système social* when he contrasted the *esprit social* with the *esprit de corps*, the division of society into corporate interests which, he said, was typical of "despotic" governments. Tyranny, he explained elsewhere, thrives on the division of men into separate groups, although he argued against Montesquieu that monarchies as well as republics could be based on virtue.[72] The political manifestation of "social spirit" was what eighteenth-century writers called *patriotisme*, devotion to the community on the highest and most abstract level. *Patrie* was the third tip of a triangle whose other two points were family and humanity.

Eighteenth-century patriotism should not be confused with later forms of nationalism. Patriotism in the earlier French sense was not exclusive but universalistic. It was described as a feeling that transcended a narrow love of country: the opposite of patriotism was not cosmopolitanism but selfishness.[73] James Rutlidge, an Anglo-Irish expatriate, described patriotism as "a virtue which leads us to find our own happiness in that of every member of the community." He saw patriotism as directly linked to a happy family life, for it was doubtful that a man without the capacity to cherish those closest to him could feel love and devotion to that more remote entity, *la patrie*.[74] *Patrie* in the sense of moral community was a term heavily used in the political disputes of the eighteenth century. Although initially favored by critics of the monarchical status quo—Jansenist dissidents and rebellious members of the high courts or *parlements*—it was adopted after mid-century by the kings themselves, who now posed as embodiments of the *patrie*.[75]

Family, humanity, and *patrie* were therefore closely overlapping categories in the discourse of social morality of the late eighteenth century. The categories most obviously missing from the texts which explored these notions were those of rank or class. Everyone deplored selfish corporate interests, and some writers mentioned in passing that the advent of *les moeurs* would entail a happy and harmonious acceptance of the social hierarchy. The more radical, like the materialist philosophes Helvétius and d'Holbach, suggested that gross inequalities of wealth were a breeding ground for moral corruption and that a measure of social leveling would speed up the promotion of morality.[76] What is most remarkable about the discourse on *les moeurs,* however, is the way in which it bypasses distinctions of social class: the triumph of social morality would not so much overcome social distinctions as make them irrelevant. The ideal promoted in these ideological commonplaces is one of emotional fusion and bonding: the submersion of social divisions in the warm milk of family feeling.

## LOVE, TEARS, AND SOCIAL FUSION: THE REDEMPTIVE FAMILY

Among the many clichés that routinely accompany the term "bourgeois," some of the most tenacious concern family life. The very word "bourgeois" conjures up images of family and domesticity, of the loving nuclear unit made up of parents and a small number of children. The typical demeanor of this group is expressively affectionate—the professed rationale for this bourgeois or middle-class family is above all the love between parents and children, spouses, and siblings, rather than economic survival (like the poor) or dynastic ambitions (like the rich). The modern cult of family love first took shape in the second half of the eighteenth century, and despite its subsequent association with social middlingness, the ideal of the companionate family appealed initially to the upper classes.[77] In France, the quintessential literary expression of this new family ethos was a theatrical genre known

variously as *drame,* or *genre sérieux,* or, mostly after the eighteenth century, as *drame bourgeois.* Given the traditional association between this
form of theater and the middle classes, and because the plots of these
plays typically revolve around hyperbolic expressions of family love,
the *drame* is a good place to explore the social meaning of family imagery in prerevolutionary France.[78]

Although a few plays in this genre were written before mid-century,
the birthdate of the *drame* is usually considered 1757, when the poly-
math intellectual Denis Diderot published a dialogue that was a critical commentary on his new play, *Le Fils naturel (The Illegitimate Son).*
The themes of the *Entretiens sur le Fils naturel* are well known to students of eighteenth-century literature: Diderot announced the need
for a new genre to fit between existing tragedy and comedy, one that
would stage the experiences of ordinary people rather than kings or
heroes and show them in everyday settings wearing ordinary clothes,
speaking prose instead of spewing alexandrine verse. In style these
plays were to be visually expressive: Diderot stressed the importance of
gestures such as weeping or falling to one's knees, which he called
*pantomime* and which he valued more highly than vocal utterance.
The subjects of these dramas would challenge the traditional primacy
of character on the French stage. Instead of Molièresque plots revolv-
ing around personifications of pride, greed, or misanthropy, Diderot
wanted a drama propelled by the tensions between different "conditions," by which he meant both social conditions (persons of different
status and occupation), and family relations.[79]

Diderot's prescriptions for the contemporary stage included a call
to "create domestic and bourgeois tragedy"—hence the later appellation of *drame bourgeois.* But the term "bourgeois" seems to have been,
under the pen of Diderot and a few others, more a negation than an
assertion of class characteristics. What Diderot seems to have meant
was that he proposed to apply the noble genre of tragedy to characters
and settings that were neither mythological nor royal nor martial—but
which otherwise could be very squarely upper-class. Significantly, his
two major plays in this style, *Le Fils naturel* and *Le Père de famille,* are
set among what seems to be a moneyed elite, and the characters, who
do not appear to work for a living, bear aristocratic stage-names like
Dorval, Clairville, Saint-Albin, and Germeuil. If the new genre adver-

tised itself as a drama of ordinary life, that life was likely to be materially comfortable and socially secure.

Even when these plays directly address issues of social class, their message is far from sounding clearly bourgeois. Possibly the most successful eighteenth-century *drame* was Michel Sedaine's *Le Philosophe sans le savoir* (1765), written as a self-conscious illustration of Diderot's theories.[80] The play is often considered the quintessential vindication of the struggling bourgeoisie, and indeed its hero is a successful merchant, Monsieur Vanderck, who appears to embody the dignity and usefulness of his occupation. It turns out, however, that Vanderck was born a nobleman but took on, out of gratitude, the name and business of his late adoptive father, a Dutchman. In the course of a scene in which Vanderck lectures his son about the merits of trade, he mentions that he knows only two occupations that he values more highly: that of the magistrate and that of the warrior—in other words, the two traditional noble callings.[81] The play ends, after the requisite crises, on the reconciliation of Vanderck's son with a young nobleman who had insulted the chosen profession of Vanderck *père,* just in time for the marriage of Vanderck's daughter to a nobleman of the robe. The final scene, a wedding feast, is a sentimental reconciliation between different types of aristocrats: nobles of the robe and the sword, and Vanderck, the noble as enlightened businessman. In good middle-of-the-road Enlightenment fashion, many of these plays poke fun at aristocratic pretensions: Sedaine's play, for instance, features a snobbish aunt who is obsessed with lineage and military careers. But while debunking aristocratic foibles, these plays did not especially promote the middle classes—they featured protagonists of every social station. The prolific and radical Louis-Sébastien Mercier, whose plays enjoyed considerable success, chose for his dramas heroes spanning the entire social scale, from the comfortably-off to the very poor.

What all of these plays by Diderot, Sedaine, Mercier, and others do share is a cult of family. Just about all of their plots include the portrayal of a highly expressive, indeed relentlessly proclaimed love between parents and children, brothers and sisters. The celebration of family bonds typically reaches a climax in the last act of the play with the disclosure of previously unknown kinship between some of the characters. Obviously, the resolution of a crisis by the revelation of a foundling or lost child's true identity is not unique to this genre or even century. What is notable is how often this device is used in the *drame* to resolve the tensions created by social differences.

The crisis in Diderot's *Le Père de famille*, for instance, is triggered by the infatuation of young Saint-Albin with a poor woman named Sophie—a love his good father tries gently to talk him out of, and his authoritarian uncle, the Commandeur, attempts to prohibit by force. The problem is solved upon the discovery that Sophie is in fact the Commandeur's niece and Saint-Albin's cousin, and the play ends with the double betrothal of Saint-Albin to Sophie and of his sister Cécile to Germeuil, a young man raised in the household as their brother. Both marriages therefore reinforce already existing family bonds, and in the last scene the good patriarch blesses the merging of these four quasi-siblings into an official family.

Mercier's most famous *drames* offer variations on such themes of recognition and the transformation of an implicit family into an explicit one which transcends social divisions. *Le Juge* is about the dilemma of a highly moral judge whose conscience tells him to rule in a dispute over land in favor of a poor peasant family and against the local count who has been his protector and surrogate father. Although the furious count at first threatens to ruin the judge, he is ultimately moved, at the sight of the pathetic peasant family, to reveal that the magistrate is in fact his son from an early and clandestine marriage. The dispute over land involving three social strata thus vanishes when the count acknowledges and joins his real family.

In these dramas the sentiments of family love extend beyond the middle and upper classes. Sophie in Diderot's *Père de famille* is destitute, and the heroes of some of Mercier's most successful plays are wretchedly poor workers. In Mercier's *L'Indigent,* a family of penniless spinners, old Rémi and his children Charlotte and Joseph, inhabit a basement in the house of a callous young nobleman named De Lys. A crisis erupts when De Lys attempts to seduce the virtuous Charlotte, first with money and then by proposing marriage. It turns out, a few plot twists later, that Charlotte is not Rémi's daughter after all but De Lys's lost sister, whom he had been trying to disinherit in absentia. Charlotte is now a wealthy noblewoman, but she chooses to marry her ex-brother, the poor worker Joseph, whom she has always loved. De Lys has a sudden change of heart as he feels drawn to the virtuous affection between Charlotte, Joseph, and Rémi; before the curtain falls, he too has tearfully acknowledged the power of family love: "Here is the first true pleasure of my life," exclaims the former debauchee, "I have felt it in your embraces."[82]

In most of these plays, the tension created by social differences is resolved through the revelation of hidden family ties, which are then reinforced through marriage. As Mercier saw it, however, marriage across social boundaries was the solution to both inequality and the feelings of disunity experienced by his contemporaries. In the preface to his *La Brouette du vinaigrier,* a play about a peddler's son who marries a rich merchant's daughter, he wrote:

> All that which mingles the different estates of society and works to break down the excessive inequality of conditions, that source of all our ills, is politically good. All that which brings citizens together is the blessed cement uniting the many families within a large state, which must look upon all of them with the same eye. That same law which forbids unions between brother and sister should prohibit the rich from marrying one another.[83]

Mercier's allusion to fraternal incest is interesting in light of the frequency of just such incestuous situations in so many of these plays. In *Le Fils naturel* Dorval and Rosalie are powerfully drawn to each other by what they take to be romantic love, until they learn they are brother and sister; in *L'Indigent* De Lys tries to seduce Charlotte, eventually revealed to be his biological sister. She in turn immediately marries Joseph, whom she assumed to be her brother just minutes before. Beaumarchais set up a similarly murky situation in his *La Mère coupable* (1789), the sentimental sequel to *The Marriage of Figaro:* the son of count and countess Almaviva, Léon, is in love with Florestine, a young woman who is the count's ward and goddaughter—and whom we soon assume to be his illegitimate daughter. She is indeed the latter, but the story ultimately reveals that Léon is not the count's son but the result of the countess's single brief infidelity. As Figaro concludes triumphantly, "to the law and to nature these young persons are nothing to one another, they are strangers to each other"; the count declares that the family will consult "under assumed names some discreet, enlightened, and honorable men of law," who will presumably sanction, to everyone's delight, this marriage between brother and sister.[84]

The language of nature speaks powerfully to us, according to these plots, but we sometimes mistake its message: we take for fraternal love that which is really romantic passion, and vice versa.[85] In this literature—and in the broader discourse of *les moeurs*—there were no foils against which the family could assert its cohesion. Because the ideals of the *drame* and more generally of eighteenth-century French liberal ideology were so doggedly universalistic, the family could not define itself *against* the threat of a lower class, a criminal element, or a foreign danger. (One exception is *La Mère coupable,* written on the very eve of the Revolution and first performed in 1792, in which the family unites in the end against an Irish villain.) Even aristocrats who stand for destructive antifamily solipsism—the count in *Le Juge,* De Lys in *L'Indigent,* the straying but finally reconciled Almavivas in Beaumarchais—are ultimately accepted into the kinship of domestic love. The combined absence of exterior threats to the family, along with the importance of marriage as the cement of the state, placed a large burden on family sentiment, which had therefore to be invested with the full power of erotic passion.

The plots of these plays offered eighteenth-century audiences a new dramaturgy of crisis and resolution. The premise of *the drame* was that human beings are social creatures involved in a network of human connections, and that the true stuff of tragedy could be found in inequalities of power or money. Such tensions could be overcome, however, by heeding the voice of nature, which leads us to the delights of family love, the most authentic human connection. The denial of social hierarchy was a central feature of the economy of eighteenth-century sentimentalism, which was dedicated to demonstrating the universal nature of our deepest feelings. The very language of sentimentalism, with its hyperbolic expressions of emotion, aimed at making inner experience visible as a basis for human connection.[86] This is why gesture was so important to Diderot and his successors: the deepest emotions were ineffable and could only be spoken by the body. A famous passage in Diderot's *Entretiens* illustrates the ways in which verbal and bodily languages of sensibility could act as a solvent upon class differences. It concerns a peasant woman whom the narrator encounters just as she has discovered the body of her murdered husband. She is clutching her husband's feet and sobbing that she never thought that these feet would lead him to his death. Diderot comments that a tragic discovery of this nature would have drawn the same words and "pathetic" gestures from a woman of any social rank: "what the artist must find is what anyone would say in a situation like this; what no-one will hear without recognizing it in himself."[87]

The *drame* can be seen as emblematic of social attitudes among the educated public of prerevolutionary France. In response to deep fears of social dissolution and corruption, these plays promoted the ideal of a community that transcended class divisions. Family love was both the means and the metaphor for that transcendence: an electrifying force manifest in bodily symptoms (tears, heavy breathing) which brought the cast together for a tear-drenched final *tableau*. There was nothing class-specific about the sentimental family as portrayed in these dramas: its nucleus could be proletarian (as in *L'Indigent*) or aristocratic (as in *La Mère coupable*), and its function within the drama was to transcend social divisions. Far from representing the ethos of a single group, the sentimental family was a way of imagining the cohesion of an entire society. At a time when older models for society—ordered, corporate—seemed increasingly irrelevant, and before the appearance of modern class, national, and historical solidarities, strong affective family bonds were the only available means for imagining an enduring social cohesion.

Yes, France did become significantly richer, more urban, more commercial, and more consumerist in the middle decades of the eighteenth century. But there is no evidence that contemporaries interpreted these changes, for better or for worse, as causes or effects of the rise of a middling or capitalist group. Later historians drew such conclusions on the basis of their experience of the nineteenth and twentieth centuries. It is impossible, however, to locate in this society any significant body of opinion that identified a rising bourgeoisie or middle class, whether to celebrate it or to revile it. Instead, economic change was understood in traditional moral terms as "luxury," a disease affecting the entire social body which bred confusion of ranks, selfishness, dissipation, and sterility. When a remedy to the bane of luxury was proposed, it was rarely couched in economic, social, or political terms. Most of the writers who denounced the evils of urban luxury did so in very general, moralistic terms, and implicitly or explicitly contrasted it with the allegedly virtuous, austere, and (in all senses) fertile world of the countryside. But the countryside celebrated as the cradle of *les moeurs*—virile peasants reaping bountiful crops while their wives suckled pudgy infants—was not a real place at all but a metaphor for a lost sense of national community.

One might object that social observers, critics, and politicians often speak in general moral terms ("family values," "restoring honor," and so on), and that this sort of idealistic universalism often serves as a decorative drape hiding real class interests. But even universalist ideologies usually involve the demonization of some group of "not us," and what is most remarkable about the discourse of *moeurs* and *patrie* in the later eighteenth century is the absence within it of identified social enemies. As the plots of eighteenth-century *drames* suggest, a society reimagined as a moral and sentimental family would clasp both the indigent poor and the reformed aristocracy—and everybody in between—into its tearful embrace. The collapse of traditional understandings of religion and the waning of the monarchy's sacred character prompted educated French men and women to seek meaning and moral community in emotionally charged understandings of family and *patrie*.[88]

For a few decades between the 1750s and the 1790s, French social observers and critics believed that the moralized nation could be remade in the image of a family. The loving nuclear family was an ideal central to this culture, not because it was especially bourgeois or middle class, but because it was viewed as both the source and the model for a new kind of universal social connection. And indeed, those who experienced the first heady months of revolution in 1789 did initially believe that brotherly love or *fraternité* was powerful enough to hold together the citizens of the new nation. The family model was to prove fragile, however, as it became apparent in short order how easily brothers could turn against one another. The French revolutionaries soon had to seek coherence in a common crusade, explicitly against aristocrats and foreigners, implicitly against the threat of violence from the plebs.

# Revolutionary Brotherhood and the
# War against Aristocracy

## 3

It used to be that we knew exactly when the bourgeoisie clattered onto the center stage of French history. It happened in May–June of 1789, as a result of the convening of the Estates General of the realm, made up of Clergy, Nobility, and Third Estate. The Third Estate deputies, for the most part well-heeled and educated professionals, rebelled against the monarchy and the two other orders. With help from members of the lower clergy and liberal nobility, the Third Estate deputies seceded and in June declared themselves, under the name of National Assembly, the sole representatives of the French nation. This, surely, was a bourgeois revolution.

Since the 1960s, the interpretation of the French Revolution as the triumph of a capitalist middle class has fallen on hard times, and today historians are arguing more than ever over whether what happened in France in the decade after 1789 should be viewed as a bourgeois revolution. One obvious question, rather astonishingly, has never been posed: did the revolutionary bourgeoisie, if such there was, ever identify itself? There is no debate about the general social identity of the revolutionary leadership, the men who were elected to the governing assemblies (Constituent, Legislative, and Convention), those who staffed the committees including those of the Terror, ran city governments, gave speeches, wrote pamphlets, and organized factions. Except for a few liberal nobles, they were practically to a man upper-middle-class professionals: lawyers above all, but also writers, journalists, doctors, engineers, and priests.[1] Did these men, in their speeches, writings, or memoirs, describe what was happening as the advent of a bourgeoisie or middle class? Did anyone else, for that matter? And if the answer is no, what are the implications for this pivotal episode?

## WHAT WAS THE THIRD ESTATE?

The obvious place to look for discourses on society in the early stages of the Revolution is in the outpouring of pamphlet literature that preceded the convening of the Estates General in May of 1789. Louis XVI and his government had called upon this ancient assembly of delegates of the three orders of the realm in a last-ditch effort to resolve France's intractable financial woes. As this huge body of nobles, clerics, and commoners had not been convened since 1614, the king's minister, Loménie de Brienne, invited public commentary on how the Estates should be convened. He and his colleagues got a lot more commentary than they had bargained for, especially after September 1788, when the Parlement of Paris, in registering the edict that convened the ancient body, declared that the Estates should follow the "forms of 1614." If this were the case, each estate would have one vote on any issue regardless of the number of deputies it contained or of the constituency it represented; as opponents of the decision quickly and vociferously pointed out, this meant that privileged nobles and clerics would always have a two-to-one advantage over commoners.

Champions of the Third Estate argued that because of the numerical and economic importance of that group in society, its representatives should be twice as numerous as those of either of the other two estates, and that the voting should be done by head rather than by order. Thousands of pamphlets were published from the summer of 1788 to the summer of 1789, many as the result of carefully orchestrated campaigns.[2] Although every point of view can be found in this mass of polemical literature, it is safe to say that the majority of pamphlets, and certainly those most influential at the time, promoted the interests of the Third Estate. Historians have traditionally viewed this literature as a reflection of bourgeois or middle-class political aspirations,[3] so we need to take a closer look at what the writings about the *tiers état* tell us about society and politics on the eve of the Revolution. The convening of the Estates General had the effect of suddenly introducing social themes into what had previously been a mostly political crisis. Whom did the three estates actually represent, and were some constituents more important than others? Did the division into three orders have anything to do with the way social distinctions really functioned in 1788–89? And what was the nature of the relationship between the Estates and the monarchy? Were the deputies going to Versailles merely to obey Louis XVI, the source of all power, or did they themselves have power invested in them as carriers of the nation's will?

The pamphlets of 1788–89 offer therefore a unique vantage point from which to gain access to ways in which their authors—members, of course, of the literate elite—imagined the social world and conceived of the link between social worth and public power. The idioms used for describing society were very much in flux by the later eighteenth century, and as a result one may find even within the same pamphlet a range of different concepts and images. Even liberal writers like Pierre-Laurent Bérenger or the future president of the National Assembly, Jean Paul Rabaut Saint-Étienne, resorted easily to ancient organic images: "The harmony of the human body is the image of that of the state," wrote the first; "The nation is the body of which the king is the head," intoned the second.[4]

Directly colliding with the body imagery is one of the most persistent themes of the pro-Third Estate literature, the quantitative claim. The point of the argument from numbers was that since the Third Estate included all those who were neither nobles nor clerics, their crushing statistical superiority ought to insure that they were given the numerical—and therefore political—upper hand in the Estates. The numbers invoked varied significantly, but any way one figured it, the numerical disproportion between privileged and nonprivileged was always staggering. The nobility should not ignore our rights, said one writer, or it will find twenty-three million of us pitted against its one million members; how dare the nobility try to speak in our name, fumed another, when "it numbers about one hundred thousand while we are twenty-five to twenty-six million strong."[5] In the most famous pamphlet of the time, *What Is the Third Estate?* the abbé Sieyès wrote of two hundred thousand *privilégiés* pitted against twenty-five or twenty-six million unprivileged citizens.[6]

The force of this claim seems self-evident to us because we are the heirs of the brand of Western intellectual and political modernity initially created by the French Revolution. But it is important to remember just how recent and still controversial such an argument was in a culture where the worth of one person was not necessarily equal to that of another. These same writers, after all, slipped easily into describing the state as a body, a metaphor to which numerical weighting is in theory irrelevant: it matters little whether a body has one, two, or thirty feet, if the organs which give it life and direction are a single heart and a single head. Numbers may speak powerfully to us, but had their importance been as self-evident in 1788, there would have been no debate at all.

Somewhere between these two views of society, the organic and the statistical, was the ubiquitous notion of the realm as family, which could serve both traditional and more radical agendas. Liberal pamphleteers resorted with surprising frequency to the image of the king as a kindly but beleaguered father mediating between feuding brothers. On the face of it, family metaphors seem to be clearly archaic in nature—by the 1780s it had been over a century since John Locke had skewered patriarchal justifications for monarchy in his *Two Treatises* (1688), and a full generation since Rousseau had published *The Social Contract* (1762). But family metaphors applied to politics did not disappear, they merely changed to accommodate new messages which could be quite radical. It was the future Jacobin Jacques-Louis David who produced in his celebrated *Oath of the Horatii* of 1785 an iconic conflation of family and social contract imagery, the three Roman sons and their sword-brandishing father oddly prefiguring the pamphlet portrayals of Louis XVI as father facing his three estates as sons. The three sons in David's painting are preternaturally identical, suggesting that in the progressive idioms of the 1780s fraternity was inseparable from equality. Family metaphors were easily pressed into service to highlight the real anomaly, primogeniture (in a family) or privilege (in a state). A monarch, said one pamphlet, "is the common father to a large family"; disasters will ensue if he continues to show "gratuitous predilections" toward some of his children. Another conjured up a parable involving four brothers, which ended on this note: "From near or far we are all brothers; we are all equal; we are all part of the same family." Yet another, attempting to work the numerical argument into family imagery, asked readers to imagine a good father with twenty-four children (one for each million French subjects, presumably), two of whom got most of the family's food.[7]

Accounts by participants in the first days of the Estates General suggest that the language of brotherhood was a great deal more than just a symbolic conceit; it was rooted in the emotional experience of participants awakening to an unexpected sense of kinship with other Frenchmen. Jean-Sylvain Bailly, who was to be mayor of revolutionary Paris from 1789 to 1791, received delegations from the nobility and the *tiers état* before the Estates met and wrote that the concert among them "brought early tidings of the grand union of the realm and the commingling of orders. These were brothers preparing, in full agreement, to take possession of their inheritance."[8] Others, like the marquis de Ferrières, recorded a more visceral, euphoric experience of national connection when the Estates opened: "O love of my country, thou didst speak powerfully to my heart. I had not known how deep was the mutual tie which binds us to the soil, to men who are our brothers; I learnt it in this moment."[9]

Imagining society as a family writ large was not a throwback to monarchical or aristocratic models, but a step into modernity inasmuch as all "brothers" were presumed equally welcome. In the first few months of the Revolution, the implicit political message of Diderot's and Mercier's *drames* seemed to be coming alive in the Estates at Versailles and then on the streets of Paris: once benighted divisions into estates, corporations, and the like were overcome, the nation would surely come together in a great familial embrace. At least one participant perceived an explicit connection between the new theatrical genre and sense of fraternal epiphany many felt in the spring of 1789. The abbé Claude Fauchet wrote that the *drame* "must inspire a new surge of interest from the majesty which the French people is right now acquiring in its own eyes. There is, furthermore, no form of theatrical instruction better suited to the fraternal creed which makes all men equal with respect to vice and virtue."[10]

In Lynn Hunt's Freudian reading of revolutionary family metaphors, the political fraternity willed into existence in 1789 would soon come of age by disposing of their father and creating their own law in his place (sisters were excluded for want of reason and moral fortitude).[11]

Family imagery thus served as a transitional metaphor, initially involving traditional obeisance to the king as good father, while allowing for revolutionary brotherhood to take shape and later break free of paternal authority. But most importantly, revolutionary brotherhood was presumed all-inclusive: not of women, of course, nor of those who deliberately refused it, but of everyone else indiscriminately. Revolutionaries dismissed social divisions into estates or corporations as artificial; instead, they naturalized and universalized citizenship by portraying it as a matter of blood ties on a national scale.

Familial, and more specifically fraternal metaphors had a universalizing thrust, as did the other theme used to identify the Third Estate as the core of the nation, that of work and productivity. The most famous expression of this theme is of course Sieyès's *What Is the Third Estate?*, with its familiar opening whiplash of questions and answers: "What is the Third Estate? Everything." To his own rhetorical question, Sieyès answers "Everything"—not the middle class, or the golden mean, or the better sort, or the saner part, but *everything*. Sieyès's first chapter, "The Third Estate Is a Complete Nation," builds on the physiocratic premise that work and productivity are the reasons for human association, and that there exists a "natural" ordering to human society according to productivity and proximity to the material world. The Third Estate includes, in descending order, first, those who work the land, second, those who process materials through craft and industry, third, those who ensure the circulation of goods, and fourth, those, ranging from intellectuals and artists to domestic servants, who provide "useful and agreeable services."[12]

Many other writers similarly defined the Third Estate as the broad range of persons who constituted the nation by virtue of productive work. Take away the clergy and the nobility, wrote Rabaut Saint-Étienne, and you still have a nation; take away the Third Estate, and all you have left is a collection of useless lords and clerics.[13] Another writer pressed the point with heavier irony: just try working your own lands, cultivating your vines, fighting your own battles, mining your own shafts, he challenged the nobility. If we commoners were to disappear, you would still have your coaches and dogs, your swords and your mistresses; the only thing you would lack, he smirked, would be food.[14] The very broad category "Third Estate" in whose name so many writers took up their pens in 1788–89 derived from the inversion of an ancient hierarchy of values. In the traditional tripartite division, the *tiers* was a huge, undifferentiated residual category, remote from divinity because of its debasing contact with the material world. The Enlightenment's displacement of divinity with nature flipped this ordering upside-down: if the laws of nature were divine in origin, then proximity to nature ensured moral and social stature.

It should by now be obvious, both from the numbers invoked on its behalf and from the importance writers like Sieyès gave to productive, physical labor, that the Third Estate was never imagined as anything like a bourgeoisie or middle class. Enumerations of its components routinely stressed its internal diversity and its capaciousness. None other than Jean-Paul Marat penned a pamphlet in 1789 which laid out a full enumeration: "The Third Estate of France is composed of the class of servants, laborers, workers; of artisans, merchants, businessmen, traders, cultivators, landed-proprietors, and non-titled rentiers; of teachers, artists, surgeons, doctors, men of letters and science, men of law, lower-court magistrates, ministers of religion, of the army on both land and sea: an innumerable, invincible legion which carries in its bosom enlightenment, talent, force and virtues."[15]

Iconographic evidence confirms the *tiers*'s eclecticism and casts further doubt on any narrow identification of third estate with a middle or upper-middle class. Around the time of the Estates General and after, an array of prints appeared for sale on the streets of Paris offering among other things visual representations of the three estates. That the Third Estate was most commonly depicted as a peasant—in rags, hollow-cheeked, "born to suffering," and carrying the rich on his back—is notable though hardly surprising; such images echoed the traditional designation of the third as *laboratores*, those whose sacrifice is toil rather than chastity or blood.[16]

Sometimes, to be sure, the Third Estate was indeed imagined as a middling or prosperous sort. One print show the Third—playing music while the other orders two dance to his tune—as a rather elegantly clad gentleman wearing a green striped waistcoat. And in "Le Réveil du tiers," the figure breaking his shackles under a looming Bastille appears to be of modest middling status, clad in brown coat, green waistcoat, and yellow breeches.[17]

There are some references to the bourgeoisie in this pamphlet literature, but of a fleeting, unsystematic nature. One author, for instance, writing in the name of a group of provincial bourgeois and seeking popular support, drew a line between two groups within the bourgeoisie: on the one hand the good, unequivocal bourgeois, the *bons et francs bourgeois,* who live from managing their lands or on the income from their professions; on the other, "those bastard [i.e., mongrel] bourgeois who, living off their rents without working, nonetheless lay claim to the regard which is owed only to useful men."[18] This passage intriguingly echoes Marivaux's remark of some seventy years earlier, that the bourgeois was "a mixed animal who takes after the great lord and the people."[19] It suggests that this crossbred creature could claim membership within the Third Estate if he engaged in productive labor, but would be cast out of the nation if he chose the parasitical ways of the nobility.

The pamphlet literature of 1788–89 was, of course, written not just, or not primarily, to describe society, but for the purposes of promoting a political agenda; paeans to the utility and productivity of the Third Estate were arguments designed to justify doubling the number of delegates and counting votes by head rather than by order. Many writers had political visions that went further still, scripts that envisioned profound changes in France's political regime through a transfer of power to the Estates. The idea that the Estates General might, on the occasion of a political crisis, transform into an assembly sharing power with the king had been articulated long before 1789, notably in abbé Mably's *Des droits et des devoirs du citoyen* of 1758.[20] In 1788–89 there was disagreement even among those who supported such radical notions about what kind of group should emerge from the newly empowered Estates. About one-third of the pamphlets published between September 1788 and May 1789 contained some argument to the effect that the three orders should unite so as actively to oppose the monarchy.[21] That position was the one advocated by the most active and influential liberal group sponsoring and producing pamphlets, the Society of Thirty. The prescription for the three orders to unite was not unrelated to the fact that the overwhelming majority of the Society were noblemen, although it had the support of influential commoners like the lawyer Jean-Baptiste Target.[22] Others, however, argued that the Third Estate alone constituted the nation, and that it would therefore be justified in taking power into its own hands. This was Sieyès's thesis. His insistence that the Third contained every socially useful element of the nation cannot be separated from his concrete political program, a play for power by the Third Estate.[23]

Sieyès's scenario was the one that was ultimately enacted, but whether the aim was for the orders to unite or for the Third Estate alone to seize political control, writers had a clear interest in minimizing differences within the *tiers état*. Any political program constructed around the Estates or the Third alone needed to emphasize the breadth of social interests that the delegates represented. But beyond the tactical necessities of the late 1780s, there were profound ideological reasons for stressing the unity of the Third Estate. If the Third was coterminous with the realm and the carrier of its political will, it could not be splintered into interest groups, for neither could that will. Writers drew variously on the tradition of political absolutism or on notions of a "general will" loosely derived either from Jansenism or from Rousseau. In any case, patriotism and the national will were firmly anchored in unitary language. Champions of the Third Estate celebrated undivided community, while damning particularism as morally or politically heinous.

If the positive definition of the Third Estate involved productivity, the negative pole defining it was privilege. Here again, the crucial text was penned by Sieyès, whose *Essay on Privileges* complements his *What Is the Third Estate?* (the former was written in the fall of 1788 and immediately preceded the latter). Sieyès and his contemporaries were well aware of the etymological origin of the word "privilege," which comes from the Latin for "private law." Privilege therefore represented much more than iniquitous taxation; it was the essence of a system in which different legalities, and therefore different "nations," were allowed to coexist. Privilege destroys all patriotic feeling, wrote Sieyès, inducing an antisocial caste selfishness in the *privilégié*, who "thinks of himself and his colleagues as forming a separate order, a chosen nation within the nation."[24] In *What Is the Third Estate?* Sieyès describes the nobility as a group that is not only outside the nation, but a fatal strain upon it, "a counterfeit people which, unable to exist on its own for want of useful organs, attaches itself to a true nation like those tumorous plants which can only subsist on the sap of other plants which they sap and dry out."[25]

Long before the French Revolution declared war without mercy on all aristocrats, in what was still supposed to be the heyday of fraternity, Sieyès and other writers created the Third Estate by pitting it against its natural antithesis, the *privilégiés*. The Third Estate, the abbé explained, is made up of citizens subject to the "common order." If you cling to legal privilege, he concluded, you opt out of the Third Estate, and therefore out of the nation.[26] To borrow a phrase from current theory, the privileged orders were "marked" and as such served to define the Third Estate as "unmarked," or normative. In the section of his pamphlet arguing that no member of the privileged orders should be allowed to represent the Third at the Estates-General, Sieyès rhetorically raises a universalist objection: was this not impeding the freedom of the electorate to choose? No, he answered, since the law reasonably excludes certain categories: children and youths, women, the destitute, servants, and foreigners. The analogy with foreigners seemed to him the most telling, since the interests of the privileged were "naturally" and intrinsically opposed to those of the commoners: "To be sure, the privileged act no less as the enemies of the common good than do the English towards the French in wartime." If seafaring cities like Venice and Genoa decided jointly to police the sea, would they invite the Barbary pirates into the agreement? This can change, Sieyès concedes, "and I wish no less than any other that the aristocrats will one day cease to act as the Algerians of France."[27]

The description of the privileged as enemy aliens extended the themes of the historical debates of the eighteenth century. The pamphlet literature that preceded the Estates General includes many historical accounts of the origins of the nobility and the Third Estate which follow Mably's interpretation in his *Observations sur l'histoire de France* (its second and final volume was published in 1788). These narratives tell the story of how the weakened later Carolingian monarchy was forced to give away fiefdoms to threatening grandees and to make those possessions hereditary; how in a period of cultural and political decline, those nobles had begun to behave as violent and predatory outlaws; how, in order to protect itself, the monarchy sought and received support in the newly enfranchised towns known as *communes* from their non-noble denizens. History showed how the aristocracy had come to set up its own "private law" in opposition to the public interest. Ignoring the fact that privilege was an expression of the royal will, such accounts set up the nobles as enemies of the monarchy, and the Third Estate as its savior and most loyal defender.

Mably's historical work was later pressed into service, under the Restoration and July Monarchy, as an argument for the historical importance and destiny of the bourgeoisie. Such was not the case in 1789, however, when the monarchy's ally was designated more generally as the Third Estate. Only on rare occasions in this polemical literature does the bourgeoisie as such come up. One finds here a pamphlet written in its name, there a fleeting reference. (In a striking passage of his essay on privilege, Sieyès comments that while the nobleman is fixated on the past, the bourgeois's gaze is on the present and future. What he means, however, is that while the nobleman is obsessed with history, the working commoner invests himself in the present and future products of his industry.[28]) The pamphlet literature of the late 1780s focused on the image of an entire nation of productive citizens, unequal in wealth and status but equal in legal rights and united in patriotic fraternity. As for the privileged, they stood outside of the nation, which they were said to threaten, but at a deeper level served to define.

The Third Estate was a sociopolitical entity which included the whole nation and was imagined as necessarily equal and undivided—in rights, that is, if not in fortune. Michel Servan, for instance, addressing the lower orders in a rather patronizing screed, puts these words in their mouths: "Declare that without equality morality is but an illusion, and justice an unsolvable problem; but do make it clear that you are not demanding equality of rank, wealth, power, or honors, which is incompatible with monarchy. . . . State that the equality you demand is that of rights."[29] Members of the Third Estate might differ greatly in wealth, but they were emphatically assumed all to have the same interests.

Two sorts of principles underlay the Third Estate's (indeed the nation's) imagined cohesiveness, drawn from two main currents of eighteenth-century French thought, the physiocratic and the Rousseauean. In the physiocratic view the principle of cohesion was nature, which governed the complementary pursuits of different groups of workers in a well-ordered society. In the Rousseauean tradition, the principle of unanimity was the law. These two strains were routinely conjoined in the pamphlet literature of the eve of the Revolution. In the pamphlets' double definition of society as productive activity and common law, social enemies cannot, by definition, exist inside society; they endanger it from the outside. They are the *privilégiés,* those who through their choice of economic parasitism and legal exceptionalism cast themselves out of the national community.

But between these two opposite though mutually defining entities, the nation and the privileged, no third group, no *via media*, was ever imagined to exist.

Portrayals and discussions of the Third Estate in the pamphlet literature of 1788–89 reveal a central and enduring feature of French revolutionary culture: the refusal to acknowledge fundamental divisions or structural conflicts of interest within the French body social. This trait is intimately related to what François Furet and other scholars have identified as the governing feature of French political culture: the absence of a concept of loyal opposition. Just as in politics there were no legitimate interest groups, only sharply opposed congeries of patriots and traitors, the social world was made up of an undivided *peuple* within the national pale, and a selfish and parasitical group beyond it. Social conflict could exist only outside the (political) nation, as a war against the aristocrat-as-enemy-alien. In order to grasp why society could be imagined in this way, it is necessary to understand that for the liberals and radicals who made the French Revolution, freedom was assumed to reside in consensus and uniformity, unfreedom in multiplicity. The standard image of tyranny in the rhetoric and imagery of the later eighteenth century was a many-headed hydra—the hydra of despotism, feudalism, federalism, and so on. It was therefore difficult to imagine a free people as legitimately divided into anything like a lower and a middling group. When the bourgeoisie was mentioned by revolutionaries, it was in most cases understood as a possibly menacing reincarnation of aristocracy.

## A PEOPLE UNDIVIDED? POPULAR VIOLENCE AND PROPERTIED CITIZENS

The preceding discussion of the Third Estate as undivided *peuple* and the revolutionary insistence on social unanimity might legitimately trigger a skeptical response from any good social historian. Regardless of high-minded rhetoric about the revolutionary people, common sense suggests that there was a world of difference between the Assembly politician who would go home to a good dinner cooked by a servant, and the man or woman whose stomach would ache every time the price of bread shot up. And surely all those involved in the Revolution must have been aware of that divide. The lived experience of social difference in 1789–1791 can be illuminated by focusing on two divisive developments: the violent acts of the Revolution's popular supporters, and the creation of a citizen militia, the National Guard, made up of wealthier elements of the population, whose central task was the maintenance of order. Did the rough "justice" of the crowd, the savage knifings and beheadings often perpetrated on members of the elites, cause the well-to-do to recoil from their popular allies? Did the corresponding repression of popular disorder by the Guard alienate plebeian activists? Were the social tensions inherent in such a situation ever articulated into an ideology of social difference?

The problem of popular violence posed itself to the deputies of the National Assembly and others of the upper classes as early as July 1789. In retaliation for his garrison's shooting of several dozen of the Bastille's besiegers, the fortress's governor, de Launay, was hacked to death after he surrendered, and his head was hoisted on a pike. The same treatment was meted out to the city official de Flesselles, and a few days later to two government officials, Foulon and Bertier, whom the mob accused of organizing starvation. For generations now, historians have argued that the leaders of the newly formed National Assembly averted their eyes from popular violence while reaping its political benefits. In response to the events of July 14, the king withdrew the troops he had been massing around Paris and recalled his dismissed minister, Jacques Necker, thereby acknowledging the power of the Assembly and its popular allies. To many deputies, apparently, such results were worth the price paid in deadly mayhem: the comment most frequently cited is that of deputy Antoine Barnave, who asked rhetorically, in the wake of the lynching of Foulon and Bertier, if the blood of the victims was really so pure.

Certainly, a measure of calculation and manipulation entered into the attitude of the political leaders toward the people. On June 27, deputy Adrien Duquesnoy confided to his journal: "[W]e are so dependent on public opinion, that of the people of Paris is so necessary."[30] Jean-Sylvain Bailly, a prominent participant in these events—he was named mayor of Paris on July 15—also said as much in his memoirs. He explained, for instance, that on July 15 the National Assembly had ordered the demolition of the Bastille, "which had been started the previous day by the *peuple,* and therefore in a very illegal manner. It was important to sanction this popular act, or rather to have it devolve from authority, so that a blind multitude should not get into the habit of usurping that authority."[31] In this as in other instances, the preferred strategy was to run ahead of the crowd to seize control (or appear to do so) of what was already happening.

Attitudes toward the people in 1789, while complex, were a great deal more positive than one might expect, even when *le peuple* engaged in harrowingly violent behavior. Admittedly, the memoirs of upperclass observers of the early Revolution do contain many a flash of primal fear in the face of what they saw as the people's animalism. Early on, in June, Duquesnoy wrote in his journal of his nervousness about the way in which the poor were being encouraged to go after the aristocracy: "A loyal man . . . must intervene between the nobility and the ferocious man who would cut their throats . . . [Egalitarian] ideas are fermenting among the people, who insult and mistreat all those designated by the party leaders . . . Heads are getting ever hotter, and from one moment to the next the people can engage in terrible excesses."[32] More pithily, Bailly noted that when the people burst into the Hôtel de Ville on July 12, the concierge was chased away and replaced by a man guarding the main hall, a rifle at his shoulder, "in his shirtsleeves, and wearing no stockings or shoes."[33]

Yet upper-class perceptions of the people and their actions remained mostly positive, if condescending. Even faced with a menacing crowd, Bailly understood that the Parisians were "rightly scared of the present and the future." He admonished the Electors, who formed and improvised city government, to calm the people's alarm and if they had to oppose its movements, to do so "only in a prudent and paternal manner."[34] As for the violence of July 1789, many of Barnave's colleagues and contemporaries found reason, as he did, to accept or even applaud it. The lawyer Adrien Colson, in letters to the steward of an aristocratic family for whom Colson also worked, recounted the storming of the Bastille with unmitigated approval. Colson characterized the fortress's governor de Launay as a "scoundrel" and "coward," described with some relish his death at the hands of the crowd, and concluded that this was indeed a *glorieuse journée*.[35] Duquesnoy's account of the storming of the Bastille expresses outrage at the shooting of the besiegers, while applauding the death of Flesselles, whom he described as a traitor to the people's cause.[36] Even the aristocrat Ferrières, writing to his sister about the four killings, refused to indict the perpetrators: "I would never have thought that a good and lovable people could have been brought to such excesses; but divine justice often makes use of human hands."[37]

Colin Lucas has described the relationship between the elites and the crowd at this stage as "simultaneous fusion and separation."[38] Appalled at the sight of what the mob could do, men like Bailly, Duquesnoy, Colson, and even the nobleman Ferrières nonetheless continued to articulate the belief that there was no essential difference between their own will and that of *le peuple*. If the latter acted in unruly or misguided fashion, it was for lack of political experience or education. Duquesnoy mused over the worst possible scenarios—that the people might get used to blood and shed "even impure blood without due process or law"; that they might try to subjugate the Assembly, adopt an "exaggerated" constitution, or secede from the rest of France. But, he concluded, "the people of Paris has feelings of generosity and honor; I believe it is enough to enlighten it as to its true interests and duties, and for the nation to learn that no part of it, no individual or corporation, no town, no province has an interest that is separate or different from that of the whole."[39] Because of this view of the political nation as a whole, the revolutionary elites were unwilling to draw a line between themselves and their plebeian allies. At most, they allowed that the crowd had been infiltrated by "brigands" or manipulated by "aristocrats." As Lucas points out, the deputies' and electors' own discourse on sovereignty prevented them from drawing such a line—in the end they remained convinced that, property qualifications notwithstanding, their own legitimacy and power were inseparable from the man in shirtsleeves and no shoes.[40] Sovereignty and *le peuple* were both indivisible.

Such lofty conceits were not easy to maintain unchallenged for long. Inevitably, and quite soon, the belief in the people's essential rightness was seriously dented by the rough and tumble of street politics. While some of the witnesses to popular violence in July 1789, such as Colson, saw the happenings in Paris, the National Assembly deputies were safely ensconced in Versailles, some twenty miles away from the bloodshed. From there, it was easy to remain Olympian about the undivided French people, but it was quite another matter when the delegates were forced to contend with *le peuple*, and a very rough segment of it, face to face. On October 5–6, 1789, a large crowd of armed Parisian workers, led by the redoubtable fishwives *(poissardes)* of the central markets, marched on Versailles to protest rising bread prices and demand the return of the royal family to Paris. This too was a violent episode and, like many of his colleagues, deputy Duquesnoy recorded scenes that chilled his blood: women reeking of fish and drunk on spirits invading the president's rostrum; men and women howling from the galleries above the Assembly: "Bread, bread, talk about bread"; and finally, the physical intimidation and death threats that ended in the decapitation of some of the royal family's bodyguards.[41]

The October days were a turning point that left many of the deputies profoundly shaken with respect to their plebeian allies. For most, it was their first direct encounter with popular violence.[42] Adrien Duquesnoy's language, for instance, changed significantly after this episode. Quite suddenly, his respect for the *peuple* gave way to censorious comments about the savagery of the *populace,* or *vile populace.* During and after the October days, he began using certain new expressions: he talked about *honnêtes gens* (honest folk) or *gens de bien* (decent folk) in contrast to the rabble and those prepared to make use of its violence.[43] On October 19, for instance, he noted gratefully the return to a "profound calm": "All of the *gens de bien* have an interest in maintaining [this calm] and those who have the forces to do so will do their best to keep it in place."[44] The expression *gens de bien* is a particularly telling one, since the word *bien* means both "good" and, in the plural, possessions. The *gens de bien* were thus both the "good" and "decent" folk and the property owners.

Property had been an issue from the time that the Estates General were convened, and it was clear that big changes were in the air. Privilege, the collective ownership of certain rights and exemptions, was an important form of property under the Old Regime, and, one pamphleteer warned readers in 1789, if you call upon "the multitude" to wage war on privilege, how can you be sure that they will not turn against all manner of property?[45] In the first months of the Revolution, some of the more conservative members of the Assembly sometimes expressed qualms on this score. In August, when the idea of a Declaration of the Rights of Man was raised, the monarchist Malouet worried about the effects of such a declaration of principle unmodified by practical qualifications. It would be better, he argued, to wait until the new constitution was in place.

Of course this had not stopped the Americans, he conceded: "But American society, recently formed, is made up entirely of property owners already accustomed to equality. . . . Whereas we, Gentlemen, have as fellow citizens an immense multitude of men without property . . . who are sometimes angered, not without reason, by the sight of luxury and opulence." Let us work gradually, through institutions, he pleaded, at narrowing the gap between rich and poor, rather than rashly granting abstract rights to the dispossessed.[46]

Questions of property, wealth, and status became conspicuous in the winter and spring of 1789–90, as the Assembly grappled with the issue of voting rights and eligibility to both local and national legislatures. Under the shock of the October days, the deputies hurried to pass a decree, on October 29, which established a distinction, previously articulated by Sieyès, between "active" and "passive" citizens. The decree established a three-tiered system. It gave the vote to men over twenty-five paying the equivalent of three days' unskilled labor in taxes; these voters chose electors who paid the equivalent of ten days' labor, who in turn chose deputies from a group paying what was known as the *marc d'argent*, fifty-four days' labor, in taxes. Even the second tier of the system would comprise only 50,000 men. The *peuple* might be undivided, but only the comfortably-off could vote, and only the wealthy could get elected. A modified version of this scheme was eventually written into the Constitution of 1791, over the vociferous opposition of the left wing of the Assembly.[47] Radical journalists kept up a campaign against the new electoral laws in the fall of 1789. In December, the journalist Elisée Loustallot thundered in the widely read *Révolutions de Paris:* "The *marc d'argent* decree has produced all of the bad decrees of which it was the germ. Already the *pure aristocracy* of the rich has been established."[48]

It was the deputy from Arras, the lawyer Maximilien de Robespierre, who articulated the most sustained and eloquent critique of the new electoral requirements, in a speech to the Assembly on January 25, 1790. Restricting the vote was, he argued, purely and simply "aristocratic." If the decrees limiting voting and eligibility rights were to remain, "What would your constitution be? A real aristocracy. For aristocracy is a state in which one group of citizens is sovereign and the rest are subjects—and what aristocracy? The most unbearable of all, that of the rich!" The proposed electoral laws were, he thundered, simply a way of recreating something like the Old Regime by exchanging "feudal aristocracy" for a new "aristocracy of wealth," thereby restoring privilege under a new guise.[49]

The reaction to Robespierre's speech by deputy Adrien Duquesnoy, a comfortably-off man of moderate opinions, is probably typical of most members of the Assembly:

> Vile and detestable incendiary, he thinks he is championing the people's interest by arming it against its natural defenders! No doubt in theory this idea that all men have an equal right to law-making is beautiful, even sublime, but how wrong it is in practice! . . . Certainly we must not substitute a new aristocracy for an old one, but where is the man who is attached to his homeland, to the earth that saw him born, if he owns nothing and can take his strength and industry, or even his violence, anywhere? There is no doubt about it, only property-owners are citizens . . .[50]

But Robespierre had anticipated this objection in his speech, asking his fellow-deputies how they could brand the poor as irresponsible beings who had "nothing to lose." Yes, he said, a small shack, ragged clothes, and paltry wages "may look like *nothing* to luxury and opulence, but it is something for the common run of mankind, it is a sacred property, as sacred, certainly, as the lavish domains of the rich."[51] At stake, as both sides understood, was a view of society later expressed in Guizot's famous admonition to the disenfranchised: "Get rich!" Robespierre put it in almost the same terms, albeit in the mode of sarcastic disbelief: "[The proposed law] gives citizens this astonishing lesson: 'Be rich at any cost, or you will be nothing.'"[52]

In traditional interpretations of the Revolution, the struggle over and eventual adoption of a set of stiff property requirements for active political participation is presented as unassailable evidence that the Revolution represented the triumph of bourgeois interests and leadership. And certainly it would be foolish to deny that a majority of members of the Constituent Assembly assumed that only men exactly like themselves—wealthy and well-educated—could responsibly represent the nation, and that these could only be elected by men not very different from themselves. And yet two aspects of this debate should be kept in mind. First, opponents of the property requirements like Robespierre and Loustallot never identified the new political elite as either middling or bourgeois—as a new elite with a distinct source of income and a clear historical identity. They designated the beneficiaries of the voting laws by the loaded term "aristocracy." And second, the deputies themselves would have denied that they were creating a new elite of any kind. To them, the differences between active and passive citizenship were quantitative, not qualitative. Unlike nobility, a matter of bloodlines and legal distinctions and therefore an essential component of one's social being, property was purely contingent, a matter of industriousness and perhaps good luck. Unlike privilege, which was rigid and juridical, property—usually conceived as landed property—was "natural," open in theory to those who, in Lockean fashion, "mixed their labor" with it.[53] A contingent matter, property could not be the basis of an essential social distinction.

## BROTHERS IN ARMS

Thus a discrepancy arose between the revolutionaries' language of social consensus (the idea of a single people, united in interests) and social practices at odds with that discourse—popular violence from below, limitations on the vote from above. A central embodiment of this tension in revolutionary culture was the National Guard, an institution initially central to the Revolution whose universalist claims were at odds with its well-to-do membership. At least at first, the National Guard, the symbol of citizenship, was often called the *garde bourgeoise,* a term which invites us to look into both its institutional origins and its social composition. Although the National Guard was created as the embodiment of a united armed citizenry, its function quickly became the maintenance of internal order. Was it therefore perceived as the instrument of the political elites?

The earliest calls for setting up a citizens' militia came from the National Assembly, during its tense standoff with the monarchy in early July 1789. On July 8, Mirabeau moved to beg the king to withdraw the troops he was massing around Paris, and to set up units of what he called *gardes bourgeoises* in both Paris and Versailles. The expression *garde bourgeoise* seems to have been the one used in the unsuccessful palavers that followed. Ultimately, the militia created itself in the course of the scramble for arms of July 12–14 and the siege of the Bastille.[54] Upon returning to Paris from Versailles, the new mayor of

Paris, Bailly, and the hastily named commander of the Guard, Lafayette, encountered a fearsome crowd of men armed with pikes, hatchets, and scythes as well as rifles. Their sole identification was the red,
white, and blue badge or *cocarde,* which had become practically overnight the sign or revolutionary allegiance. In his memoirs, Bailly regarded the creation of a citizen militia a "barrier against despotism"
equal in importance to the capture of the Bastille.[55] Most contemporary accounts of July 14 concurred, ranking the formation of the
Garde Nationale just behind the destruction of the fortress as the second most important outcome of that glorious day.[56]

In the days after the fall of the Bastille, the new force was at last
authorized by the monarchy, and hastily organized. The new National
Guard of Paris was 31,000 men strong, with service in it a duty for all
men between the ages of twenty-five and fifty, *except* for workers, artisans, servants, and the homeless.[57] The actual composition of the
Guard was more diverse than this regulation (and others following it)
suggest.[58] In some districts of Paris and many provincial centers there
simply were not enough men of property to make up a plausible force,
and in most places wealthy men were allowed to hire replacements
instead of serving. But the numbers we have and contemporary descriptions still do suggest that National Guard membership was skewed
toward the upper reaches of urban society. Records show that the rank
and file were heavily populated by the wealthier elements of the
artisanal world (retailers and skilled workers like jewelers), with a liberal sprinkling of *bourgeois de Paris* and professionals.[59]

Contemporary descriptions reinforce the numerical data.
Duquesnoy wrote somewhat defensively on July 18: "It is important to
note that in the Parisian militia there are a large number of very
respectable [*honnêtes*] men, some of the best citizens in the city, chevaliers of Saint-Louis, chevaliers of Malta, very good bourgeois,
financiers, priests, lawyers, monks, all very well disciplined and no
more apt to abandon their situation than are the regular troops."[60]
The marquis de Ferrières, upon learning that his brother-in-law and
another nobleman had been named to head their local militias, expressed satisfaction at what he termed an alliance between the nobility
and the *haut tiers*—the "higher Third Estate."[61]

And then there was the matter of the uniform. By August of 1789, the ragtag army of men wearing cockades had been replaced by a smartly clad militia: royal blue jackets with white facings and linings, scarlet piping, white waistcoat and breeches, not to mention the gaiters, buttons, and seasonal variations. Along with a rifle, the whole getup could cost fifty livres, easily a month's salary for an unskilled worker.[62] Bailly, by then mayor of Paris, wrote in his memoirs that he "ardently desired" that the guard be clad in uniform: "I thought that these townsmen [*bourgeois*] in different clothes carrying only rifles were not sufficiently imposing to our crowds of brigands . . . The magistrate and the armed forces must wear distinctive signs, otherwise the people see in the magistrate or the soldier only their neighbor or their comrade."[63]

In some quarters at least, this strategy seemed to have seriously backfired. In the summer of 1789, workers in several Parisian districts protested the decree which excluded them from membership in the guard. One Eugène Gervais, a servant, was arrested for incitements to violence after he allegedly declared that "the *garde bourgeoise* and all those who wore the uniform were all j.f. [*jean foutres,* buggers] and that ten thousand servants could take all the j.f. with their blue suits and white facings and make them dance; that all the *bourgeois* [in this context, probably "bosses"] were j.f., with no exceptions . . . that there were sixty thousand servants in Paris who could get together with the workers in different trades, and then you'd see all those j.f. go hide away at home with their f[ucking] uniforms."[64] The guards' uniforms were a loaded social and political matter because they later became the very literal equivalent of full citizenship: a ruling of 1790 established that since the cost of the outfit far surpassed the minimum amount of taxation required for active citizenship, anyone who had bought a uniform would be automatically placed on the voting rolls.[65]

Matters of terminology seem further to reinforce a view of the Garde Nationale as a reflection and instrument of the urban elite. In late June and early July of 1789, the expression most commonly used in calls for and discussions of an urban militia was *garde bourgeoise,* the "bourgeois" or urban guard.[66] Once the new force was set up it was named, on July 16, the Garde Nationale, but the older designations of *garde bourgeoise* or *milice bourgeoise* remained in use in the following weeks, even months. The lawyer Adrien Colson, in the letters he wrote home, was slow to change the names; by mid-September 1789 he was collapsing old and new together and calling the force the *garde nationale bourgeoise.*

The latter expression was technically an oxymoron, because the essence of what people thought of in the eighteenth century as a "bourgeois" militia was a unit for the defense of a specific urban locality. Since the Middle Ages, most French towns had formed such units on a temporary or permanent basis for the defense of the community. From a real military role these troops had been reduced to internal policing and ceremonial functions, the towns' dignitaries parading proudly in their uniforms, sashes, and plumed hats on official occasions.[67] These militias were bourgeois in the sense that they embodied the political power of the bourgeoisie as urban citizenry, as described in Chapter 1. Just as the eighteenth-century dictionaries equated bourgeoisie with urban citizenship, and gave examples of the "bourgeoisie rising" or "taking up arms," a chronicler of the early Revolution such as the marquis de Ferrières could write in July that "the bourgeoisie has armed itself, thirty-thousand strong."[68] Any significant political activity in an urban context was considered, at this point, "bourgeois." And no doubt this longstanding identification of militias with the power of French towns' ancient *bourgeoisies* had been reinforced by the popularity of Mably's recently republished *Observations sur l'histoire de France.* In the twelfth century, amidst the mayhem of "feudal anarchy" the towns, Mably had written, "became little republics" in which the bourgeois exercised communal authority and "divided themselves up into militia companies . . . became masters of their towns' fortifications."[69]

Urban militias, then, offered two sets of connotations which, after 1789, were at odds with one another. On the one hand, they stood for citizenship and the defense of a common good; on the other, they represented the local and particular interests of a multiplicity of different urban worlds. Not surprisingly, in the course of its rapid transformation from *garde bourgeoise* to Garde Nationale, the new Parisian militia embraced the first set of meanings while relinquishing the second. The Guard became a national institution in fact as well as in name, in the weeks after July 14, when units modeled on the Parisian one sprang up in towns and villages.[70] The so-called Great Fear, the wave of rural unrest that broke over France in the second half of July, was a main precipitant for the creation of units. "Crowds of brigands have overrun the nearby provinces," wrote Ferrières on July 28; "Everywhere people are taking up arms; the bourgeois militias are looking to the safety of towns."[71] But while the older bourgeois militias had evoked local particularism, the National Guard evolved, in the first year of the Revolution, into a central—for a while *the* central—symbol of classless political fusion.

The National Guard unit quickly became the archetypal setting for a powerful symbolic gesture, perhaps the central political ritual of the Revolution's beginnings, the oath of brotherhood. In the first twelve months of the Revolution, National Guard units acted out thousands of times, all over the realm, the gesture which symbolized the founding of the new order, the fraternal oath. The occasion very often was a conjoining of forces for purposes of common defense, sealing the agreement by means of elaborate ceremonies which centered on oaths of brotherhood and loyalty.[72] In November 1789, for instance, ten thousand Guards from eastern France rallied on the Plaine de l'Étoile where they ceremonially vowed, "upon their hearts and their weapons, before heaven," to defend one another as "brothers in arms."[73] Long after the brotherly euphoria of May–June 1789 had given way, for the deputies and their plebeian allies, to anger, fear, and hard-headed politics, National Guardsmen rekindled the spirit of the Tennis Court Oath for audiences all over the realm.

The oath was a natural gesture for Frenchmen of this period and not just (or not primarily) because it evoked a revolutionary tradition of contractual thought that reached back, via Rousseau, to Hobbes, Grotius, and the like. The juridico-political culture of the Old Regime was predicated upon the swearing of oaths, which the guardsmen's vows both evoked and superseded: the oaths of workers joining their sworn trades or *jurandes,* those of professionals like doctors or lawyers to their *ordres,* a whole range of vows from the oldest vassalic rites to the recently devised secret oaths of the Freemasons.[74] Within this corporate structure the king represented the principle of unity, binding together and arbitrating among the myriad oath-bound communities. With the displacement of kingship as the central principle, all of these particularistic covenants were redirected toward that more abstract unifying principle, the nation. The revolutionary oath derived from older corporate oaths, yet at the same time it repudiated the principles upon which the older gesture rested. Where Old Regime vows were based on local, social, and professional particularism, the revolutionary oath rejected all of these. The text of a March 1790 oath in western France, for instance, explicitly negates all competing allegiances among participants: "Being no longer Bretons or Angevins but French and citizens of the same empire, we renounce all our local and private privileges as unconstitutional."[75]

Besides universalism, the other distinguishing characteristic of the revolutionary oath was its designation as fraternal; it was an oath between brothers, an endless reenactment of the scene prefigured in Jacques Louis David's *Oath of the Horatii* of 1785, with the king-father still, in 1790, presiding. Chroniclers of the French Revolution have not really noted the strangeness of the concept of *fraternal* oath. These were not oaths that made participants into brothers—those who took them were presumed to be brothers already. And siblings who either literally or metaphorically share the same parents and the same blood are, arguably, the only people in the world who do not need an oath of loyalty. The oxymoronic fraternal oath reflects a moment of transition in the Revolution, when the force of family love was first acknowledged to be insufficient to bind the nation together. It was all very well before 1789, and even in those heady first weeks, to imagine a community bound by sentimental kinship writ large, but almost from the start it was obvious that such sentiments could not simply be presumed to exist. Hence the importance of a gesture which forced participants into explicit endorsement of the Revolution, and the spread of a ritual which oddly conflated kinship and political will, blood ties and the law.

The fraternal oath was associated with the National Guard more than with any other group in the Revolution, and it explicitly conveyed a rejection of differences—social, local, or occupational—within the *patrie*. The culmination of a year's worth of fraternal oath-taking occurred on July 14, 1790, when the grandiose Festival of the Federation saw the convergence on Paris of tens of thousands of guards from the provinces who, at a rain-soaked ceremony, echoed the vow pronounced by Lafayette of fidelity to Nation, Law, and King. The same set of contradictions inherent within the Guard itself ran through this one-year anniversary of the Bastille's fall.

The presiding spirit and ideology of the festival were harmony and unity, endlessly proclaimed in allegory and symbol: female embodiments of concord, clasped hands, triangles whose points were Law, King, and People.[76] The scene tirelessly evoked in prints preceding the event was that of people of all classes, from nobles to paupers, all physically toiling to make the Champ de Mars ready for the great event. Contemporaries seem to have been struck above all by the idea of thousands of men converging on Paris; much of the commentary at the time focused on the dynamic coming together rather than the static oath.[77] If modern nationalism is, as Benedict Anderson has argued, "a new way of linking fraternity, power and time meaningfully together," the Festival of the Federation was a significant event in the birth of French nationalism.[78] Yet the pattern of exclusions which characterized the Guard as an institution marked the festival as well. As Mona Ozouf points out, two important parties were excluded from the festival. One, named often and explicitly, was the aristocracy, the negative pole defining the people's unity. The other excluded party was not named but was defined through the topography of the festival: the common people actually stood outside the perimeter of the festival, beyond the closed ranks of armed guards encircling the festival's active participants: the king, the political notables, and the National Guard.[79] But as Ozouf remarks, nobody seems to have thought anything of this: "[N]either of the two exclusions defining [the festival] was experienced as such; neither seemed to harm the national spirit celebrated by the festival."[80]

This denial of social difference might be accounted a shallow and transitory phenomenon, reflecting the euphoria of the Revolution's beginnings. But the adamant belief in unity did not abate; if anything it got more entrenched, and served, paradoxically, as the basis for a whole series of exclusions. Let us remain in the same place—the Champ de Mars in the west of Paris, where the Eiffel Tower now stands—and jump almost exactly a year forward, to July 17, 1791. On that day, the National Guard opened fire on a group of popular militants who had assembled to sign a petition demanding the abolition of the monarchy. The Guard killed about fifty people, mostly plebeian members of radical popular clubs. This event, known as the Champ de Mars Massacre, the culmination of a summer of growing tensions following the closing of government workshops and the royal family's aborted flight, has usually been considered the first instance of open class warfare within the ranks of the revolutionaries.

Contemporary commentary on the massacre, however, did not match what later historians have assumed. Certainly, there were many spontaneous outbursts of popular anger at the Guard, and especially at its commander Lafayette, in the wake of the killings. The police arrested a man distracted with grief and anger who tried to raise a mob, yelling "Down with the *habit bleu,* burn the *habits bleus.*" They rounded up a group of journeyman cobblers who were shouting that "the National Guard had killed people, that they were *gueux* and *coquins* [wretches and scoundrels], that their *habits* should be torn off them and that none should be left in existence." Working women threatened to kill the "blue uniforms" with stones and knives.[81]

Such sentiments are reminiscent of the rantings of the servant Gervais against the National Guard in the previous summer, and together they show plenty of scattered hostility to the battalions of better-off folks who policed them. The interesting matter, however, is that such sentiments never congealed into any sort of antibourgeois ideology, indeed any recognition whatsoever of class antagonism. As David Andress has shown, even the radical newspapers of Gorsas, Marat, and Loustallot refused to condemn either the National Guard or their popular antagonists, arguing that alien conspirators had infiltrated the crowd and provoked the massacre. Whether constitutional monarchists or newly minted republicans, journalists and politicians refused to read the Champ de Mars Massacre as a social conflict; they placed the blame instead on elements foreign to society, traitors, conspirators, aristocratic renegades. The people could only be one (plebs and Guard together) and politically pure. Ironically, this very insistence on unity and blamelessness would serve soon to justify multiple exclusions of those who were said not to conform. "The protesters of July 1791," Andress concludes, "were victims less of a class war than of the belief that class war was impossible."[82] Even when confronted with the starkest instance of what seems to us to be social conflict—and murderous conflict, at that—neither side chose to see the events of July 17 as such. Workers did express rage at the Guard and its leaders, but not the sort of anger that translated into awareness of separate social interests. As for politicians and journalists right across the political spectrum, they always located division *outside* of the legitimate nation.

## DEFINING THE ENEMY:
## NOBLE AND BOURGEOIS ARISTOCRATS

This was the paradoxical logic of the Revolution's social imaginary: that the denial of conflict in society, the refusal to acknowledge divisions in the nation, was the trigger for ostracism and in some cases persecution.[83] The logic governing revolutionary culture was different from the familiar process of scapegoating. Revolutionaries did not say to their perceived enemies: you are responsible for all of our problems. Rather, they held that citizenship was a matter of will, of implicit or explicit oaths of loyalty. Any sign of division implied that some person or group had refused that act of will, thereby opting for outsider status. The response to any form of strife, from parliamentary opposition to street violence, was therefore the identification of the persons or groups who, in deed if not in words, had demonstrably chosen not to belong. Of course the war which began in 1792 provided the Revolution with authentically foreign enemies, but there was always a need to locate an internal foe. This was the role individuals and groups fell into under the catchall term "aristocracy."

Aristocracy proved a convenient term because it coupled political meaning with an obvious social referent. The revolutionary elites, all of them trained in the classics, were well aware that the word did not mean nobility but government by an elite. From the start, however, the term attached itself most stubbornly to noblemen. In the early days of the Revolution, in the Estates General and the National Assembly, the two main groups in contention were identified as Democrats (the progressives), and Aristocrats (mostly conservative noblemen). The initial division into Estates reinforced the perceived connection between the social and the political: Duquesnoy wrote in May that "in the Third they speak only of aristocrats, in the Nobility only of democrats; that is the war cry."[84] Under the pen of the marquis de Ferrières, this dichotomy endured well into 1791. In the spring of that year he wrote, in a "pox on both your houses" spirit: "The Aristocrats are hoping for the arrival of five or six [foreign] armies. The Democrats are behaving like fools, they have no common sense."[85] While the aristocrat remained in place as main foe throughout the revolutionary years, his antagonist would quickly become that universal, normative group, *le peuple* or *la nation*.

The term *aristocrate* long survived, of course, the legal eradication of both feudalism and nobility. The former was famously destroyed in the extraordinary session of the National Assembly that lasted through the night of August 4, 1789. The latter was abolished a few weeks before the Festival of the Federation, on June 19, 1791. The details of the session of June 19 demonstrate once again how connected were, for the revolutionaries, the two realms we call "the social" and "the political." The discussion began with Alexandre de Lameth pointing out that provincial Frenchmen arriving in the capital might be offended by the statue of Louis XIV on the Place des Victoires, which portrayed the French provinces as manacled slaves at the king's feet. Thereupon an obscure deputy, melodramatically announcing "This day is the tomb of all vanities," proposed the abolition of nobility, a suggestion eagerly seized by others, including such blue bloods as Lafayette and the viscount de Noailles. In short order, the deputies endorsed the abolition of hereditary nobility along with that of titles, coats of arms, and liveries on personal servants. In a second decree they voted to remove the figures of the chained provinces from the statue of Louis XIV.[86]

The conjunction of the statue business with so drastic a social measure as the abolition of ancient nobility may appear odd to us, but did not seem incoherent to deputies used to considering the social and the political together. The Sun-King's military and administrative tyranny over the French provinces was reflected in the social claims made possible by hereditary rights and trappings, the custom of decking grown men in liveries that advertised one's lineage. The only deputy to speak out against the motion, the abbé Maury, pointed this out: "In France nobility is intrinsic to the constitution, . . . if there is no more nobility there is no more monarchy."[87] Although most would not have foreseen it in 1790, the future was of course to prove him right.

Within the first year of the Revolution legal and fiscal privilege, corporate and hereditary status, and all outward symbols of social preeminence were abolished. Particles in people's names melted away for both nobles and upwardly mobile commoners (Georges d'Anton became Danton again). Attitudes and habits did not, of course, change overnight. The marquis de Ferrières wrote privately to his wife that the June 19 decision was absurd, "for they can't keep a person from being his father's son, and nobility will be transmitted as before, by tradition."[88]

Ten days later he noted that although at the theater the duchess de Luynes's servants announced her simply as madame de Luynes, "in society things go on as before."[89] In contrast, commoners who resented nobles were delighted by the decree. Edmond Géraud, a student from Bordeaux devoted to the new ideas, wrote home to his equally *patriote* father: "You must surely have learned with joy of the charming little decree which so casually strikes down all of those vain ornaments, old titles, fine coats of arms, all of those splendid names, all that was invented to flatter the vanity of our miserable aristocrats."[90]

Patriots like Géraud applauded the measure; philosophical nobles like Ferrières accepted it as inevitable. By the summer of 1790, most of those diehards likely to protest the abolition of nobility had fled the country anyway. The menace of nobility did not go away, however. It remained rhetorically alive through the use and abuse of the word *aristocrate,* which caught on and endured as one of the key elements in the revolutionary lexicon for several reasons. For one thing, the term had the advantage, as an insult, of harsh guttural consonants that allowed one to spit it out more effectively than the more euphonious *noble* or even *privilégié.* And most people knew the difference between a noble and an aristocrat: not everyone could be a *ci-devant,* but just about anyone could be guilty of the sin of aristocracy.

Anyone familiar with the French Revolution is aware of the term *aristocrate*'s ubiquitousness, of its labile and capacious nature. From the first few months of the Revolution, the term was lavishly sprinkled throughout the "patriot" newspapers put out by men like Camille Desmoulins and Élisée Loustallot, often coupled with its favored antithesis, *peuple. Aristocrate* was employed indifferently to name the Old Regime elites—nobles, clergy, and officers—as well as those, like financiers, who had too much money or earned it in the wrong way, or those, like lawyers, who were too educated or too clever. The term referred to social status and social advantages, then, but was equally characteristic of political beliefs and behavior: aristocrats typically schemed and plotted, working behind the scenes to undermine the political activity of the deputies who carried out the people's will.[91]

It was evident even to those without much sophistication that the word "aristocrat" was a very loose term, something of a negative slogan. Coachmen berated their sluggish horses by calling them *aristocrates,* and young Géraud, who usually displayed the humorlessness of the True Believer, did note that anything Parisians were in the mood to complain about became "aristocratic": "Even the students in the Academy of Drawing accuse their pencils of feudalism when they are too dry."[92]

The mythical aristocrat was the necessary other, the flip side of the ideal of fusion into a great national family. To quote Simon Schama: "[A]ll the images of incorporation presupposed counter-images of denial: obstinate anticitizens who, refusing to sink their differences within the revolutionary community, had to be extruded from it . . . Increasingly such outsiders were identified by the treasonable epithet 'aristocrats.'"[93] Even at the time, contemporaries sometimes noted the term's vagueness, as well as its ideological usefulness. As early as November 1789, the newspaper *Révolutions de Paris* noted: "The word *aristocrate* has no less contributed to the Revolution than has the cockade. Its meaning is today very wide; it is applied to all those who live from abuses, who are nostalgic for abuses, or who wish to create new abuses."[94]

Unquestionably, the term "aristocrat" was applied more to nobles than to any other group. Thanks to historians like Mably, noble claims to separate bloodlines were easily turned back against them: if they were indeed the descendants of Frankish warriors from the forests of Germany, then they did not belong anyway. Certainly the accumulating threats posed by emigration, foreign war, and domestic counterrevolution did much to keep up the demonization of noble aristocrats as enemy aliens throughout the Revolution. But for all that aristocracy attached itself primarily to nobles, the epithet stuck to other groups as well, as the stigma of elitist separatism.

It is revealing to note, then, that while the notion of bourgeoisie is largely absent from revolutionary discourse, when it does appear it is often shackled with the damning qualifier "aristocratic." On February 10, 1791, the Girondin newspaper *Le Patriote français* published a lengthy letter from one of the group's leaders, Pétion, to his colleague Buzot, deploring the political fissure between the bourgeoisie and the people: "[T]he third estate is divided, that is the cause of all our problems. The bourgeoisie, that numerous and wealthy class, has broken from the *peuple;* it thinks itself superior to them, on a par with the aristocracy which disdains it and waits only for the best time to humiliate it."[95] But *bourgeoisie* was only one term among many. The expression *honnêtes gens* (decent folk), for instance, which Adrien Duquesnoy contrasted with "the rabble" or "the mob," was used later in the Revolution by the Girondins and then the Jacobins as a term of abuse for enemies on the right. The Girondin Marie-Jeanne Roland, for instance, in a 1790 letter, scathingly equated *honnêtes gens* with "the quadruple aristocracy of priests, lesser nobles, big merchants, and lawyers."[96]

The growth of the popular movement in the early 1790s naturally turned up the volume of the rhetoric castigating social distinctions based on wealth. The minutes of meetings in the sans-culotte bases (called sections), as well as stories in popular newspapers and pamphlets, reveal a relentlessly dualistic view of the sociopolitical world: on the one hand good sans-culottes, embodiments of *le peuple,* on the other an enemy who took multiple forms under the single umbrella term, "aristocrat."

The speaker at the section du Mail on May 21, 1793, offered this definition of the latter: "Aristocrats . . . are all the rich, the big merchants, the hoarders, the river-jumpers, the bankers, the brokers in the shops, the pettifoggers, all those who have something. We must banish them from the land of freedom." A petition from another section in December of that year denounced an unpopular decision as "the product of the priestly, noble, parliamentary, financial, and bourgeois aristocracy; everyone had a hand in it, except for the *peuple.*"[97]

Such statements point to the social and economic beliefs of the sans-culottes, as they have been memorably described by Albert Soboul: fiercely egalitarian, anticommercial, work-and-family centered, deeply suspicious of anyone too rich or too prominent.[98] It is in their statements that the expression "bourgeois aristocracy" recurs most systematically in revolutionary discourse. Soboul suggests that in occasionally designating the bourgeois as their enemy, some of the sans-culottes were prescient, anticipating the rise of a class with interests opposed to theirs. But on the very next page, Soboul quotes one of their number contrasting the poor sans-culotte with "a class of what was formerly called bourgeois."[99] The bourgeois was clearly a creature of the past rather than the future. And what is one to make of the instructions given to all local governments in the Lyon region, describing the achievements of the popular revolution: "If the bourgeois aristocracy had survived, it would soon have spawned the financial aristocracy, and the latter would have produced the noble aristocracy"?[100]

Popular political discourse, while occasionally ruder or more extreme than that of the elites, shared many of the same assumptions. Robespierre's language and beliefs were, no doubt, closer to the views of popular militants than were those of most politicians within the ruling assemblies. He wielded the same clatter of dichotomies, opposing popular virtue to the corruption of the rich, the powerful, the all-purpose aristocracy. Like the sans-culottes, he often ran through the familiar litany of aristocracies—bourgeois, municipal, noble, ecclesiastical, commercial—and not infrequently used the expression *aristocratie bourgeoise* or its variant *bourgeoisie aristocratique*. But neither in the rhetoric of the popular clubs and sections nor in that of the Jacobin leader does the bourgeoisie occupy a special place. It is but one item in a list of groups making up the many-headed monster of social egoism and political reaction: nobles, rentiers, patricians, rich merchants, town oligarchs, clerics, the English, and assorted *honnêtes gens*.[101]

The bourgeoisie occupies no especially prominent place in this lineup of enemies, nor does the Manichean contrast between a unified people and its many-headed foe leave any room for intermediate groups, social or political. Neither a temperate middle class nor the rising elite of the future, the bourgeoisie remained, in the revolutionary years, trapped in what had always been its role in the social imaginary: that of lackluster understudy to the nobility. Revolutionary discourse was from the start fixed in dualistic patterns pitting a virtuous and unified people against a shape-shifting but equally singular enemy, the aristocracy. Where social elites were concerned, the conceptual legacy of the Revolution was to prove exceptionally tenacious. Any group that sought to mark itself off and wield power was from now on viewed with suspicion as a possible reincarnation of the hated nobility.

The allegedly bourgeois French Revolution, at least in its first few years, produced no language or ideology justifying a middle- or upper-middle-class leadership. Wherever one expects to find defenses of a non-noble propertied elite, the search proves elusive: glorifications of the Third Estate emphasized that group's working-class component; the National Guard took oaths on behalf of an entire nation's sense of fraternity; property requirements for voting were never justified—as they were in England in the 1830s—on the basis of the virtues of a separate middle class.[102] In fact, judging from the language of revolutionaries, one would be tempted to label the French Revolution anti-bourgeois. Inasmuch as the Old Regime category of "bourgeoisie" meant urban citizenship, that notion dissolved because it was enlarged. As Jean-Sylvain Bailly put it, Frenchmen such as he were no longer bourgeois now that they were citizens. But the bourgeoisie had also been a legally privileged elite group, and as such was abolished outright. One of the Revolution's most enduring linguistic legacies was to attach the taint of despised privilege to the word "bourgeois." The revolutionaries' articulation of the threat of a bourgeois aristocracy prefigured the ubiquitous identification of a bourgeois enemy in nineteenth- and twentieth-century French republicanism.

But while the bourgeois was reviled as the self-serving enemy of an idealized *peuple,* such was the power of the latter concept that no idea of a middle class distinct from a bourgeois elite emerged either. In French revolutionary culture, the social and the political were completely coterminous: just as the French people—working, productive, prorevolutionary–*were* the nation, an aristocrat was a compound social and political enemy. For this reason, as François Furet once pointed out, the contest for control and legitimacy between the governing assemblies and the popular sections and clubs was never understood as middle-class versus working-class politics, but as claims to *represent* the people versus claims to *embody* it.[103] In the Revolution's first years, then, we cannot locate, any more than in the social imaginary of the Old Regime, any distinct pro-bourgeois or middle-class ideology. But the turbulent first years of the Revolution were also important for the features of French public culture which they did create, such as the sacredness invested in an undivided *peuple* and the moral importance of the state. When the dust settled down from those first years of upheaval, what appeared was not a triumphant capitalist elite, but a vastly expanded and glorified state bureaucracy.

# The Social World after Thermidor

## 4

The period between the fall of Robespierre and Napoleon Bonaparte's coup is sometimes called the bourgeois republic. The forms and ideals of republicanism were preserved between 1794 and 1799, but under a regime led by men of property who unambiguously denounced Jacobin excesses as they dismantled and disarmed the popular movement. A time when leaders struggled to maintain power against the twin threats of royalism and Jacobinism, the years of the Directory offer a good vantage point from which to examine the social consequences of the Revolution, both as historians have described them and as contemporaries saw them. What is left of the once universally accepted idea that the French Revolution brought the bourgeoisie to power? As the country recovered from the worst years of violence and repression, how did political leaders and legislators hostile to the nobility and suspicious of the plebs understand their own social position? And how did intellectuals of the generation that lived through the Revolution understand the social dimension of what their nation had just experienced?

## A SOCIAL REVOLUTION?

Until the 1960s, historians in France quarreled over whether Danton or Robespierre was the real hero of the Revolution, and their counterparts in Britain and the United States disagreed as to whether the events of 1789–1799 were admirable or appalling; but nobody questioned the metahistorical significance of what had happened in France as the eighteenth century came to a close. A triumphant bourgeoisie, buoyed by nascent capitalism and inspired by the Enlightenment's message of freedom and self-determination, had snatched power from a decadent aristocracy and a monarch who governed in the interest of the privileged few. The Revolution's causes were deep and structural, and while it did not have to happen at that exact time and in that exact way, a massive and probably explosive readjustment was bound to be the consequence of the contradiction between expanding capitalist wealth and remaining feudal sociopolitical structures.

That this view, derived from Marx, held such complete sway for over a century after around 1850 is understandable. It seemed as solid and impregnable as a massive brick house, securely connecting everything from the Atlantic trade to the writings of the philosophes to the Constitution of 1791. It is no wonder that some historians today want to believe that the house is still standing, however drastically remodeled. Yet breaches in the foundations first appeared in the 1950s, when a British scholar, Alfred Cobban, began to point out that French feudalism was a misnomer, that capitalism was marginal to this society, and that the revolutionary bourgeoisie included almost nobody remotely like a capitalist.[1] Soon other British and American revisionists were attacking the Marxian orthodox scenario of bourgeois revolution, shaking it with pronouncements such as the American historian George Taylor's famous conclusion that the French Revolution was "not a social revolution with political consequences, but a political revolution with social consequences."[2]

The revisionists argued that the deep structural causes conventionally assigned to the French Revolution were hard for historians to locate. Not only was there very little capitalist development of any sort (industrial, commercial, or financial) in prerevolutionary France, there were no irreducible differences in resources, aspirations, or beliefs between the noble and non-noble elites in this society. Rich commoners were already like nobles in some respects—owning land and real estate, for instance—and wanted to be like them in others: those who were financially successful could and did acquire offices in the administration, more land, a chateau, a title, even a son-in-law from an authentically noble family. So it had gone for generations, and so it went still in the 1780s.[3] The crisis that broke out in 1789 was not social in origin but political, a fiscal and financial muddle gone awry through egregious mismanagement, and which happened to coincide with a disastrous harvest. And, as Colin Lucas shrewdly suggested, if the Revolution looked like a social conflict, that was largely the result of a political decision: by convening the Estates General according to the benighted "forms of 1614," by bringing together nobles in silk suits and plumed hats with lawyers and writers in dingy garb while dithering over who would get how many votes, the monarchy imposed the appearance of a social struggle onto a purely political mess.[4] One troubling implication of the revisionist argument is that the Revolution was accidental and evitable: given a better ministerial team or a plentiful harvest in 1789, the whole thing could have been avoided.

This view of the Revolution as a political accident left many scholars in the field deeply skeptical—not just for ideological reasons, but because the revisionist argument is profoundly counterintuitive. Given widespread agreement that the French Revolution was the founding event of political modernity not just in France and Europe but for much of the rest of the world, how was it possible to assign to so great an event such (relatively) trivial, contingent causes? While some revisionists were merely engaged in a work of demolition, others tried to rescue the significance of the event by arguing, in the manner of George Taylor, that the Revolution had narrow political causes but large social consequences—or as Colin Lucas put it, "the Revolution made the bourgeoisie even if it was not made by the bourgeoisie."[5] To this day, many scholars who claim some allegiance to the Marxian model argue that even if the French Revolution was not the outcome of growing capitalism, it fulfilled its assigned role in history by clearing the ground for free markets and economic individualism. The political, in other words, begat the social.

But "political" is not necessarily synonymous with "accidental" or "superficial," let alone "trivial." This realization prompted a methodological shift in the field in the 1980s, toward a view of 1789 and after as a revolution in "political culture."[6] The reassessment grew out of an incipient reaction against the conventional notion that the social was deep and the political shallow; that politics was the brittle icing atop the substantial cake of economy and society. If one defined politics in terms that encompassed more than elites jockeying for government positions, it might be possible to think of the political as something deep, structural, culturally complex, as a domain that had defining power over large areas of human life.

Of the two foundational works in the political culture vein, one was French and written in the mode of provocation, the other American, more detached and eclectic. François Furet's *Interpreting the French Revolution,* first published in France in 1978, took on every Marxian and indeed mainstream republican piety with the gusto of a former Communist Party member gleefully repudiating his former acolytes and former self. It is hard not to read a measure of iconoclastic delight into such statements of Furet's as "[N]othing resembled French society under Louis XVI more than French society under Louis-Philippe."[7] Furet's point, derived from Tocqueville, was that the French Revolution, which brought about no profound social or administrative change, was remarkable above all for generating the *illusion* of change. What needed explaining was not the causes and consequences of what Furet dismissed as a nonevent, but the language through which the revolutionaries powerfully convinced themselves and posterity that the crisis through which they were living was a fundamental rupture. In denying to the Revolution any transformative role in either social or political structures—as Tocqueville had pointed out, why get rid of a king to acquire an emperor?—Furet trained the spotlight onto what historians had long taken for granted: the peculiarly abstract, absolutist, Manichean framework in which the revolutionaries explained what they were doing. Where historians had either embraced their language as heroic or reviled it as proto-totalitarian, Furet—admittedly no fan of Jacobinism—suggested that what mattered was to show the cultural logic of revolutionary discourse, and to explain the power it needed to fill the void left by the removal of divine-right monarchy.

The real legacy of the French Revolution, in Furet's view, was therefore not a change in social life or even in the deep structures of power, but the creation of a potent political tradition in French and Western culture. While Furet had a very large axe to grind against the Communist establishment in the field, the same was not true of his most influential American follower, Lynn Hunt.[8] Hunt's *Politics, Culture and Class in the French Revolution* (1984), an exploration of rhetoric, imagery, symbols, and political actors, accomplished several tasks beyond fresh readings of new evidence: it defined and gave currency to the object "political culture"; it sought to give a social dimension to Furet's argument by connecting the new politics to changes in political personnel; and it made the point implicitly but forcefully that Furet's approach and insights could be put to creative use by a historian unambiguously sympathetic to the Revolution. While Furet confined himself to brilliant rereadings of traditional political sources—the writings and speeches of leaders—Hunt showed that the political could be defined very widely indeed, to include everything from the composition of village councils to the way ordinary men and women wore their clothes. Hunt's approach promised a new way of combining the social and the political, reversing conventional views so that politics defined and drove social identities rather than vice versa.

An approach as temperate and inclusive as Hunt's still sparked resistance in many quarters to the new emphasis on politics and culture. Even some historians with up-to-date agendas proved unwilling to concede that what happened in 1789 and after was not a bourgeois revolution in some sense of the term. In fact, recent years have seen something of a backlash in the form of several works by prominent scholars which appear defiantly to resurrect aspects of the old interpretation.[9] The most avowedly Marxian of these neo-orthodox approaches is that of Colin Jones. Rather than tinker like other scholars with the definition of bourgeois, or claim that the Revolution put capitalism in a time-bomb that would detonate sometime after 1830, Jones goes back to basics with the bold claims that capitalism, at least of a commercial variety, had in fact been developing in France for several decades before 1789 and that yes, this was a bourgeois revolution in the traditional sense of the expression.[10]

Other historians who stop short of Jones's full-blown interpretive nostalgia nonetheless reassert versions of the belief that what drove the Revolution were the social interests and ambitions of the non-noble elites. William H. Sewell's recent rereading of Sieyès's *What Is the Third Estate?* is unabashedly titled *A Rhetoric of Bourgeois Revolution.* Sewell argues that the famous pamphlet had a crucial mobilizing effect, in the first few weeks of the Revolution, on the bourgeois members of the Third Estate by providing them with an identity and ideology, and by setting up a specific (and successful) program for their seizure of power. Sewell explains that his use of the label bourgeois is not Marxian: "I use the term bourgeois in a different, more diffuse, and more eighteenth-century sense as signifying a class of urban, well-to-do property owners."[11] It was this group that the abbé, armed with a solid command of political economy, recruited to his cause by convincing them that their identity as the nation's quintessentially productive members demanded mobilization against a parasitic aristocracy, while at the same time allowing them to forget—Sewell calls this a "rhetoric of amnesia"—that they too were the beneficiaries of countless legal and social privileges. Sieyès, he concludes, "had what was perhaps the most thoroughly 'bourgeois' vision of any of the great revolutionaries" in that he rejected both aristocratic principles *and* classical republicanism in favor of the language of political economy.[12] Sewell's elegant analysis suffers in its social terminology from the problem of circular reasoning that bedevils much post-Marxian discussion of the bourgeoisie: if one begins by redefining what one means by the labile term "bourgeois" to fit one's object of study, one can later conclude that bourgeois ideology, interests, and politics have at last been pinned down.

Even if it is possible to locate a distinctive non-noble social group and to demonstrate that its members engaged in effective political activity, this does not necessarily amount to describing a bourgeois revolution. One of the most important recent works on the subject is Timothy Tackett's exhaustive study of the deputies to the Estates General and the National Assembly in the first year of the Revolution.[13] Analyzing the backgrounds of hundreds of deputies, Tackett at first seems to bring grist to the Marxian mill by showing that the Third Estate deputies had much different backgrounds from those of men of the other two orders, and especially from the Nobility's delegates. The members of the *tiers état* were a lot less wealthy than their noble colleagues, but also better educated and more experienced in local government. Many of the Third Estate deputies entered the Revolution with social experiences that predisposed them to harbor suspicion or resentment of nobles; conversely, while most were initially sympathetic to the people in general and their constituents in particular, their experiences in the summer and fall of 1789 soon made them turn away in horror from the violence. But having done some serious damage to the revisionist claim that nobles and bourgeois were not all that different, Tackett backs off from a neo-Marxist position: what turned the delegates into revolutionaries, he concludes from their own writings,

was not a social program but the volatile dynamic of revolutionary politics, the "political dialectic of action and reaction between factions."[14]
Both Sewell and Tackett strive to get back to the Revolution's recently
neglected social component, and both go out of their ways to identify
a politically active and effective non-noble leadership. Ironically,
though, both of them start with questions about the social—regarding
Sieyès's rhetoric or the identities and experiences of the deputies—
only to slide back into the political. Both end up with analyses in which
social experience and rhetoric are the means to purely political ends.

The bourgeois revolution remains elusive in part because the Revolution's social goals were met so quickly and with relative ease. Feudalism was dispatched, at least in principle, on the night of August 4,
1789; nobility was abolished within a year; and the Revolution then settled for the longer haul into its obsession with political traitors, including those it called aristocrats. In the process, this political upheaval
produced no ideology of social middlingness, no paeans to bourgeois
or middle-class virtues. The Revolution of 1789–1799 cannot be called
culturally middle-class, nor were its economic origins or effects clearly
favorable to a bourgeoisie. The upheaval slowed down all French industry except that directly related to war and provoked a collapse of
foreign trade, which did not regain its prerevolutionary level until after 1830. Where the rural economy is concerned, the consensus is that
by splitting up some of France's larger estates and establishing a dura-
ble system of partible inheritance, the Revolution increased access to
and investment in small-scale rural property—at the most it increased
the landholdings of the group of rich peasants who are sometimes
called the "rural bourgeoisie."[15] Historians of all stripes have long
agreed that the Revolution made France a more, not less, agrarian
country.

There is one area, however, in which a case could be made for calling this a bourgeois revolution, namely, the sociology of political and
administrative personnel. There is no question that starting in 1789 a
lot more men of non-noble and even quite modest background gained
access in large numbers to local and national structures of government. Lynn Hunt's social analysis of the "new political class" of the
French Revolution yields results that could easily be pressed into the
service of a classic Marxian view. On the national level, as has long
been known, the deputies of all the successive revolutionary assem-

blies were for the most part professionals: lawyers, administrators, doctors, clergymen, writers, and the like; merchants and other commercial types made up at the very most some 15 percent of the total. The same was true, roughly, of departmental administrations, but on the municipal level the picture is rather different: merchants and manufacturers were conspicuous on the revolutionary city councils of larger, commercially oriented towns such as Marseille, Bordeaux, Toulouse, or Amiens. And in smaller towns and villages artisans and shopkeepers were numerous. (There was change over time as well, as the period of the Terror saw an increase in men of lower social status in most local administrations.) The change away from Old Regime administrative personnel was dramatic, as noble participation declined quickly and all but disappeared by 1792, while wave after wave of "new men" of middling and modest backgrounds took power locally.[16]

The city of Paris, for instance, acquired a new political class, as David Garrioch has shown in a richly documented recent study. The Revolution accelerated a process that had begun earlier in the eighteenth century: the decline of local lineages that had exercised power in the context of the parish institutions of a single *quartier*, and the rise of a citywide elite of new men, a mixture of prerevolutionary notables, political leaders from the Revolution, and the new rich who had benefited from the abolition of the guilds and the sale of Church land. Although new economic opportunities did play a part, Garrioch concludes that "The formation of the Parisian bourgeoisie was not primarily an economic phenomenon . . . It owed much to political struggles and to political institutions and ideas, religious and secular."[17]

Calling what happened in 1789 and after a "bourgeois revolution" is at worst misleading, and at best imprecise. Inasmuch as the expression in its classic sense designates a movement powered by capitalist growth and resulting in a massive shift of economic regimes, it does not, by most accounts, apply to the French Revolution. Recently, historians who accept this verdict have nonetheless suggested that the broad shift of power between 1789 and 1799 from Old Regime elites to a new group of men with a different worldview and aspirations (antinoble, meritocratic, well-educated, and so on) can be equated with the advent of a bourgeoisie. But as Lynn Hunt points out, the term "bourgeois" applied to this development is not so much wrong as hopelessly vague.[18] Once the concept of bourgeois revolution is cut loose from a Marxian framework, it loses its interpretive power and becomes a rather toothless descriptive phrase. Recent research conclusively shows a renewal in both political culture and the structure of local and national political elites in the years after 1789; because both these developments were intimately connected to shifts in social resources and new understandings of the social world, they challenge us to think in new ways about the relationship between the social and the political. The post-Thermidorean years, when political passions began to recede and leaders attempted to normalize revolutionary gains, are a good place to explore the longer-term cultural legacy of the Revolution's more heroic and violent days.

## IN THE WAKE OF THE TERROR:
## PATRICIANS, PLEBEIANS, BARBARIANS

The regime which followed the Reign of Terror in 1794 and lasted until Napoleon's coup in 1799 is sometimes known in France as *la république bourgeoise,* in contradistinction to the previous Jacobin regime.[19] Where the national leadership was concerned, the new regime was no more and no less bourgeois than its revolutionary predecessors. In reaction against the violent popular uprisings of the spring of 1795, the men of the National Convention did draw up a new constitution which broke with revolutionary precedent by setting up two legislatures (the Council of Five Hundred and the Council of Ancients) and a five-man executive Directory. But the members of the new assemblies were no different sociologically from their predecessors (they included, in fact, many who had served in previous assemblies): they hailed from the educated property-owning classes, and two-thirds to three-quarters were lawyers and other professionals.[20]

What did distinguish the politicians of the Convention from their predecessors in the Revolution was an open hostility to the goals and institutions of radical popular politics. The tone was set, for the Thermidorean period, by the events of the Spring of 1795 known as the Germinal and Prairial uprisings. Already dispirited by the fall of the Jacobin leaders, the Parisian working poor were further stricken in the winter of 1794–95 by one of the worst frosts on record. Government bread subsidies, which had staved off the worst of famine in the winter, were running out by spring, and the poor felt utterly betrayed by the men who had brought down Robespierre. On April 1 and May

16, 1795, tens of thousands of sans-culottes marched on the Convention, angrily demanding "bread and the Constitution of 1793," but on both occasions were forced to back down. Some remaining Jacobin leaders were arrested and later executed or deported, and the Convention forced popular militants to surrender their weapons.

The sans-culotte movement was effectively silenced, but inflation, misery, and the hard lessons of six years of Revolution kept fear and resentment alive. By the mid-1790s both the rulers and the ruled were ready to acknowledge what their predecessors had so long denied: that there was a chasm between haves and have-nots, and that it ran right through the group of those who supported the Revolution. On June 23, 1795, the moderate leader François Boissy d'Anglas introduced a committee report on the new constitution with a speech that sounded like a battle cry against the poor:

> We must be governed by the best; the best are those who are best educated and most interested in the maintenance of the laws: now, with very few exceptions you find such men only among those who, owning a piece of property, are devoted to the country that contains it, to the laws that protect it, to the tranquillity which maintains it . . . The man without property, on the other hand, requires a constant exercise in virtue to interest himself in a social order that preserves nothing for him . . . A country governed by non-proprietors is in a state of nature.[21]

Following upon these principles, the Constitution of 1795 restricted effective voting rights to citizens owning or renting property worth between 100 and 200 days' labor. The directorial electorate was thus reduced to 30,000, about half the size of that established by the Constitution of 1791. The Revolution had produced its most elitist regime to date.

The view from the other side of the social divide was just as stark. Starting in 1794, the radical journalist and future conspirator Gracchus Babeuf sounded the themes of social warfare from the pages of his newspaper, *Le Tribun du peuple*. As early as December 1794, Babeuf stated in the plainest terms that the republican government had been snatched from the people by an elitist minority:

> I am willing to believe that [both parties] want the republic; but each wants it on his own terms. One side wishes it bourgeois and aristocratic; the other says that they created it, and would have it remain popular

and democratic. One wants the republic of one million, which was ever the enemy, the tyrant, the exploiter, the oppressor, the leech upon the twenty-four [million] others . . . the other party wants the republic for those twenty-four million who laid its foundation and cemented it with their very blood . . .[22]

The numbers invoked are very similar to those in the Third Estate literature of 1788–89: twenty-four million members of the *peuple* versus a million of the selfish privileged. Babeuf was prone to describing the conditions of 1794–95 as a replay of 1789, a similar popular outburst against manifest iniquity. He employed the term "aristocracy" to designate the social enemy, but with a big difference from previous usage: instead of being located outside the polity, the aristocracy was now at its core. What is this "aristocracy of wealth," he asked, this "dividing line between the *peuple* which pays and that which does not?"[23] Indeed, the sentiment seems to have been widespread around 1795–96 that the new rich were no better than the *ci-devant* aristocracy. "Look at this Directory," wrote Babeuf's associate Buonarroti, "does one not, in its insolent display, numerous guards, in its hauteur and fawning courtiers, recognize the court of the Capets?" Nor was the sentiment limited to radical intellectuals, as a police report from 1795 suggests: "Heads are getting hotter and dispositions more bitter against wealthy farmers and great merchants now accused of harming society more than the former nobles ever did."[24]

Babeuf's rhetoric drew upon the familiar aristocracy/*peuple* division while drastically shifting its location. Where the struggle against aristocracy had always been waged at the border of the polity, to defend it against a defining enemy, Babeuf proclaimed that the struggle was now inside the state, the republic, in the Revolution itself. "What, exactly, is the French Revolution? An open war between patricians and plebeians, between rich and poor."[25] Although some identification of the social and the political endured (bourgeois/aristocratic versus popular/democratic), the location of social struggle inside the polity had the important consequence of beginning to delineate the social as an entity distinct from the political. The erstwhile tensions between rich and poor citizens could no longer be dismissed as the work of manipulative traitors; they were the outcome of flawed institutions within the republic.

While Babeuf was busy locating the enemy within the nation rather than beyond the pale, the members of the governing Assembly were engaged in an opposite move, that of defining at least some of the poor as alien. One of the most popular tropes of the post-Thermidorean period was the denunciation of "vandalism."[26] The term was coined in 1793 by abbé Grégoire in a series of reports denouncing the desecration of monuments, both religious and secular, by political extremists, and it was picked up by Robespierre and his followers as a rhetorical weapon against de-Christianizers of the extreme-left-*enragé* persuasion. But the theme of vandalism and its cognates ("Gothic," "barbarous") really came into its own during the Thermidorean period, when it served the men in power as a discursive means of distancing themselves from the Reign of Terror. In accusing their enemies of vandalism, the Jacobins and then the Thermidoreans were picking up on a central idea of the Enlightenment, that tyranny rests on ignorance. Earlier in the century, enlightened antifeudal writers like Mably had accused the aristocracy of the post-Carolingian centuries of having all but destroyed French civilization—and why indeed would these men, brutal warriors from beyond the Rhine, have any interest in preserving it? The new Vandals, for the Thermidoreans, were the men of 1793–94, those who had presided over the destruction of some of the nation's most important monuments, and sent geniuses like Lavoisier and Condorcet to their deaths.

Because of the association of tyranny with ignorance, the individual most frequently excoriated as a Vandal was Robespierre. To anyone familiar with Robespierre's deep classical learning and remarkable command of language (not to mention his fastidious dress and manners), it comes as a surprise to read contemporaries denouncing him as "an ignorant but ambitious man who little by little succumbed to a shameful barbary," or "a man of crass ignorance," a book-burner who seethed with jealousy of the learned.[27] But while Robespierre was singled out as Head Vandal, motifs of barbarism and vandalism attached themselves most naturally to the uneducated and violence-prone part of the nation, the lower orders. Vandalism had been promoted by Robespierre's local emulators, the Thermidorean leaders believed—men who had emerged from low down on the social scale to impose their *canaille* (vulgar, crude) style upon the nation. "I can still see them," wrote Jean-François La Harpe in 1794, "those brigands calling themselves patriots . . . with their grotesque clothing which they said was the only garb for patriots, as if patriotism could only be ridiculous and filthy; with their crude manners and brutal speech, as if coarseness and indecency were the essence of republicanism."[28]

The problem facing republican leaders in 1794 with respect to *le peuple* was not new, for it had preoccupied their predecessors in the Revolution as well. Brutal and destructive acts committed by the poorer classes had to be attributed to forces outside the Revolution, though it was manifest that such barbarism was in fact located inside the nation. At the height of the Revolution, the usual reflex for explaining such things came into play: if supporters of the Revolution committed unspeakable acts, that could only be because essentially good people were the prey of plotters, of a *complot vandale* (Vandal plot) by counter-revolutionaries who abetted the violence.[29] To the Thermidoreans, the *peuple* had been misled in the past by the Jacobin "cannibals." Intent on denouncing Jacobinism, aware of stark social divisions in their society, yet still firmly committed to the principle of the people's unity, the post-Jacobin leaders were forced to walk a fine line. Witness the tension within Boissy d'Anglas's ranting against "those men of fierce look, pale complexion, and angry words who excite the people's resentment against that part of itself which they perfidiously call the *gilded million*."[30] If there was a plot to turn the people against a part of itself, this time its instigators, the men with pale faces and wild eyes, were clearly not aristocrats.

Directorial leaders assumed that the people was neither barbaric nor civilized but malleable. Just as it could be led astray by iconoclastic leaders, it could be taught and molded, especially by a regime which prided itself on its creation of institutions of learning like the École Polytechnique, the École Normale, and the Institut. As Bronislaw Baczko concludes, "The anti-Vandal discourse combined with pedagogic discourse legitimated a sharp division of roles between the civilizing power and a people in need of being civilized."[31] The people, then, was no longer a given but a work in progress. The Thermidorean preoccupation with vandalism, while still formulated within the context of assumed social wholeness, opened up the possibility of thinking of the lower orders as essentially different and threatening, in need of education and control.

The political elite in the post-Thermidorean period adopted an ambivalent attitude toward the plebs, one which bespoke the acceptance of some social distance. But while keeping the people at arm's length, the leaders also kept their distance from the former nobility. Indeed, the Directory's latter-day revival of antinoble legislation is puzzling to anyone who believes, as did Babeuf, that the country was governed by a neo-aristocracy no better than the old one. The most drastic legislation, that of November 29, 1797 (9 Frimaire year VI), deprived most nobles of many civic rights (an earlier draft of the law had suggested that they all be deported), but there were other hostile pieces of legislation, including one barbaric measure in 1799 which allowed for the taking of four noble hostages every time a patriot was murdered or damage was caused by a royalist attack.[32]

These laws could not have been more explicit in their treatment of nobles as enemy aliens by sole virtue of their bloodlines, and in fact this period saw a curious revival of the racial arguments against nobility. Echoing his themes of a decade earlier, Sieyès returned to the motif of the Frankish origins of the French nobility, this time with much more open racial overtones. (Benjamin Constant apocryphally quoted Sieyès as saying around this time: "If a person is not of my kind, he is not my fellow man; a noble is not of my kind, therefore he is a wolf and I can shoot him.")[33] A deputy glossed past historical abuses by saying: "They treated us like beasts of burden; they had extinguished the flame of art and science; they had established their reign on that of ignorance and barbarism. That is how we were treated for centuries; there you have true proscription and robbery."[34]

The context for the new laws and the renewed debate about nobility was a specific political development, the coup of 18 Fructidor (4 September 1797), a military action by the Directory's generals which undid the royalist and conservative republican majority returned by the elections of March 1797.[35] Obviously, the Directory's leaders and their left-leaning allies had a political interest in arguing that the nobility was in its essence committed to destroying the French people, and should be treated like a political, military, and racial enemy. It is interesting, however, that the same language used to denounce popular vandalism was turned, a few years later, back against the nobility. Historians have often described the politics of the period from 1794 to 1799, the repeated military actions to counter Jacobin or royalist majorities and shore up the political middle, as a *politique de bascule* (see-

saw politics, a balancing act). Because of the enduring overlap between the social and the political, this seesaw dynamic also applied to
the social world, and was expressed in a need to contain and condemn
both the poor and the former nobility.

The Directory is conventionally tagged bourgeois for several overlapping—and often unexamined—reasons: the political reaction
against Jacobinism, the social identities of its leaders, the regime's restriction of the electoral base, and its defensive espousal of middling
politics. Certainly, in the years after the Terror, the political leadership
was more prone than previously to assert, often in strident tones, the
importance of substantial property ownership, and the education that
was assumed to go with it, for active participation in the political process. (Hence the designation of the quintessential political enemy as
the Vandal, a creature who attacks both property *and* culture.)

Yet the Thermidoreans also continued to assert that they represented the people, all of the people. Boissy d'Anglas denounced wild-
eyed radicals as folk who wanted to turn the people against a "part of
itself." In the course of early debates in the Thermidorean Convention
concerning a law aimed against Jacobin societies, deputies who supported the measure draped themselves in the mantle of republican
universalism to denounce the societies as aristocratic throwbacks to
the regime of corporate particularism. There is considerable irony to
arguments such as those of the deputy Bourdon de l'Oise: "What are
popular societies? A collection of men who select one another, just as
monks do . . . Aristocracy begins wherever a group of men, in communication with other such groups, promotes opinions other than those
of national representation."[36] Another deputy addressed directly the
question of where *le peuple* was located, voicing the position shared by
most of his colleagues: "*Le peuple* is not in these societies. Sovereignty
dwells in the universality of the nation. . . . The safeguard of freedom
resides in the noble and determined sentiments of the entirety of the
French."[37] In the struggle over political representation between the assemblies and the street, the legislators won out. They did so by denouncing as dangerous to the republic both aristocratic traitors *and*
popular radicals. In opposition to those two breeds of dangerous factionalism, the Directory claimed to represent "the universality of the
nation."

A standard response to the sort of universalist claims made by directorial politicians is that they are simply a veil covering class-specific self-interest. Historians have been aware of the fact that the Revolution produced no bourgeois or middle class ideology as such, but that has not prevented them from finding such beliefs in various convenient places. William Sewell, for instance, confidently tags Sieyès a spokesman for the bourgeoisie because the abbé spoke the language of political economy and praised productivity—a conclusion that only makes sense when based on the debatable assumption that political economy and productive ideals are essentially and necessarily bourgeois concerns. The more common argument, however, involves the notion of bourgeois universalism: the claim that upper-middle-class men of the Constituent and Legislative assemblies, the Convention, and the Directorial assemblies promoted their own interests as a propertied bourgeois elite while concealing self-interest under the language of social unanimity and universal rights.[38]

Historians allege that bourgeois leaders espoused individual rights, free trade, antifeudalism, meritocracy, and the like ostensibly as a boon to every citizen, while they themselves would be the principal beneficiaries. This argument extends the curious yet widespread assumption that the bourgeoisie is the one class that lives in constant self-denial; that its motives are so perfectly heinous that it can never—at least in the French context—speak its own name. It also implies an astonishing level of blindness on the part of contemporaries: even if the bourgeoisie refused to name itself, why was it almost never identified by those it victimized, the working classes and the aristocracy?

Those who see the French Revolution as bourgeois are driven to espouse some version of the notion of universalism when it comes to ideology. Yet as a theoretical tool, this view of ideology has come to appear rather blunt and rusty. One need not espouse Jacques Derrida's position that there is "nothing outside the text" to be skeptical of arguments that assume a sharp distinction between the hard facts of social and economic interest and the decorative froth of ideology. As Lynn Hunt has pointed out, it is ironic that both the Marxian position and Furet's anti-Marxian stance treat language as a mask or veil: in the former case rhetoric conceals class interest, in the latter case the "discourse of rupture" hides the truth of sociopolitical continuity.[39] Both views carry clear judgmental implications, the first in condemning bourgeois selfishness, the second in denouncing revolutionary self-delusion. More recent approaches (including my own) eschew the assumption that language either reflects or conceals some hard-and-fast reality, preferring to approach discourse as a system whose internal patterns need to be decoded on their own terms.

All of which is to say that, in this instance, we should not view the insistence that governing bodies fully embodied an undivided *peuple* as a cynical cover-up for upper-middle-class interests—or, for that matter, as admirable idealism. Rather, we need to interpret those claims as part of the enduringly powerful (in France) assumption of a complete congruence between the republican state and the people, the belief that popular will is located in and expressed through central political institutions. The refusal to acknowledge and act upon social divisions and competing social interests (*"Le peuple* is not in these societies. Sovereignty dwells in the universality of the nation"*) was the strength of republican governments before 1870, but also their undoing.[40] We should not conclude, however, that directorial politicians held views identical to those of their pre-1794 predecessors. Their open antagonism to popular politics, their eagerness to recognize Jacobin Vandals as well as wolfish emigrés as their enemies, implies at least a distinct consciousness of social position, something which, following Anthony Giddens, we could call class awareness, as opposed to class consciousness.[41] And their refusal to acknowledge class divisions and social competition as constitutive of the state does not mean that they ignored other kinds of social issues in other contexts.

In the years after 1794, the legislature received hundreds of petitions from individual citizens asking for redress from the perceived injustices of revolutionary family law. Petitioners claimed that by instituting divorce and equal inheritance, and granting civil rights to illegitimate children, the Revolution had unleashed chaos in families and therefore throughout society. The dialogue between these constituents and their deputies represents a crucial area in which relations between the state and society were negotiated and, in the process, defined.[42] The petitioners complained, as one might expect, that easy divorce encouraged fickleness in wives, that egalitarian inheritance gave women too much power, that strict laws governing bequests undermined paternal authority and upset family strategies. The petitioners, who all claimed to be good republicans, argued in favor of laws which upheld the social order as they saw it, and against the disruptive revolutionary family legislation of the early 1790s.

In response, the Thermidorean and Directory legislators rolled back some of the most controversial family legislation, and in the process hammered out their views of the relationship between the family, the law, and the polity. The deputies defined their role as that of rebuilders of family structures shattered by extreme revolutionary legislation; they were proponents of positive rather than natural law. "Why are we talking about *equality, reason* or *nature?*" asked deputy Jean-Denis Lanjuinais in 1795. "These vague and undefined words, if we apply them to private property, there would be no more property, there would be no more society."[43] These debates over matters of family law turned into an important arena for the deputies to define their view of their own role as legislators and governors—specifically, they repudiated a disembodied equality or general will and argued instead for justice and the social interest. In upholding, as they generally did, the rights of the family over those of the individual, they rejected the particular interest of individuals such as women or illegitimate children.[44] The deputies thus invoked family unity as a universal interest, and used their status as legislators to arbitrate within and between families.

Looking back to the decades before the Revolution, we see interesting patterns of cultural continuity and change. As was the case in the prerevolutionary period, the Directory saw great uncertainty about the ultimate source of social connection. Where prerevolutionary writers had proposed the sentimental family as the model for social connection, and revolutionary culture promoted fraternal love in military trappings, Thermidorean leaders no longer had faith in the power of affective bonds. They returned to the family as the obvious universal model and source of cohesion, but this time the ties were those of positive law, not the cement of expressive affect. In the end, faced with deep divisions in wealth and ideology, post-Thermidorean legislators created the illusion of a level playing field by choosing the universal family as their main social object and interlocutor. In doing so, they implicitly recognized a social object distinct from politics, a field of competing interests in need of arbitration, not on the basis of abstract ideals but through more pragmatic approaches to local justice and the greater social good. But if legislators dealt with the social at close range, in the context of family disputes, were there others who took a longer view of what the Revolution had wrought?

## HISTORICAL CHANGE AND THE NEW ARISTOCRACY

The French Revolution transformed understandings of history in Europe. By demonstrating the possibility of astonishingly rapid and drastic change, it offered whole new perspectives on the past to those who lived through it and in its aftermath. For several generations of thinkers, including such figures as Friedrich Hegel, François Guizot, and Karl Marx, the Revolution was an illumination of past and present, and a model for future change. Contemporaries thus struggled to assign meaning to what they had lived through, and it is notable that among those who witnessed the Revolution in France, none assigned a primary role to an industrial or commercial bourgeoisie, or even to the professional upper-middle class. Reading the texts of the 1790s and early 1800s, one is struck once again by the endurance and elasticity of the category "aristocracy": both historical analyses and more abstract works of political theory remained anchored to the twin concepts of democracy and aristocracy.

This was true of one of the earliest and most sophisticated attempts to make sense of what happened in the years after 1789. Were one to look for a perfect embodiment of the revolutionary bourgeoisie, Antoine Barnave would qualify as an excellent candidate. The scion of a prosperous and highly educated Protestant family from the province of Dauphiné, Barnave began his revolutionary career as a Third Estate deputy and became one of the leaders of the moderate Feuillant group in the Constituent Assembly. As the Revolution lurched leftward, Barnave retired to his provincial home in 1792, but was arrested, tried, and executed in 1793. While in provincial exile and in prison, he wrote an interpretation of the Revolution, *De la révolution et de la constitution,* which is often viewed as an early instance of historical materialism.[45]

Barnave's account does indeed seem precociously modern in that he interprets the Revolution in the context of epic changes in the socioeconomic evolution of humanity: first pastoral independence; then the consolidation of agrarian property, which brings the landed aristocracy to power; then the development of cities and movable commercial wealth, and with it the final advent of *le peuple*. "Just as the possession of land elevated the aristocracy, industrial property brings about the ascendancy of the people; it acquires its freedom, multiplies, begins to influence [public] affairs."[46] Although Barnave is sometimes considered a forerunner of Marx, the difference between them is immediately apparent: the advent of "industrial property" promotes a whole people, not a bourgeois elite. Barnave bases his analysis on forms of property, not modes of production. He sees no logic of accumulation or exploitation at work in the postagrarian world—on the contrary, in his account commercial wealth promotes democracy in both the economic and the political order: "[I]ndustrial and movable property is therefore the foundation of democracy, just as territorial property is the foundation of aristocracy."[47]

Barnave does recognize that in some contexts the accumulation of commercial and industrial wealth will produce something which he calls, significantly, a form of aristocracy. Such is the case, he admits, in long-established commercial societies such as Venice, the Low Countries, and the Hanseatic towns. In such settings, "a new aristocracy, a merchant and bourgeois aristocracy may, it is true, arise by means of this form of wealth."[48] Although he tags this new elite an aristocracy, he is at pains to point out that it has nothing in common with the old "equestrian and feudal" elite whose power was based on land ownership and warfare. But Barnave could not imagine a separate identity, or new words to describe the ascendancy of these people (he does once refer to them once as "rich capitalists").[49] Their political-cultural fate, depending on the setting, is to be absorbed into one of the two great older models: in a commercial republic, with nobody above them, they will "become aristocracy"; in a traditional monarchy, they will stay subordinate to the old feudal-military elite and thus will "remain democracy."[50] Barnave's sociopolitical imagination was framed by the great binary patterns of the early 1790s. Although he was able to describe the emergence of a capitalist group, he could not conceive of the sustained existence of such a middling elite. They would necessarily get sucked upwards or downwards.

While Barnave in 1792 could still contemplate with equanimity the emergence of "the people" and "democracy" as political forces, they were not so easy to accept for those writers of the later 1790s who had taken the full measure of the instability of democratic rule and the violence of popular politics. By 1795 it was no longer possible to believe in Rousseau's dream of the unmediated sovereignty of the people's will: somebody had to govern, and those in charge should naturally be chosen from society's best. The challenge for writers and thinkers of liberal inclination in this period was to determine the proper relationship between the national interest and the new political elite.

One of the most astute liberal commentators on the Revolution was Germaine de Staël, the daughter of Suzanne (a prominent *salonnière)* and Jacques Necker (Louis XVI's most popular minister). A member of the pre- and postrevolutionary social and political elite, Staël embraced the Revolution and republicanism, although she left France during the Jacobin ascendancy, between 1792 and 1795.[51] Staël's major works of commentary on the French Revolution reflect both her republicanism and her suspicion of popular or Rousseauean politics. The pamphlet she wrote in 1798, *Des circonstances actuelles qui peuvent terminer la révolution,* defended the Directory's policies and institutions in response to a royalist upsurge in 1797, which was followed by a Jacobin backlash in 1798. In her text Staël is at more pains to distance herself from Rousseau than from royalism. The opening pages of her tract repudiate the idea of direct popular democracy as an unworkable chimera, and the heart of her discussion is a philosophical defense of a restricted system of representation like that of the Directory.[52]

Staël believed that true democracy was impossible in a large state such as France, and that the huge single assemblies favored under the Revolution were counterproductive: if anything had been learned from those disastrous years, it was that such bodies would necessarily fall prey to factionalism and eventual tyranny. The issue she wrestled with in her pamphlet was that of the meaning and form of a true representative system. Representation, she wrote, is not a mathematical formula, nor is its essence oneness or omnipotence, nor yet does it yield a miniaturized image of the nation; rather, it is "the political combination which causes the nation to be governed by men chosen and combined in such a manner that they possess the will and the interest of all."[53] What mattered was not strict proportionality, but a system set up in such a fashion (through division of functions, numerical balance, and so on) that the interests of the people's proxies could only be those of the nation. Businesses, she added by way of illustration, are able to set up shareholders in such a way that each has a vested interest in the health of the whole, and nations should be able to do the same.[54]

Staël's ideal of representation is obscure, clearer in what it rejects than in what it aspires to. But elements of an explanation can be found in her repeated references to the ideal political class, what she calls a "new aristocracy." She shared with many intellectuals of her generation a belief that the most vicious aspect of the Old Regime social system was not oligarchy but heredity. Like her lover and collaborator Benjamin Constant, Staël saw the recent upheaval in France as the last in a series of revolts which had, in succession, felled theocracy, slavery, feudalism, and most recently, hereditary nobility.[55] The goal of the Revolution, toward which the directorial government was still working, was that of "substituting a natural aristocracy for an artificial one." The Revolution's leveling of the playing field simply made it possible for this natural elite to emerge: "Political equality is nothing but the restoration of natural inequality. All hereditary distinctions are nothing but artificial inequality, which sometimes accords with but often contradicts natural inequality."[56]

Staël's endorsement of oligarchy includes, as one might expect, an adamant defense of property as a necessary precondition for active public life. She repeatedly asserts her belief in the Republic while arguing that oligarchy in no way contradicts such principles. "What, they will say, republicans running after fortune! You want property!—No social order can do without it; you must therefore seize the influence it commands."[57] If electoral principles based on property were to recreate a new aristocracy of a different sort, so be it: "[R]epublicans must become rich, and the rich republicans."[58] One finds similar sentiments in Benjamin Constant, who likewise advanced the classic arguments for property as a basis for political participation, a principle, as we have seen, repeatedly invoked under the Directory and inscribed in practice into the Constitution of 1795.[59] The meaning of such attitudes has long been considered self-evident. It seems predictable that after the defeat of the old aristocracy and the rout of the popular movement a new non-noble elite would move in and stake its claim to the social and political leadership of the nation. It follows that the Directory was the first in a series of transitional regimes in which, prior to the advent of full-blown capitalism, a mixed elite of nobles and non-nobles, a group known collectively as *notables,* united in their passion for landowning and their social conservatism, prepared the move to a squarely bourgeois, capitalist social order.[60] Where social elites are concerned, the Directory is usually taken to be the first act in the half-century-long rule of the *grands notables*.[61]

But if the likes of Staël, Constant, and other leading intellectuals of the turn of the century were speaking for such an elite, their attachment to principles of republicanism and popular sovereignty may look anomalous. Even after it seemed that the Republic had disappeared for good, Germaine de Staël maintained her belief in it, famously clashing with Napoleon, who expelled her from France for being a political troublemaker. Her major statement about the French Revolution, *Considérations sur la Révolution française,* completed shortly before her death in 1817, reproduces much of the Revolution's discourse about itself. "The French Revolution," the book begins, "was one of the great epochs of the social order."[62] This social epic, as it unfolds in her pages, pitted "the nobility" against "the nation." And what was, and is, the nation? She variously enumerated its components as "writers, capitalists, merchants, a large number of proprietors, and a mass of people employed in the administration," or as "merchants, men of letters, proprietors and capitalists"; the eighteenth century, she wrote, had discovered this "nation" where before there were only "nobles, priests, and *peuple.*"[63]

In her later work Staël no longer wrote so insistently of the need for a new aristocracy to rule the nation. The purpose of the two works was different, of course, but the return of the old monarchy and its blue-blood allies in 1815 no doubt also did much to change her rhetoric. One may even construe as emergent middling consciousness her equal abhorrence of privilege and heredity on the one hand, and of what she described in the strongest terms as repulsive popular excesses on the other.[64] Indeed, in her earlier *Des circonstances actuelles* she referred to "[t]he middling class [*classe mitoyenne*] which carried out the Revolution in France."[65] But beyond fleeting references, her work contains no sustained analysis or apologia of a separate middle group. While her writings unequivocally condemned popular violence and explicitly rejected theories of direct popular rule, her vision of society even in 1817 remained encased in the massive political dichotomies of the revolutionary era: aristocracy versus nation, nobles against people, privileged versus third estate.

The same, generally speaking, can be said of Staël's contemporary Antoine Destutt de Tracy, the founder of the intellectual movement known as Ideology, which is often considered the final blast of the Enlightenment, and which also was to fall afoul of Napoleon.[66] For Destutt, as for Staël and Constant, differences in social systems were inseparable from differences in political regimes, and Destutt's preferences were similar to theirs, albeit articulated in more formally analytical terms. In his critique of Montesquieu penned in 1807, Destutt quarreled with his famous predecessor's classification of governments and argued that only two broad principles lay behind different states: "I will divide all governments into two classes . . . one of these I denominate *national,* in which social rights are common to all; the other *special,* establishing or recognizing particular or unequal rights."[67]

Destutt asked his readers to look beyond the superficial organization of governments to their underlying principles, to distinguish between governments whose ultimate sanction derived from divine right, conquest, or heredity, and which therefore worked in the interests of a subgroup, and those whose purpose was to serve society as a whole. The latter form of government—which Destutt very clearly preferred—could exist as a direct or representative democracy, but the people's interests could also be entrusted to an aristocracy or even a hereditary monarchy.[68] What mattered was the principle animating a "national" government: "the maxim, that all rights and powers belong to and emanate from the people or body of the nation."[69] Like Staël, Destutt and many of his fellow Ideologues were both republican and elitist. The articles in their journal *La Décade philosophique,* while warning against excessive patrician or plutocratic power, dreamt of an aristocratic republic where, as one article put it, "the inequality of talents would serve to further the equality of happiness."[70]

How should we understand the apparently self-contradictory views held by intellectuals of the directorial years when they proclaimed their republican convictions yet frequently argued for a nonhereditary form of aristocracy? The usual answer—that such ideas represent a form of proto-bourgeois ideology—imposes a teleological Marxian cast on the writings of the postrevolutionary generation. The new elite that Staël and her contemporaries had in mind appears to be one generated not by economic accumulation but by administrative and political success. If, wrote Staël, you want to substitute a real aristocracy for a factitious one, you should introduce strict rules for promotion within the administration, so that nobody could head the state without having moved steadily upward in public service. "Only true merit will secure this succession of elections," and "since respect always follows from comparison and degree, a hierarchy of power will secure all the advantages of arbitrary distinctions in birth and rank, without any of their drawbacks."[71] The call for promotion within the administration was also taken up by the *Décade philosophique,* which drew upon the example of the Roman *cursus honorum* to argue for what they called *gradualité des fonctions:* the principle of gradual advancement within administration which would result in true excellence at the top.[72]

Writers in the early 1800s, like most historians today, believed that the Revolution had performed a massive ground-clearing function: it had abolished archaic social and political institutions and thus allowed for the emergence of something new. But what was that new thing? Only since Marx's generation has the assumption been that the most important social consequence of the Revolution was the opening up of economic opportunity and free-market-happy individualism. The works of the Revolution's contemporaries offer a much different impression. Even a historian like Barnave, attuned to the change in economic regimes, saw collective well-being and democratic power, not plutocracy, emerging from the shift from an agrarian economy to a commercial one. In the view of prominent liberals like Staël and the Ideologues, it was in the realm of administration and government that the Revolution cleared the ground for competition. Political equality made for a pure meritocracy, the "inequality of talent," whose most important result was to yield a new elite of brilliant and dedicated public servants.

## HONOR AND THE STATE

If intellectuals looked to the administration as the source of a new elite, they had good reason to do so, given the huge changes in the nature and size of bureaucracy that the Revolution had brought about. The Revolution certainly did not create the state bureaucracy, which had evolved for centuries and was greatly expanded under Louis XIV. The royal bureaucracy did, however, show many of the hallmarks of a premodern administration. Though merit and skill were certainly not discounted, the system relied heavily on personal credit and connection, and the monarch usually chose his top functionaries from a limited number of great dynasties. Jurisdictions often overlapped and functions were ill-defined, problems that no amount of well-meaning reform in the 1770s and 1780s was able to clear up. Nor did the early Revolution witness any major changes: France remained a constitutional monarchy and until 1792 its bureaucracy barely expanded. Some of this stagnation was due to the abstract idealism of those early years, a time when it was assumed that the role of the state should be limited to the drafting and publicizing of rational, self-evident legislation.[73]

All of this changed after 1792, as France became a republic, entered a major and lengthy foreign war, and endured for several years a state of national emergency. The modern French administration came into being over the course of the 1790s, in the tumultuous years of the Terror and Directory. The size of the staff employed by the French state grew in the 1790s from under 50,000 to a quarter of a million by the time Bonaparte took power. While the Directory saw a slight decrease in the size of the national bureaucracy, the period was important in entrenching the administration created at the height of the Revolution, stabilizing its size and functions, beginning the process of education and selection that was to prove so important in later generations.[74] When Staël and Destutt talked of creating a new aristocracy of talent, they were describing a process that was actually taking place.

Alexis de Tocqueville famously argued that the change of regimes in 1789 and in subsequent revolutions was much more apparent than real: "[E]very time that an attempt is made to do away with absolutism, the most that could be done has been to graft the head of Liberty onto a servile body."[75] His argument may hold as far as the underlying nature of ultimate power is concerned—with "king" becoming "people" and then "emperor"—but there is reason to believe that he was mistaken with respect to the nature of state bureaucracies. The Revolution of 1789 saw not just a change of personnel and an increase in its size, but also a profound transformation in what state bureaucracies were about. Under the Old Regime, bureaucracies were private preserves in aristocratic hands. This was particularly true of the finance administration, where officials in charge of collecting tax revenues and handing them over to the state used their position openly, quasi-officially, for private speculation and profit. (They often made so much money investing tax revenues that they were major lenders to the perpetually cash-poor monarchy.)[76]

What the Revolution put an end to was the overlap between private business and state function: it did not just expand and rationalize the administration, it also made public service truly public. To quote John Bosher's classic study, "[A]n aristocratic system, based on personal position in a social hierarchy, became a bureaucracy with an administrative hierarchy in which the organization of public functions took precedence over the claims of individual officials."[77] The revolutionary transition in the financial administration was therefore, as Bosher's subtitle has it, one "from business to bureaucracy," a decisive move away from a system in which administrative positions were personal business assets. This, as Bosher himself noted a generation ago, posed a problem for anyone wanting to see the Revolution as the advent of capitalism. The Revolution took government out of the hands of private entrepreneurs to build "a national business machine out of men and paper . . . so far improved that it furnished the wealth necessary for twenty years of war against nearly the whole of Europe." The industry of government went through a revolution far more thoroughgoing than any branch of manufacturing.[78] No wonder intellectuals saw the new elites as public servants, not captains of industry.

Napoleon perfected the new governmental machine bequeathed to him by the Directory, ensuring its continuity, regularizing the mechanisms for career advancement, and creating an elite corps of high officials, known as *fonctionnaires*, who were selected on the basis of their personal loyalty to the emperor.[79] And it was under his aegis, first as consul and then as emperor, that the highest social distinctions were deliberately attached to state service. After seizing power, Bonaparte was well aware of the need to anchor his regime by defining and, if need be, creating a social elite committed to its survival, which he famously called the "masses of granite." To this end, three different schemes were tried in succession (and eventually overlapped): the identification of an official group of *notables*, the invention of a civic distinction, the Legion of Honor, in 1802, and eventually the creation in 1808 of an imperial nobility.[80]

Napoleon Bonaparte, his associates, and his legislature struggled on all of those occasions to define the criteria on which social distinction should be established: wealth, merit, birth, or some amalgam thereof. All of these criteria eventually were used in combination, but what emerges most strikingly is Napoleon's personal hostility to wealth alone as a standard of distinction, and the prominence of state service as the single most important basis for recognition. At the instigation of the ubiquitous Sieyès, the *notables* were selected on the basis of wealth according to the standard assumption that only the rich had the freedom and education to devote themselves fully to the public good; it is remarkable, then, that by 1810 over one third of the group consisted of public servants such as military officers, judges, and administrators.[81] As for the Legion of Honor, it was devised by Bonaparte specifically as an antidote to what he perceived as rampant materialism, and instituted in the face of considerable opposition from critics who complained that honor was a feudal throwback. It was to be the ultimate award to those who served the state well, in the administration or in the military.[82]

The creation of a new nobility might at first seem like a repudiation of an open meritocratic elite, but it meant to counter the fact that the Legion of Honor was fast evolving into a purely military distinction. The decree establishing the new titled elite did specify that nobility would be conferred on the basis of merit, and promoters of the law were quick to point out that even in the Old Regime nobility had as much to do with distinguished service to the state as with genealogy.[83] Wealth was never disregarded, and the imperial state made sure, through gifts of land, that new noble families could sustain their status. But though money and property usually undergirded the position of the new elites, they were never sufficient criteria or justification for status in the eyes of the emperor. What Napoleon restored in 1808 was not some benighted feudal caste, but the Old Regime's tradition of conferring high status on men and families with strong records of service to the state.[84]

In the aftermath of the Revolution, the social group that expanded most conspicuously *and* was invested with the greatest social recognition was that of civil servants, especially those in the highest ranks. Such a group represented at this time in France the central social norm, and the bourgeoisie was construed as its exact antithesis. This contrast was articulated by a German contemporary of the French Revolution and Napoleonic state, Georg Wilhelm Friedrich Hegel. In works very much influenced by the French Revolution, such as the *Philosophy of Right* (1821), the historian and philosopher wrote of the nec-

essary division of society into different estates with different relationships to a state which embodied the historical triumph of reason.
Alongside a passive peasantry and a barely nascent proletariat, Hegel
distinguished various estates among the elites. The estate *least* qualified to rule is the bourgeoisie, since burghers are by definition given
over to the pursuit of private gain, and therefore least equipped to
serve the *res publica*. The realm of the bourgeois is the private—private
life and private profit. The universal class, by contrast, is the bureaucracy, its business devoted to and motivated by the general interest
embodied in the state. Society, like the individual, is marked by the
postrevolutionary split between—he used the French terms—*bourgeois*
and *citoyen*.[85]

In the aftermath of Thermidor, the fiction of an undivided *peuple*
proved hard to sustain. The need for the directorial government to
keep both Jacobinism and royalism at bay was matched by its corresponding suspicion of the poor as coarse and destructive Vandals and
of nobles as enemies of the fatherland. Under these conditions, one
might expect an ideology of social middlingness to emerge, but that
did not happen: the cult of *juste milieu* was still a full generation and an
empire away. The leaders of the Directory did not, any more than their
revolutionary predecessors, claim to govern in the name of any social
group. Their perception of the social focused not on class but on family: rather than looking to a segment of society to provide stability or
seeking to arbitrate between social groups, they fixed upon restoring
and strengthening familial ties. Republican ideals endured, though
they were quite different from those of 1792–1794. Leading intellectuals and social commentators clung to their belief in a state that embodied the national interest, but the republic they idealized was now to be
led by a new aristocracy of means and talent: an elite whose vocation
was service to the state. And indeed the period from 1793 to 1815
saw the birth of the modern French civil service—vastly expanded,
trained, and educated, dedicated to the public good. This group was
to become in the nineteenth century France's central social norm and
ideal, and its implicit centrality has to be understood if one is to
make any sense of the widespread revulsion against an imagined bourgeoisie.

# The Political Birth of the Bourgeoisie, 1815–1830

## 5

It is tempting to say that the French bourgeoisie was born of the thrust of a dagger on the night of February 13, 1820. The knife was wielded by a lone working-class fanatic named Louvel, and it pierced the heart of the duc de Berry, nephew of Louis XVIII and the Bourbon dynasty's only hope for perpetuating its male descent. The point is not, in this overly simple scenario, to imply that this fatal blow caused the bourgeoisie to spring out of a box like some genie—in any event, the duke's widow miraculously produced an authenticated male heir seven months later. Rather, the assassination of Berry proved a boon to the so-called Ultra party, the clamorous reactionary wing of Restoration politics, accelerating and magnifying a shift to the right which had begun some months earlier: the press was muzzled, election laws were restricted, and the left was soundly defeated in the next round of elections.

In the process, members of the center-left political grouping known as the Doctrinaires, previously central to Restoration politics, were forced to the margin and into oppositional stances. From the floor of the Chamber of Deputies and the lecture halls of the Sorbonne, men such as Pierre-Paul Royer-Collard, Augustin Thierry, Prosper de Barante, and François Guizot told their political enemies and their mesmerized students the story of France's bourgeoisie. The seeds of liberty and progress in France, they said, first germinated in the medieval free towns or *communes,* havens of civilization in a landscape of feudal violence. The bourgeois of these towns were the monarchy's best allies against the brutal pretensions of feudal grandees, and in return for their help Louis the Fat and other Capets granted the towns charters that ensured their inhabitants' freedom. Louis XVIII had also given the French a Charter, the 1814 constitutional document which the Doctrinaires embraced as an ideal compromise between past and present. Was it not obvious in 1820 who were the monarchy's most loyal supporters? And did not history clearly show, even in the midst of a reactionary backlash, who the winners would inevitably be?

Of course these histories of bourgeois ascendancy had many more sources, both deep and proximate, than just the political crisis of 1820. They drew most obviously on eighteenth-century histories like that of Mably, and their authors' sense of the importance of history in general, of social conflict as a motor of change, had been immeasurably sharpened by the nation's experience of the Revolution and Empire. Furthermore, while France in this period still had not experienced anything like large-scale industrialization, the urban population grew steadily in both relative and absolute terms in the first half of the nineteenth century, most dramatically in the capital: Paris had 43 percent more inhabitants in 1831 than in 1801.[1] Even if ideas about society are driven by political rhetoric, linguistic representations are still bounded by what appears credible in a certain social landscape.[2] It simply made more sense in 1820 than in 1780 to claim that the urban bourgeoisie was in the vanguard of historical change.

Granted that Guizot and his colleagues did not pull their narratives of bourgeois advent out of thin air, the fact remains that politics did play a decisive role in creating the most positive and successful characterizations of the bourgeoisie in French history. The situation of France after 1814 was such as to ensure plenty of rancor between members of the former ruling elite who returned, bitter and vindictive, from years of exile, and the men committed to gains made in the Revolution, even as they repudiated its radical excesses. The ideological stakes were high, as each side justified its claims to lead the country and denounced its opponents as dangerously reckless by pointing to the lessons of history: the Ultras were accused of bludgeoning their way into power as their German aristocratic forbears had done in the dark ages, the liberals were charged with once again playing to the rabble to get their way. In the 1820s a script for bourgeois ascendancy emerged from the writings of political economists and historians, and from the rough and tumble of political life itself.

## HENRI DE SAINT-SIMON:
## INDUSTRY WITHOUT BOURGEOISIE

One of those figures who, like Lafayette and Talleyrand, bridged the old and new regimes, Claude-Henri, count of Saint-Simon, played a pivotal role in reworking older concepts of society for a postrevolutionary world. A writer who glorified "industrialism" while reviling "the bourgeoisie," an aristocrat claimed as an inspiration by both bankers and socialists, Saint-Simon drew on the Physiocrats but turned their theories upside-down. He injected historicism into social analysis, and his work was a prime source of inspiration for the liberals he came to despise.

Born in 1760, Saint-Simon had an impeccably aristocratic pedigree; there is a beautiful irony to the fact that this fervent champion of industrialism descended from the Duke of Saint-Simon, the snobbish chronicler and gossip famous for scorning the court of Louis XIV as a lair of "vile bourgeoisie." In the course of a life that spanned the Age of Revolution, Saint-Simon turned up in all the right places: tutored by d'Alembert as a boy (or so he claimed), helping the Americans at the battle of Yorktown, awaiting execution in 1793 in the Luxembourg Prison, making and losing a fortune during the Directory, hosting Ideologues in his salon, pursuing Germaine de Staël, acting as surrogate father to Augustin Thierry. His writings span a period from the early 1800s to his death in 1825, with the most important clustered around 1820.[3]

Earlier in his writing career, Saint-Simon described society in conventionally ahistorical terms, as made up of the property owners, the propertyless, and a floating group of intellectuals. His views in the 1790s partook of the anxiety about possible social warfare that pervaded the directorial years: the only way the propertied could avoid defeat at the hands of the rabble, he argued, was to recruit to their side the class of *savants* whom Saint-Simon already viewed as a kind of secular priesthood.[4] In the wake of Empire and Restoration, however, the count's views of society changed considerably, taking on a decisively historical quality.

Saint-Simon's Restoration writings have a "feudal class" and an "industrial class" facing off, with an "intermediate class" wedged in between them; this may look like a modern upper-middle-lower scheme, but in fact it is not, since people we would consider members of the middle classes can be found in both the "intermediate" and the "industrial" categories. Saint-Simon's works contain many discussions of the historical genesis of these groups. In *L'Organisateur* (1819–20), for instance, Saint-Simon explained how the two main classes came into being. Under the old (medieval) system, spiritual power was "papal or theological," while temporal power was "feudal and military." The principal means of enrichment for nations under this regime was warfare and plunder, and "industry"—by which he meant both agriculture and manufacturing—was subordinate to these ends.[5] Feudal-military society naturally spawned authoritarian political regimes, since a system geared toward warfare demands a passively obedient population, just as the primacy of religion in the spiritual realm calls for blind, unquestioning faith.[6]

Yet even within this martial and theocratic world, as early as the eleventh century another universe was taking shape, that of the two great "positive capacities," science and industry. "Since then these two systems have coexisted and struggled, sometimes silently, sometimes openly, with the result that the first gradually weakened while the second grew increasingly strong."[7] The historical turning point was political: in the eleventh and twelfth centuries, the kings of France began to grant freedom to some towns and their inhabitants in return for, or in anticipation of, their help in containing turbulent feudal grandees. This was the famous *affranchissement des communes,* an event of towering importance to Restoration liberals. "This *affranchissement* laid the basis for industrial capacity since it endowed the latter with a social existence independent of military power."[8] Eventually, urban industry generated inventions such as gunpowder, which made warfare dependent upon science and technology, paving the way for the gradual but inevitable rise of industrial society.[9]

With Saint-Simon, have we finally arrived at a narrative of rising bourgeoisie? One might be tempted to jump to that conclusion given the ways in which his account prefigures Marx's, with a new economics and a new social world taking shape in the interstices of the old. But Saint-Simon differs from Marx—and for that matter from his predecessor Barnave—in the importance he grants to political agency in his account. The event that touched off change initially was not the pressure of a new form of wealth (commerce in Barnave, capitalism in Marx), but an act of political will, the Capetian kings' decision to grant freedom to some of their urban subjects. Like many of his liberal contemporaries, Saint-Simon was eager to find in the French past confirmation of the argument that commoners, not benighted Ultras, were the monarchy's natural allies and most reliable supporters.

Even more importantly, Saint-Simon's industrial class cannot be equated with a middle class or bourgeoisie in any sense of those terms; it is simply too capacious. To describe this group he uses such phrases as *les sciences, les beaux-arts, les arts et métiers* (sciences, arts, and crafts), *savants, artistes, et artisans* (scientists, artists, and artisans), or *agriculteurs, manufacturiers et commerçants* (agriculturalists, manufacturers, and tradesmen). In short, anyone who engages in productive work.[10] The group can also be defined by those it does not include, and whom Saint-Simon once famously tagged the drones as opposed to the bees: the royal family, the court, the entire administration, the clergy, and all landed proprietors.[11]

It is tempting to see in Saint-Simon's industrial class a blueprint for a capitalist bourgeoisie, since the writer shows a clear predilection for the leaders in the sectors he enumerates: the heads of manufacturing, commerce, banking, and agriculture. Yet agriculture, while not the object of special concern, is clearly part of industrial society, suggesting that Saint-Simon's use of the term "industry" remained close to its meaning as work. At the same time, the category encompasses, besides captains of industry, the people termed "artists" under the Old Regime: masons, locksmiths, cobblers, bakers, and their ilk. In fact, allowing for some updating and a more elaborate historical framework, Saint-Simon's industrial class is very similar to the catchall Third Estate as described by Sieyès and other pamphleteers in 1788–89.

There is one important exception, however: the group Saint-Simon refers to most often as *légistes et métaphysiciens* (men of law and intellectuals), the leaders of the revolutionary Third Estate, who are summarily rejected from the industrial class. These men, spinners of words and theories, are actually given a class of their own; it is they who make up the intermediate class. The term "intermediate" can be understood in several ways, none of which denote social middlingness. These men are social and historical mediators; in their various incarnations—as Old Regime *parlementaires,* revolutionary rhetoricians, Napoleonic administrators, and liberal politicians—they helped to bring about the demise of the old world of theocracy and warfare. They are not real "organizers" of society, just brokers of transition, and their influence can and has become nefarious: having no idea of the substance of the world, they mistake words for things, and form for content. To Saint-Simon, this group belongs more to the past than to the present, as suggested by one of the monikers he used to designate it: *la féodalité de Bonaparte* (Bonaparte's feudal class). From philosophes and magistrates to Jacobin lawyers to Bonaparte's ennobled bureaucrats, these were all the same group, a new form of aristocracy which would, its historical mission accomplished, simply stay around to bicker with the older nobility.[12]

It was in the existence of this noxious class of theorists that Saint-Simon found the answer as to why industrial society had not developed as it should have. The industrial class was made up of all those who had any tangible good to contribute to society. Internally diverse and unequal yet harmonious, *la classe industrielle,* encompassing all things good and useful, was a universal class destined to take over and become *la société industrielle.*[13] Why, then, had it not already done so, now that the class of feudal warriors had been disposed of for good? The problem was politics, and within the political arena, the refusal of the intermediate class of rhetors to bow out once their historical role had been fulfilled. Having no other role to play, the lawyers, speech-makers, and administrators posed as representatives of the new society. They colonized the Chamber of Deputies, impeding the rise into politics of real industrial leaders. In fact, Saint-Simon shrewdly argued, it was precisely because they themselves were a "bastard" intermediate group that they thrived on the hybrid nature of a regime such as that of the Restoration, and had no interest in causing it to change in any fundamental way.[14]

The brilliantly eccentric Saint-Simon is a pivotal figure in the transformation (in some ways) and reinforcement (in others) of understandings of society in France. Drawing upon the political economy of the Physiocrats, he transformed it in ways that signaled just how much things had changed since 1789. Gone was the worship of mother earth, the good farmer, and all the images of fecundity associated with them; instead, Saint-Simon enshrined the groups dismissed by the

Physiocrats as "sterile": technicians, manufacturers, industrialists. Even more importantly, the count took the work of the Physiocrats and historicized it. Groups were defined by the nature and value of their work, but no longer arranged on some atemporal grid: there were those whose time was past, and those whose day was coming. Born and bred in the age of Enlightenment, Saint-Simon moved beyond the century of his birth by showing how only Turgot and Mably together could give meaning to what had happened between 1789 and 1815. Saint-Simon's enormous influence on the liberal historians of the Restoration is beyond doubt, for he served as employer, mentor, and father-figure to no less a figure than Augustin Thierry.[15]

For all of Saint-Simon's innovations, and of his worship of industrialists and industrialism, his view of society confounds the usual— Marxian or Anglocentric—expectations. To begin with, it harks back to prerevolutionary and revolutionary understandings of society, as articulated most famously by Sieyès: a productive "universal class" reminiscent of the Third Estate opposite a useless privileged minority. In the tradition of such revolutionary views, Saint-Simon does not identify any middle or upper class as a model or a natural elite, beyond assuming that the various occupations making up the industrial class will spawn their own leaders. On the contrary, the group which in his scheme looks most like a middle class is cast as the villain of history, the self-serving intellectuals who made the Revolution such a disaster. His terminology for this group, which he viewed as an offshoot of feudalism, shifted over time, until finally in 1823 he began calling it "bourgeois."[16]

While singing the praises of industrial society, Saint-Simon thus continued the revolutionary tradition of casting aspersion on any separate elite within the true nation. As was the case in Jacobin language, he used the term "bourgeois" to mean some form of nefarious aristocracy, the natural enemy of the nation's productive forces. Saint-Simon's intellectual legacy for the nineteenth century was thus a dual and contradictory one. His historical narrative of industrial emancipation directly inspired the so-called Generation of 1820, the group of men who sought to give the bourgeoisie a myth of origins and a claim to political leadership. Yet Saint-Simon's own denunciation of the liberal elite in the Chamber of Deputies—and indeed of any group's claim to a superiority not based on tangible work and practical science—fits more easily into a republican-socialist tradition which would soon embrace the renegade aristocrat as one of its own.

## THE POLITICS OF THE PRESENT:
## ELITES AND ELECTIONS

The Restoration government ushered into France by the European powers in 1814—and briefly interrupted by Napoleon in 1815—should not be regarded as a simple reactionary backlash.[17] The Charter of 1814 maintained the Revolution's essential gains—legal equality, most civil liberties, careers open to talent—and the aging Louis XVIII was shrewd and cynical enough to realize that his rabid supporters on the right could cause as much trouble as his enemies on the left. (In response to an Ultra-royalist electoral triumph, the king once evoked the story of the man who prays for divine help to climb onto his horse and finds himself propelled over the steed onto the ground on the other side.) The opposition from the far left was neither vocal nor organized early in the regime, as the Hundred Days left Bonapartists and Republicans marginalized and demoralized. The more substantial "liberal" opposition, the Doctrinaires led by Royer-Collard, eagerly embraced most elements of the political status quo: king, Charter, and English-style constitution.

These were the men, on the right and left, who argued on several occasions over the mechanics of the regime's voting laws. Their heated debates bring to mind the old saw about politics being all the more acrimonious when the stakes are small, for the issues had to do with the possibility of adding a few tens of thousands of voters to France's minuscule legal electorate. The Charter of 1814 gave France a constitutional monarchy in which power was shared between the king, a 262-member Chamber of Deputies, and a Chamber of Peers appointed by the monarch. The deputies were elected for five years by voters over age thirty, paying three hundred francs in direct taxes; eligibility to serve came at age forty and a tax of one thousand francs. By virtue of this system, an electorate of at most one hundred thousand chose deputies from a potential pool of about ten thousand. In a country of about 35 million, 99 percent of the population were excluded from active participation in legal politics. These electoral provisions were initially suspended in the crisis conditions of the Hundred Days. Under a different set of rules set by royal fiat, and with liberals in disarray, the elections of August 1815 returned an arch-reactionary chamber, the so-called Chambre Introuvable. This body soon proved such a political liability that the king dissolved it in September 1816, calling for a vote on the original electoral law, which had the support of the Doctrinaire group.

The arguments around this electoral law, which took place in the Chamber of Deputies in December 1816 and January 1817, offer a good vantage point for examining discourses on society within the political sphere. In the end the liberals (as the Doctrinaires were often called) prevailed, and the law was adopted; the sharpest, most vivid rhetoric came from deputies on the right resisting the law. One of the features of the proposed legislation was a prescription for the elections to take place in each department's chief urban center or *chef-lieu*, an arrangement the Ultras feared since it might result in the over-representation of urban liberal interests. Whereas in actuality the law called for a few hundred very respectable men to represent quiescent provincial towns, the Ultras warned their listeners that what was in store was the recreation of revolutionary mobs and imperial armies. Imagine the electors converging on small towns, said a deputy named de Cardonnel: "[W]hat confusion, tumult, and chaos . . . what occasions for trouble and disorder! . . . What a field opened up for intrigue!" A like minded colleague darkly concurred: "*Then* try to count on police forces; they would be like drops of water only hastening the conflagration."[18] Clausel de Cousergues invoked the names of the terrorist Barère and the man he called in the royalist style "Buonaparte" before concluding: "Nobody is unaware of how foreign to the spirit and the interests of monarchy are such large assemblies."[19]

The conservatives had to evoke these urban convergences and resort to crowd and army imagery to make the case that the proposed law was dangerously democratic, because they could not, given the stringent electoral requirements, plausibly argue that it pandered to the poor or opened the door to the rabble. Curiously, they also made the opposite case, suggesting that the liberals were setting up a system that would recreate a form of privilege. Ultra leader count Joseph de Villèle argued at the outset of the debate that the law created a "privileged class" and played to its interests. And for what purpose? The three-hundred-franc electors, Villèle said, could not be independent.

Situated between the upper and lower classes, "they have only the be-ginnings of a fortune, a fortune still to be made," and therefore were especially vulnerable to pressure from local administrations, them-selves dependent on the ministry.[20] Liberal ministers like the law's sponsor, Joachim Lainé, were using the self-interest of the middle classes to further their own designs.

Another Ultra deputy made the point more bluntly: the law creates a privileged group, he said, because its ultimate effect would be to un-dermine the "disinterested" influence of property. Without it, he went on, the nation would be made hostage to the self-interest of members of the *classe moyenne:* "I gladly add my voice to those who praise the do-mestic virtues of the middle class. But these can be found in other classes; and what are needed here are not domestic virtues but public ones." The history of the Revolution proved just how dangerous these middling types could be. Having perfected neither their fortune nor their education, they went around preaching on the basis of *demi lumières* (half understanding), with the catastrophic results seen in the 1790s. These are the men who want revolutions, he concluded, be-cause they are on their way up and, unlike the wealthy or the poor, have everything to gain and little to lose from drastic change.[21]

The Revolution, these deputies argued, had ushered in an era of isolation and egoism, as reflected in the push to make the electoral sys-tem a matter of cold arithmetical calculation. In response to this per-ceived state of affairs, the Ultras trotted out the concepts and buzz-words of the embattled Old Regime aristocracy: honor, aristocratic mediation (Montesquieu's "intermediate bodies"), the need for a corporate, organic social organization.[22] But most interesting is their characterization of the middle class—in reality the tiny group of those paying 300 francs in taxes—as inherently unstable. A stable social orga-nization necessitated a constellation of vertical ties, "relations of pa-tronage, kindness, respect and mutual need [which are] a source of peace in political assemblies."[23] Nothing more volatile could be imag-ined than a self-interested, venal, and ambitious middle class.

The liberals in response defended their law, although one would be hard pressed to find much coherence in their explanations of its social justification. The law's sponsor, Lainé, spoke of the importance of commerce and the need to have it represented along with landed property; another deputy produced a classic definition and praise of "the middle class in whom reside all of society's vitality, which perfects agriculture and multiplies industrial resources, causes commerce, arts and sciences to flourish, manages and regulates society through its administrative and judicial work."[24] But for others the law simply represented an extension of the principle of aristocracy, and especially of an aristocracy of state service. Royer-Collard, the liberal group's quasi-official leader, opened the discussion by insisting that "in spite of its democratic appearance, [this law] cannot erase the great forms of superiority which make up natural aristocracies and which strengthen all governments." Both he and his colleague Camille Jordan stressed that voting was not a right but an important function (*magistrature et service public*) exercised in the nation's interest.[25]

For still others, the law's justification lay in its combination of social with political goals. This electoral legislation was, of course, laid out in the Charter, which to its defendants expressed the perfect compromise between the past and the present, a political system which ideally combined all of the interests of society: "The inferior class must be protected and defended, but neither act nor direct. . . . This is true democratic monarchy, made up of the elite of the former Third Estate, reborn through the introduction of both ancient and new forms of superiority, of both real and conventional claims to preeminence."[26] The electoral law and the Charter together defined an ideal of "democratic" constitutional monarchy, one which was assumed to include the nation while excluding the poor and truly middling.

The issue was, indeed, and probably for the first time in French history, the nature and status of a middle class, the *classe moyenne* or *classe intermédiaire*. The debate of 1816–17 makes clear, of course, that the argument still was about rankings rather than numbers, since the group under consideration made up about one third of one percent of the population—it was middle or intermediate in status, perhaps, but very far from covering any real social middle ground. Conservatives revived in the course of the debate the fears which, in any hierarchical framework, are caused by the middling or mobile. It would be folly, they argued, to entrust so much of the nation's political welfare to a group by definition unstable—men who were ambitious, on the move, "half-rich," "half-enlightened." To the liberals, on the other hand, the intermediate class paying three hundred francs' taxes was one leg of the perfectly stable tripod made up of peers, deputies, and monarch. But reading these debates, one is mostly struck by the overall absence of a real, sustained defense of a middle class by the Doctrinaires at this date. While their foes went on the attack, evoking Bonaparte, mob rule, and the lack of public spirit among the commercial classes, liberals hid behind the Charter, the monarchy, and vague notions of natural aristocracy. It would take a political reaction and outright defeat for stronger, more positive statements of social identity to emerge.

That political reaction occurred in 1820, precipitated by the murder of Berry. The king's principal minister, the liberal-leaning Elie Decazes, had come under heavy pressure from the increasingly vocal right wing of the governing assemblies and was cooperating with Villèle on a new and more conservative electoral law when the assassination occurred. The government immediately censored the press and unleashed the police, and Louis XVIII was forced to dismiss his chief minister (Decazes, one contemporary said, had "slipped in the blood").[27] By May the stage was set for debate over the so-called Law of the Double Vote: the electoral colleges would now be based in rural districts rather than towns, and the richest rural electors (most likely to be conservative) could vote again on the departmental level to fill 172 newly created seats in the Chamber of Deputies. The law was eventually adopted and produced the desired effect in 1820 and in partial elections thereafter, so that by 1823 there were only nineteen liberal deputies left in the Chamber.

The debates over the new law, from May 15 to June 12, 1820, became the focus of political life. The entrance to the Palais Bourbon was mobbed by students and young employees who would jeer or applaud loudly at the news relayed by their messengers from inside the Chamber.[28] Now that the liberal newspapers had been shut down, left and center-left deputies used the parliamentary sessions as their principal means of public expression. Hence the speeches they gave went beyond the issue at hand to become treatises on history and on the philosophy of government.[29]

Nonetheless, politics did profoundly shape their utterances. The agonistic nature of the circumstances led the liberals to speak of the middle class as a group defined by the hostility of an aristocracy which sought to deprive it of political rights. For unlike in 1817, discourse about the middle class was this time explicit and focused. Deputies spoke of the *classes moyennes,* equating them unproblematically with the "industrious" or "industrial" classes. Deputy Martin de Gray, for instance, delivered a characteristic tirade on the very first day of debates:

> The preponderance of the middle class is the living essence of the new France; it is necessary because physical and moral forces belong to [that class]; because the weight of both wealth and ideas are on its side; it is both reasonable and fair because the interests [of the middle class] are the same as those of the whole body of the people, and it has a particular stake in the maintenance of the established order.[30]

Another liberal angrily challenged the argument that large landowners were the only group with a strong interest in the maintenance of political stability: does not the man who invests movable capital in the land have as much or more of an interest in the status quo? Does not the merchant whose goods lie in warehouses, the capitalist with heavy investments in industry, the manufacturer employing dozens of workers?[31] These were the men, the essence of the nation, whom a benighted aristocracy was trying to keep away from the voting urns. "And why these relentless attacks of the aristocracy against the industrial and working class of society?" asked Martin de Gray. "Why? Because [the aristocracy] knows how patriotic are men of commerce and industry; how in all times and places they have always fled despotism and promoted liberty."[32]

Here, at last, in the speeches delivered in the midst of full-scale political reaction, we encounter a language of middle-class identity. Deputies argued against the proposed electoral law of 1820 on the grounds that it represented an aristocratic attempt to disenfranchise an industrial, commercial, and manufacturing *classe moyenne*. The most striking aspect of the political language of 1820, however, was the constant recourse to historical argument. In the years after 1815, given the forces competing in the public arena, reference to history was inevitable. But such allusions had remained muted in the debates of 1817, with conservatives obliquely raising the specter of popular mayhem and liberals responding that the electoral law reflected the Charter's transcendent, timeless synthesis of the French nation's different components. By 1820, the rhetoric was much different. This time the liberals made a spirited defense of the middle class rooted in history, and produced vivid denunciations of the law that hinted at violence, domination, and counter-revolution. The speeches opposing the electoral law of 1820 are awash in historical references to everything from the Gauls and the Romans to Napoleon, via Pascal and Louis XIV. The arguments fall into clear patterns, however, framed by the same broad assumptions. One of these, and the most grandiose, was that current political realities (king and Charter, middle-class ascendancy, aristocratic reaction) stood at the end of a long and irresistible historical evolution.

Some of the most resonant passages to this effect can be found in the celebrated speeches of Doctrinaire guru Royer-Collard, which enjoyed an afterlife in the editions collected and published by his colleague and disciple Prosper de Barante. In 1817 Royer-Collard had supported the liberal election law using ahistorical Aristotelian language. The voting requirements wisely entrusted political responsibility, he said, "to a middle class which all interests could take as their natural representative; above it one finds a certain need for domination of which one must be wary; below, ignorance, habit and need, and therefore inaptitude for the functions under consideration."[33] Two years later, he justified middle-class ascendancy in the framework of history, not philosophy: "Centuries have prepared it; the Revolution proclaimed it."[34] And in his most famous speech on May 17, 1820, he concluded an oration which had begun with the Middle Ages: "Rivers do not flow back up to their sources; events once unfolded do not revert to nothingness. A bloodstained revolution had changed the face of the earth; upon the ruins of the old society felled with such violence, a new one had grown up, led by new men with new principles."[35]

The Revolution presented liberals with an especially delicate intellectual and rhetorical problem: how to claim it as a positive, progressive force, while repudiating the violence so deeply feared and abhorred by all members of the governing elite. Two kinds of attitudes were adopted, sometimes inconsistently. For instance, Royer-Collard flatly stated in the same speech that the Revolution's crimes "were not necessary," but later offered an apparently deterministic account of why the mayhem occurred: the Revolution suddenly created a new society, which like all new and conquering peoples was barbaric; it took a generation for this new world to recover the principles of law and legitimacy that undergird a fully achieved civilization.[36]

Because of the issues of violence and regicide, the Revolution was most often evoked either fleetingly or obliquely, an unavoidable but usually implicit reference in the context of 1820. In a gloss on the regime instituted by the Charter, Royer-Collard made the point that the Chamber of Deputies "is the Nation standing before the throne and the aristocracy, the Nation in the very state in which it received the historical designation of *communes.*" And, he added, in an echo of countless pamphleteers in 1789, once you remove monarchy and aristocracy, "what is left of the nation . . . is essentially homogeneous."[37] The term *communes* as applied to the Chamber of Deputies was especially useful given its evocative multivalence. It suggested a kinship between the Chamber and the English House of Commons, a safe, uncontroversial equivalence at this point. But the term served especially to establish a lineage that reached back first to the revolutionary Third Estate, often called the *communes* in 1789, and beyond that to the medieval towns known as *communes* which were granted their freedom by the medieval kings.

"The Revolution completed the emancipation of the *communes*":[38] the Revolution was not a beginning but a culmination whose logical extension was the compromise of 1814. This was the liberals' historical trump card. By moving very far upstream in history and locating their own historical origins in the Middle Ages, they reduced the Revolution from a cause to a consequence, and claimed justification in the inevitability of a process begun not thirty years but seven centuries beforehand. "The first lineaments of the Charter were traced by Louis the Fat, when he emancipated the *communes,*" Royer-Collard explained; "they became ineradicable once Philip the Fair convened our ancestors in national assemblies . . . It was then that silently began, later to break out on the day appointed within the course of centuries, the legitimate but terrible struggle of rights against privilege."[39] Liberal deputies like Jean Joseph de Courvoisier painted in glowing colors the pride and power of the medieval burghers, with their courts and militias, their powerful provosts. "Henri IV bore the title of bourgeois of Paris," he recalled. The real usurpers were the nobles, who eventually compensated for the irresistible decline of feudalism by invading the towns and robbing the middle classes of their rightful honors and functions.[40]

History served not only to link the claims of the liberal party to a social and political narrative of bourgeois ascendancy, but also, and more pervasively, to bring the weight of the past to bear upon what was described as a dangerous and retrograde bid for aristocratic power. Liberal speakers did not hesitate to describe what was happening as a resurrection of feudalism. Martin de Gray interpreted the proposed electoral law as a beachhead for a full-scale revival of feudal law: "The French soil," he dramatically concluded, "land of liberty and glory, would be gradually subject to *mainmorte* and its people to serfdom."[41] Equally common, and just as dramatic, were constant references to the history of aristocratic plunder and conquest, along with intimations of foreign domination. Many a speaker equated the events of 1820 with the ancient conquest of Gaul by the men from the North; the "aristocratic party" is set to do it again, de Gray thundered, "to once again conquer Gaul and seize all of its land, its factories and shops, all of the commercial and industrial wealth of the new France."[42] Royer-Collard argued that the "double-vote" law represented a "political pleonasm," the reintroduction of privilege into a system based on legal equality. Privilege, historically, amounted to a tribute which the victors demanded of the vanquished. To try and reimpose it was "not only a violation of the Charter, not only a coup d'état against representative government; it is a coup d'état against society; it is a revolution against equality; it is a true counter revolution."[43] Returning to the arguments of prerevolutionary historians, liberal deputies insisted that the threat of violence and lawlessness came from reckless grandees, not from the peace-loving heirs of the medieval burghers.

The liberal Doctrinaire position was therefore based on a conception of history which cast the emancipation of the medieval towns as the defining moment in the French past, and the bourgeois as the embodiments of the true French nation. But the Doctrinaires' justification of a highly restricted franchise seems at first to contradict historical arguments championing the middle classes. Royer-Collard, Barante, and their followers insisted that they spoke in the name of the French people, in defense of the first modern government—the Charter of 1814—to represent perfectly the interests of the French nation as a whole. Yet throughout the Restoration they promoted and defended an electoral system accessible only to the very rich, one which clearly excluded a vast majority of people who could reasonably be considered middle class. How did they explain this apparent paradox?

The answer can be summed up in the concept of *capacité*, which Royer-Collard defined at some length in another of his celebrated speeches during the 1820 electoral debate. Society is made up of two elements, he explained. In its material aspect, society can be seen as the strength and will of individual persons and groups; from a "moral" (what we would term intellectual or spiritual) point of view, society exists in the "rights resulting from legitimate interests."[44] If you base society upon the materiality of human needs and wants, you will end up with either popular or authoritarian government (these two being essentially varieties of despotism); if you build society upon "moral" considerations, then the basis for your government will be not power but well-understood "rights and interests."[45] The latter was obviously what the speaker and his colleagues favored. French society was made up of two main "interests," he explained, two separate "political conditions," the aristocratic and the popular, represented by the two chambers of government. Each of these being internally indivisible, and the first governed by the principle of heredity, how was representation of the popular interest best managed?

The solution lay in the two "capacities" established by the Charter, the right to vote and to be elected. These capacities, based on income and education, were aimed at defining a group able to see beyond the material world of competing interests, to grasp a Platonic ideal of the whole. Once capacity was defined and identified in a person, questions of numerical representation became moot: "There is in that respect neither majority nor minority in the nation, only unity and unanimity."[46] To those who might object that the restriction of electoral rights fostered a new kind of privilege, Royer-Collard answered that "this proves that a person is not cured of the notion of popular sovereignty, since they reason within the framework of that sovereignty and cling obstinately to the notion of representing persons, instead of rising to an understanding of the representation of rights and interests."[47] The capacity to elect and be elected was based not on some crude mathematical formula but on a man's ability—as determined by income and education—to rise above the interests of a subgroup in society and act on behalf of the whole: "The justness and merit of representation comes primarily . . . from the elector's special aptitude to perceive undiluted the interests of all."[48]

In sum, there is little in Royer-Collard's argument that suggests a commitment to the interests of the middle class, or of any other class for that matter. Indeed, he explicitly dismissed class-based politics as

dangerously fettered to the realm of matter. The stringent electoral requirements established in 1814 were aimed, he believed, at defining a
category of citizens for whom voting or running for office would be
not a right but a special function or duty based on a presumed ability
to transcend self-interest. The scion of a Jansenist family, Royer-Collard quoted Pascal ("Reread the first two *Provinciales,* Gentlemen; reread them, I beg of you") to establish an equivalence between "capacity" and "grace," qualities or states he deemed sufficient, indivisible,
and absolute.

If Royer-Collard did not clearly define and defend the middle class,
neither, at this time, did the politician and writer most commonly associated with the concept of "middlingness" in French history, François
Guizot—the man of the *juste-milieu,* whose most frequently quoted
statement remains his injunction to the disenfranchised: "Get rich!"[49]
In 1820 Guizot was too young—still only in his thirties—to stand for
election to the Chamber of Deputies, but he penned his thoughts on
the political climate and issues of the day in an 1821 pamphlet, *Des
moyens de gouvernement et d'opposition dans l'état actuel de la France.* Certainly there are many passages in this text which, taken out of context,
sound like predictable celebrations of the ever-rising middle class. In a
chapter entitled "The New Interests," Guizot admonished the deputies
to stop worrying about the alleged revolutionary proclivities of the
middle classes, and co-opt them instead: "You want to cure France of
hatred of the nobility; become a bourgeois government." This still nascent group will not be a source of trouble but of strength: "Far from
fearing the influence of the *classe moyenne* take on that influence; help
it to spread and to strengthen . . . Instead of fearfully holding down
the upward movement of this class, give it assistance."[50]

But assistance to do what? Not to go forth as captains of industry,
but to become high servants of government. This class on the rise,
Guizot writes, "does not ask for privilege, it demands contests."[51] Louis
XIV, famous for opening up his administration to talented commoners, is repeatedly invoked. Framing these arguments about co-opting
the best talent from the "new interests" is a view of government as a
transcendent moral force. Echoing his directorial predecessors—such
as Madame de Staël—as well as many contemporaries, Guizot reiterated the familiar argument that political "equality" means not popular
government but a system in which a "natural aristocracy" would take

over leadership of the nation. "Superior" men will inevitably form a "superior" government, which is anything but the "servant" of the people: Guizot explicitly and indignantly rejected arguments for minimal and subordinate government.[52] The national leadership he wanted for France was a state greater than the sum of its parts, a government "which is the essence and manifestation of all social life."[53] Do not insult our nation, he proclaimed, by telling it to knuckle under to the authority of paid retainers and lowly clerks: "Do you think that in obeying Buonaparte, France was submitting itself to a salaried servant?"[54]

The model presented in Guizot's writing is starkly different from stereotypical depictions of the bourgeois as bustling *homo economicus*. His ideal is not one of competition and self-interest but of carefully managed self-improvement (by way of emulation) aimed at public service. His pamphlet hammers away at the vital importance of "the general interests," repeatedly condemning their opposite, "individual interests," as a recipe for defeat. It was "individual interests" that had undermined the parliamentary session of 1820 and engendered the hated electoral law, the same "individual interests" that had brought down the government of the Directory.[55] Although he uses the conventionally derogatory spelling of the name Buonaparte, Guizot clearly admires Napoleon's achievement in making the state something more than a sum or balance of petty interests. The implicit ideal for Guizot, as for Royer-Collard, was a sort of Bonapartism without a Bonaparte, a system in which the energy, intelligence, and idealism of a Napoleon will be found not in a single, necessarily tyrannical being, but in a multitude of electors, delegates, and civil servants.

In his revisionist study of Guizot's political thought, Pierre Rosanvallon insists that the history of the French "liberal and democratic imaginary" must be kept separate from any account of capitalist development. Guizot and his followers, Rosanvallon believes, reacted against contractual thought, which had been discredited, in their view, by the Revolution. Nor did they believe that the market could, as suggested by Adam Smith and others, provide a basis for social life. Indeed, this was their quandary in a nutshell: "How to imagine the social beyond the two archetypes of body and market?"[56] How could one conceive of the relationship between the social and the political in order both to break free of traditional hierarchies and to avoid the corrosive effects of self-regard? The answer, Guizot believed, lay in "reason" as embodied in *capacité*.[57] Society generates superior beings able to envision political interests in general, transcendent terms. The stated ideal of the Doctrinaire group as a whole, and of Guizot in particular, was therefore less the promotion of an economically defined bourgeois than the creation of an elite political caste devoted to the interests of the entire nation, a new and natural aristocracy of talent, ready to devote itself to the good of all.

In the electoral debates of 1816–17, and even more of 1820, definitions and support of a bourgeois class make their first significant appearance in French history. In the earlier debates the liberals rebuffed Ultra attacks by invoking concepts of natural aristocracy and laying heavy emphasis on their devotion to king and Charter. In the debates of 1820, with political reaction in full swing, liberal rhetoric was more pointed and social identities more sharply defined. This time many deputies did sing the praises of a hard-working, productive *classe moyenne* as the nation's best source of wealth and political stability. But what is remarkable about the sociopolitical rhetoric of 1820 is the overall resistance to economic definitions of the middle class. The leading liberals did present themselves as champions of a bourgeoisie, but defined that group as the possessor of the skills and intelligence necessary for selfless devotion to the state, rather than owner of the means of production. Most of all, the bourgeoisie was a group forged by the nation's history. What entitled them to lead the nation was not industrial initiative and enlightened self-interest, but the fact that they embodied the plurisecular triumph of reason and administrative "capacity" over the aristocracy's alleged cult of violence and heredity.

## THE POLITICS OF THE PAST: THE BOURGEOISIE GETS A HISTORY

One of the consequences of the political reaction of 1820 was the migration of leading liberals from direct involvement in politics to the broader and more detached contemplation of history. François Guizot, who had held positions in various ministries and the Council of State starting in 1814, returned to teaching history at the Sorbonne in 1820. The closing down of the liberal newspaper *Le Censeur européen* that year forced Augustin Thierry to publish in another paper, the *Courrier français,* and ultimately to abandon journalism for sustained historical projects, most notably his 1827 *Lettres sur l'histoire de France*. This is not to say that politics alone "created" historical discourse by closing itself off to liberal voices. There is abundant evidence of the public's intense interest in history under the Restoration long before the crisis of 1820. Historical painting, heavily oriented to medieval and Renaissance themes, had been going strong since the end of the Empire. The genre produced a string of tableaux teeming with authentic detail, ranging from pious conservative images of Bayard, Joan of Arc, Lady Jane Grey, and Charles I, to sentimental illustrations of Walter Scott's works.[58] Scott's enormous popularity in France, which propelled him to bestseller status in the 1820s, also predated the political reaction. Between 1812 and 1825, while the annual publication of all books in France doubled, that of historical works more than tripled.[59]

The event that first triggered the great spate of liberal historiography of the 1820s, long before the political reaction set in, was the publication in 1814 of the count of Montlosier's *De la monarchie française*. François-Dominique de Montlosier was a liberal aristocrat, a supporter of constitutional monarchy who, though he fled the Revolution and settled in London, harbored no sympathy for Ultra royalism. Montlosier was much more of an enthusiast for feudalism than for monarchy. No doubt because of his indecipherable ideological makeup, the count was asked by Napoleon to write a history of France aimed at establishing the Empire's legitimacy by linking it to the monarchy of old, a text which would serve as a basis for national reconciliation. To the emperor's dismay, Montlosier completed in 1807 a history designed to inflame rather than quell social and political divisions. In *De la monarchie*, Montlosier revived the eighteenth-century paradigm of French history as a struggle between two "races," the Franks and the Gauls. His narrative chronicled the warriors' domination of the "ancient people" with their feudal institutions, and the gradual undermining of their power by their former tributaries, the Third Estate, in alliance with the monarchy. The Revolution, the ultimate seizure of power by these "new people," was just the latest episode in an unending struggle between two antagonistic races and their irreconcilable cultures and values.[60] Little wonder that the members of Napoleon's examining commission were not thrilled with the work, which they returned unpublished to its disappointed author. The return of the

Bourbons in 1814, however, provided Montlosier with the perfect opportunity to get his manuscript into print. His work was not all that flattering to the monarchy, but its celebration of feudalism and its nostalgia for aristocratic power fit right in with the vindictive mood of the returning emigrés and other Ultra types.

The book naturally caused a stir among liberals as well. Both Thierry and Guizot were incensed by it, but also certainly inspired by it. Indeed, many passages from Montlosier, removed from their overall framework, could very well have been written by his enemies: "We shall see a new state taking shape amidst the ancient state; a new people amidst the older one . . . We shall see a doubled state, a doubled people, a doubled social order march apace with one another, then attack one another, then become locked in relentless struggle."[61] Much of the liberal historiography of the Restoration reads like Montlosier turned upside down.[62] The count's pro-feudal writing provided a model that was successfully adapted for liberal ends: it emphasized medieval history and the emancipation of the *communes*, it revived eighteenth-century debates about monarchy and aristocracy, but gave equal importance to a third major actor, the "new people" of the towns. Above all, Montlosier explained the Revolution as the outcome of a history that stretched back centuries in time, and located the motor of French history in an ongoing deadly contest between nobility and Third Estate. (Previous conservative commentators on the Revolution, most notably abbé Barruel, had argued that the whole thing was a plot by Freemasons and other godless types, and was therefore both accidental and avoidable.)[63] The new historians, Montlosier and his antagonists alike, assumed that history was driven not by the actions of kings or the progress of ideas, but by the spasms of a struggle within one nation between two enemy "races" or "classes." Montlosier should receive some credit for beginning to give the Third Estate a historical identity.

The loudest, most eloquent calls for the Third Estate to mobilize and continue its historic struggle came from the pen of Augustin Thierry, the young historian who, when still in his teens, served as secretary to Saint-Simon. In 1817 he began to publish in the liberal *Censeur européen* some of the writings which would later make up his *Lettres sur l'histoire de France,* and which ring with the political passion of a man in his early twenties. "There are only two nations left: the men of freedom and the men of power; those who would live by working on things, and those who would live by working on men."[64] He called the youth of his generation to arms from the pages of his paper, as did Guizot from the lecture halls of the Sorbonne. In 1818 he wrote of the Third Estate: "Those saviors of the arts, they were our forefathers; we are the sons of those tributaries, of those bourgeois whom the conquerors devoured as they pleased . . . Memories of virtue and glory are attached to their name, but those memories are dimmed because the history which should have recorded them was paid for by our fathers' enemies." In the wake of the 1820 reaction, he once again sounded themes of identity, pride, and victimization: "We are the sons of the Third Estate, the Third Estate which came out of the communes, the communes which were havens for serfs, the serfs who were vanquished in the conquest."[65]

For his bourgeois heroes, Thierry claimed not only superior virtues, but the creation of their own history: like Guizot, he argued against the conventional view that the kings of France, starting with Louis the Fat in the twelfth century, took the initiative of freeing certain towns because they needed the bourgeoisie as allies. The townsmen wanted their freedom even more than the kings wanted allies, and they took it, if necessary by force of arms: "[A]ll this was the work of the merchants and artisans who made up the population of these towns." The kings merely came along and claimed credit for acts of self-emancipation which served their own political purposes.[66]

Fully endorsing a version of French history as the struggle between two peoples, Thierry did not hesitate, in his historical accounts, to depict violence graphically, including brutalities carried out by his burgher-heroes. He recounts in detail, for instance, the Laon uprising of 1112, sparked by the bishop's revocation of the town charter. Thierry shows his readers the bourgeois "armed with swords, pikes, crossbows, clubs and hatchets" massacring nobles to the cry of "Commune, commune!", invading the episcopal palace where the bishop was hiding in a barrel, and hacking him to death despite his pleas for mercy.[67] Thierry neither minimizes nor apologizes for the violence. He ends with considerations linking this episode to the pattern of other "national revolutions"—the peaceful desire for freedom which is granted, then taken away; the violation of trust by old rulers which prompts popular fury and the desire for revenge.[68] Revolutionary violence, he implies, does not stem from bestial or lawless inclinations; it is inscribed in the very pattern of upheavals which further the development of modern society.

Thierry uses the term "bourgeois" to designate the heroes of his history, and in many cases it is clear that he has in mind the legally defined bourgeoisie of the old regime, the leading burghers of medieval towns. But just as often his account blurs the line between wealthy and poor members of the Third Estate. He prefaces his work with praise for the "patriotism and energy" of both "the middle classes and the popular classes," as seen in countless uprisings by both the bourgeoisie and the peasantry.[69] He ascribes the "republican" leanings of twelfth-century towns to their "merchants and artisans," and he admits that these towns varied from the proudest old cities to "conglomerations of serfs and vagabonds to whom kings and lords granted asylum on their lands."[70]

This inclination to regard the Third Estate as unified in its basic desires and destiny probably came from Thierry's background as a disciple of Saint-Simon and acolyte of other prophets of "industrialism." The periodicals Thierry contributed to in 1817–1820, L'Industrie and Le Censeur européen, espoused the views of Saint-Simon about the inexorable growth and inevitable triumph of industrial society, and the link between industrial organization and political freedom. As a result, Thierry's view of society was fundamentally dualistic, in the tradition of the Revolution of 1789: there were two groups in society, the conquerors and the conquered, the men of plunder and those of industry, the advocates of tyranny and those of freedom.[71] While he recognized bourgeois leadership of the Third Estate in history, his industrialist scheme was committed to the idealization of a working, productive, and unified nation.

Although Thierry and Guizot are often described as sharing the same ideology, the differences in their understanding of, and preoccupation about, the bourgeoisie are in fact significant. In the years after the publication of Thierry's Lettres, Guizot offered a series of lectures at the Sorbonne (1828–1830), which he later published as the History of Civilization in Europe and the History of Civilization in France. Guizot's work covers much of the same ground as Thierry's—with a heavy emphasis on medieval history and the inevitable freeing of the *communes*—and, frequently citing the earlier historian, makes many of the same points. Guizot echoes Thierry, for instance, in his insistence that the bourgeoisie of the *communes* seized their own freedom rather than passively receiving it from the medieval kings. But Guizot's historical hero is not the undifferentiated Third Estate, but a smaller, distinct middle class caught between a tyrannical aristocracy on the one hand, and a dangerously violent lower class on the other.

Although he draws directly on Thierry, Guizot is considerably less idealistic and sanguine about what the medieval *communes* were really like. The violence of the communal uprisings becomes in his interpretation much less heroic and a lot more alarming. Read Thierry, he told his students, and you will see that the "freedom" of those times was mostly "lugubrious and deplorable."[72] Although they won independence from the exactions of feudal lords, the bourgeois did not hang on to their hard-won freedom, because the fear of popular violence always led them to seek out another powerful protector, a monarch or local lord.[73] Guizot's medieval towns are no republican havens but complex societies riven by inequalities. The majority of their inhabitants, he wrote, were ignorant and brutal, and soon inequality led to the formation of a *bourgeoisie supérieure*—a rich elite facing off against a *population ouvrière*. "The communes soon found themselves divided between a high bourgeoisie and a population that was subject to all the errors and vices of a rabble."[74] The towns never became as prominent as they ought to have, because the political impulses they harbored were the "blind, frenetic, ferocious" democratic instincts of the poor, and the timorous passivity of the upper bourgeoisie.[75]

Unlike Thierry, Guizot was not an advocate of industrialism, nor was his understanding of history in any way oriented toward economic determinism.[76] He did not rhapsodize about industry, commerce, and manufacturing as the lifeblood of the nation; those activities were of little interest to him. He believed that the Third Estate drew its historical strength from another source, as he explained in his history of French civilization:

> Those judges, bailiffs, provosts, seneschals, all of the officers of the king or the great lords, all of those agents of central power in the civil order soon became a numerous and powerful class. Now, most of them

were bourgeois; and their number, their power, operated for the bene-
fit of the bourgeoisie, making the latter more important and more extensive by the day. Of all the origins of the third estate, this one
may have contributed more than any other to its conquest of social supremacy.[77]

In his historical work, as in his political commentary, Guizot emphasized the power of ideas, not of economics: to him the French Revolution was an ideological, not an economic struggle.[78] He accordingly
vested the greatest historical importance in a class of educated officials
rather than in an industrial or commercial bourgeoisie.

Guizot's historical works show a keen awareness of class divisions
within the non-noble core of the nation, an attachment to the principle of natural aristocracy, reverence for administrative rather than economic leadership, and devotion to the future triumph of reason as the
accomplishment of historical destiny. Again unlike Thierry, he identifies the bourgeoisie specifically as the upper stratum of the Third Estate, defined as much by its fear of popular violence as by its hostility
to aristocratic privilege. Lecturing on the eve of the Revolution of
1830, he chides the bourgeoisie for its lack of political initiative and
courage. As Rosanvallon argues, Guizot saw it as his mission to give the
bourgeoisie, as he understood it, a history, a memory, and a political
culture.[79]

The historical writing of the Restoration period represents a crucial
turning point in the history of the French social imaginary. The political conditions of the Restoration, and especially the period after 1820,
were the context for a fusion of two intellectual pursuits which had
been separate in the eighteenth century, history and political economy. Needless to say, the new history owed a great deal to the recent
experience of the Revolution and the swings in political regimes which
followed it. The term "class" finally came into its own: it no longer had
the limited meaning of a scientist's arbitrarily defined category, but expressed something organic and dynamic, which grew and changed
over time.[80] The modern French understanding of class initially derived from the longstanding view of the nation's history as a struggle
between two races or two peoples, of which the Revolution and Restoration were the most recent episodes. Ironically, the first use of the ex-

pression *lutte des classes* (class struggle) came from the pen of the monarchist Montlosier.[81]

It was in the Restoration that the idea of class became decisively associated with the concept of class struggle, and that historians like Guizot began to write of social conflict as a source of change and progress rather than a tragic flaw in the nation's history. Increasingly, other historians, François Mignet and Adolphe Thiers, for example, suggested the open-ended nature of such a struggle, and foresaw it as continuing in the form of contests for power between richer and poorer elements of the Third Estate.[82] At the same time, Guizot was formulating a view of class that had little to do with ancestral blood-feuds but rather was bred of the common experiences of a large and scattered population. After the emancipation of the *communes*, he wrote, "[T]he country was full of men in the same situation, possessed of the same interests and the same manners, which would necessarily form a sort of link among them, a sort of unity which was to give birth to the bourgeoisie."[83] From such analyses sprang a complete rereading of the Revolution as a decisive episode in this social struggle rather than an ahistorical battle between good and evil.

Although the terms *classe moyenne* and *bourgeoisie* were now used in something close to their familiar modern meaning, none of the Restoration politicians and historians actually formulated the definition of the bourgeoisie which has been the standard one since Marx: a capitalist, non-noble elite united in its relationship to the means of production and its individualist and materialist values. The elements of Marx's definition were all available by the 1820s, but belonged to different traditions. On the one hand, industry without bourgeoisie was featured in the writings of Saint-Simon and his disciple Thierry. Proponents of industrialism understood the bourgeoisie as the extension of the revolutionary Third Estate, itself an undivided group of "industrials," those who worked and produced, on the land or in factories, in workshops and in banks. On the other hand, Guizot's view of the bourgeoisie came out of the prerevolutionary tradition of honorable state service and the postrevolutionary ideal of a natural aristocracy of talented and reasonable men: bourgeoisie without industry. One of the reasons why no ideal of bourgeoisie ever really took hold in France may well be that it was undermined by the opposite pulls of these two

traditions, the universalism of industry and the elitism of a neo-aristocracy of state service.

## POLITICS AND CLASS

By 1830, notions of middle class and bourgeoisie and claims about
the importance of this group were prominent as never before in
French public culture. The role of political discourse—debates over
election laws, highly politicized historical narratives, the ideological
polarization of the times—was crucial to the creation of this language
of class. To emphasize the political is not to discount other, more traditionally conceived bases of class formation, such as economic and demographic changes. Yet one could argue that where the genesis of
middle-class identity is concerned, political discourse is more crucial
than it is for other groups.[84] "Middle class" and "bourgeoisie" are such
vexed, amorphous categories that they can hardly congeal as identities
without the help of the concrete stakes, institutions, and language of
politics.

The most thorough recent study of a segment of the French middle
class supports such a view. David Garrioch's work on the Parisian bourgeoisie between 1690 and 1830 focuses on the elites of one Parisian
manufacturing district, the gritty faubourg Saint-Marcel, over the
course of this crucial century and a half.[85] From his deeply researched
investigation of the leading families and citizens of Saint-Marcel,
Garrioch concludes that this period saw a transformation from *bourgeois de Paris* to "Parisian bourgeoisie." The city was initially dominated
by tight-knit groups of families entrenched in the neighborhoods and
parishes where they had lived and intermarried for generations. This
system of very local power was initially undermined by the absolute
monarchy but decisively destroyed by the Revolution, as entirely new
institutions of local government were set up, and new men from outside the parish stepped in to take control of them. From then on,
there was no turning back. Many of the old families remained prominent in the district after the Revolution, but their children were more
likely to marry and settle outside of Saint-Marcel. New educational institutions—directorial *grandes écoles* and imperial *lycées*—were forging a
citywide elite.

Garrioch certainly emphasizes the importance of economic and

sociocultural changes to explain the disappearance of the parish-
based lineage and the rise of a citywide elite. Both capitalism—the demands of larger-scale commerce and manufacturing—and the consumer revolution of the eighteenth century play a large part in the
story he tells.[86] But in the end, the single most important factor in the
creation of this new, commanding citywide bourgeoisie was what he
terms "the tutelage of the state." "Above all," he writes, "it was the state,
created by the Revolution, that acted as midwife for the new local
elite."[87] Under the Empire and Restoration, the state was in firm control of local notables, down to the welfare committees and parish ves-
tries, appointing men of demonstrated loyalty—as well as local prominence—to the *conseils d'arrondissement,* the Chamber of Commerce,
school administrations, and leadership of the National Guard.[88] Certainly many factors went into the choice of, for instance, each one
of Paris's twelve mayors and twenty-four deputy mayors: local stature,
personal reputation, family connections and so on. But in the end it
was the state which picked and shaped this elite, bestowing functions
which brought with them honor and prestige along with tangible signs
of prominence such as fancy uniforms and the ribbon of the *Légion
d'honneur.* Garrioch concludes unambiguously: "The formation of the
Parisian bourgeoisie was not primarily an economic phenomenon . . .
It owed much to political struggles and political ideas, religious and
secular."[89]

Hence statements of bourgeois consciousness under the Restoration
were likely to be framed in terms of cherished political institutions
rather than in connection with manufacturing or commercial pride.
One of these documents was the Charter of 1814, which provided a
rallying point for liberals eager to prove their respectability and attachment to the Bourbons. A ringing defense of the new elites by deputy
Baignoux, written in 1829, combines praise of commerce, industry,
and "moderate" or "natural" social inequality with a tribute to the
Charter.[90]

An even greater symbol of bourgeois identity was the National
Guard, especially after it was disbanded in 1827 by the much-detested
Charles X for alleged hostility to the regime. Charles Comte, a prominent liberal journalist, produced that year a history of the Guard, pref-
aced by unconvincing announcements that his was an objective, unbi-
ased project.[91] Comte begins with the familiar story of the Guard's

birth in the shadow of the besieged Bastille, but then proceeds to emphasize the Guard's heroism in protecting the well-to-do from the violent excesses of the *classe ouvrière*. During the October 1789 invasion of Versailles by the mob, the National Guard "dispersed the brigands and saved the court and the bodyguards"; the National Guard was again present when the mob invaded the Tuileries palace in 1792, courageously containing men and women who brandished sabers and bloody animal entrails on the end of their pikes.[92] Even on the eve of the fall of the monarchy, "there were national guards who courageously devoted themselves . . . and dared to defend the monarchy, the one established by the constitution."[93] Reorganized in 1814, the Guard had many a noble commander, Comte pointed out, vigorously refuting those who tagged it a "revolutionary institution."[94] The work ends with a scathing indictment of the regime—"worse than the old regime"[95]—which had disbanded the Guard. The high point of the Guard's history was also the high point of French history, the Festival of Federation, when, under Guard leadership, national harmony and disinterestedness prevailed.

It was much easier to proclaim allegiance to the Charter or the National Guard than to commerce or industry. Not only did the former institutions symbolize a high-minded devotion to the general good over selfish pursuits, they were also a lot more specific and tangible than nascent economic developments, and they suggested a concrete political program.

The goals of the bourgeoisie seemed to have been attained on July 30, 1830, when the seventy-three-year-old Lafayette, erstwhile commander of the first National Guard and symbol of moderate revolution, bearing a large tricolor flag, embraced Louis-Philippe d'Orléans, future king of the liberals, on the balcony of the town hall of Paris, in the presence of a jubilant crowd. Textbook wisdom has it that the Revolution of 1830 consecrated the triumph of the bourgeoisie. But the "bourgeois monarchy" lasted only eighteen years, and those years witnessed turbulent worker protest and harsh intellectual and literary indictment of an unworthy, philistine elite. By calling itself bourgeois, François Furet wrote, the Orleanist monarchy "substituted the fixed target of the state for a mobile and elusive reality."[96] In postrevolutionary France politics was a dangerous game, and those who claimed their social identity from any given regime were in great danger of falling by the wayside when it did.

# The Failure of
# "Bourgeois Monarchy"

## 6

Louis-Philippe d'Orléans, who accepted the French throne in 1830, was known as "the bourgeois king," and his regime has been remembered as a quintessentially middle-class monarchy. France was the only country in Europe where a monarch ruled explicitly in the name of the bourgeoisie, and therein lay a significant historical irony: it was precisely because the government acquired this label that political opposition to the regime, as well as more nebulous forms of cultural discontent, easily crystallized around antibourgeois themes. If Restoration politics gave birth to bourgeois identity, the so-called July Monarchy (1830–1848) reversed the process, making it forever impossible to govern in the name of such a group.

Historians have long treated the bourgeois monarchy of the 1830s and 1840s as an inevitable phase in France's transition to its own brand of modern democracy. A popular view of French history construes the nineteenth century as an extended replay of the original Revolution: the Bourbon Restoration mimics the Old Regime, the reign of Louis-Philippe echoes the constitutional monarchy of 1789–1792, the radical republicanism of 1848 is capped by Bonapartism as in 1793 and 1799, and the nation finally settles into its moderate republican destiny. Having tried to rush through history in a decade, the French then took a century to get things right. One of the problems with this view is that it overlooks the obvious contingencies that went into the choice of a regime and ruler in any given moment of transition: France could well have remained a republic in the decades after 1848, just as it might have become a constitutional monarchy in 1870, had any plausible pretender been at hand. In 1830 Orleanism was just one strain in the swirl of ideologies that fueled anger at the Bourbons; it was far less popular and potent than republicanism and Bonapartism. The cries that rang out on the streets of Paris in July 1830 were mostly Bonapartist slogans, and when Louis-Philippe finally emerged as the symbol of orderly and progressive rule, he did so surrounded by revolutionary emblems: tricolor flags and cockades, the elderly Lafayette, the hastily reassembled National Guard.[1] It took some time for the regime to acquire the characteristics which have since dogged it in the historical literature and caused it to be perceived as a reign of middlingness, compromise, and narrow self-interest.

One feature sharply differentiates the July Monarchy from the revolutionary constitutional monarchy set up in 1789: the Orleanist regime of Louis Philippe explicitly invoked a social group, the bourgeoisie, as its main constituency and source of support, whereas the eighteenth-century revolutionaries never acknowledged any division between richer and poorer members of the Third Estate. The irony is that the very move that was supposed to give the regime strength and legitimacy in 1830 was a major source of its instability and eventual demise. The political legacy of the July Monarchy was not bourgeois cultural hegemony but the exact reverse: the Orleanist regime was a crucial moment in the crystallization of an antibourgeois strain central to the construction of modern French political and cultural identity.

## HOW BOURGEOIS WAS THE BOURGEOIS MONARCHY?

That King Louis-Philippe became the embodiment of middle-class moderation was, in genealogical terms at least, a surprising development. As the heir of the Orléans branch of the French royal family, he descended from a long line of political troublemakers and sexual profligates, and under other circumstances, having a Jacobin regicide for a father might have been perceived as an alarming pedigree. But the monarch initially projected the sort of reassuring homeliness that led Honoré Daumier to immortalize him as a pear, and he understood the value of symbols: his coronation was a low-key affair in the Chamber of Deputies, he made much of being a family man, and he walked to work bearing that emblem of respectable modern self-sufficiency, an umbrella. Historians routinely label the July Monarchy bourgeois because they conflate this image of the umbrella-toting monarch with other features of the regime. First, the conventional view is that 1830 marks the start of France's real leap into the industrial age, a notion conveniently illustrated by the fact that two of Louis-Philippe's main backers, both of whom headed ministries after 1830, were honest-to-goodness capitalists: the banker Jacques Lafitte and the industrialist Casimir Périer. Second, the Doctrinaire group led by Guizot, now securely at the helm of the nation, immediately enlarged the electorate while proclaiming themselves men of the sane and stable middle, the *juste milieu*.

Each one of these facts taken separately raises problems, as does the presumed link between all of them. Take the question of the electorate, for instance. The electoral reform of 1831 lowered the tax qualification from 300 to 200 francs for the right to vote, and from 1,000 to 500 francs for eligibility. The result was the enlargement of the electorate from 100,000 to around 167,000 (and later to a quarter of a million), out of a population of about thirty-three million.[2] Since barely one adult male in twenty five had the vote, this hardly meant an extension of electoral rights into the heart of society, and indeed, as one might expect, this enlarged electorate was still dominated by wealthy landowners: 55 percent of the electorate drew most of their income from the land; others combined land-owning with professional and administrative activities.[3] Guizot and his colleagues had certainly extended the vote to more members of the upper-middle class, but they still viewed the act of voting as a function rather than a right, the prerogative of an educated elite rather than of a middling mass.

If this small and wealthy electorate fails to qualify as a real middle class, was it a Marxian industrial elite, a capitalist bourgeoisie? The view that the Orleanist regime was carried into power by the rising tide of capitalism is questionable in light of the last two decades' worth of work by economic historians.[4] Economic growth continued in the early nineteenth century at a rate of somewhere between 2 and 3 percent a year, but the 1830s prolonged the eighteenth-century pattern of incremental growth linked to steady if modest population increase and slow urbanization. If anything, growth was slower in the nineteenth century than in the prerevolutionary decades because agricultural prices were depressed for most of the period, and the economy suffered from sharp recessions in the late 1820s and later 1840s. For most of the duration of the July Monarchy industrial structures remained unchanged, shaped by cheap labor and fragmented markets in which merchants still parceled out labor to indigent families working at home.[5] Although the country's largest cities—Paris and Lyon—grew dramatically between 1800 and 1850, the demographic increase was mostly in the number of poorer workers who had little effect on consumer demand.[6] In the first half of the nineteenth century, no great changes affected the basic structures of agriculture, industry, or banking. The most important qualitative change in the economy came about in the 1840s, with the creation of France's major railway lines and the expansion of canal networks. These developments were soon to lead to the integration of markets, but their effect was felt mostly in the decades after 1850.[7]

If France experienced an industrial revolution (a label that has become the object of controversy), this happened under Napoleon III, not Louis Philippe. A recent overview concludes: "In many respects the economy of the eighteenth century, characterized by market fragmentation, a low-productivity agriculture, and small-scale manufacturing dependent on water and wood for power survived until the 1840s."[8] Still, one might ask, even in the absence of a dramatic change in the economy, is it possible that the nation under Louis-Philippe included more middle-class people than it ever had before? Predictably, the answer to that question is as elusive as the definition of middle class. According to Adeline Daumard's exhaustive thesis on the Paris bourgeoisie, the number of middle-class Parisians grew in absolute but not in relative terms in the first half of the century: the more comfortably-off were still vastly outnumbered by the poor.[9] Surveying the entire country in the nineteenth century, Daumard again concludes that the difference in wealth between rich and poor remained static over the course of the century, and that, if anything, the big fortunes increased while middling fortunes slumped.[10] After several decades' worth of painstaking research on the social middle during France's allegedly bourgeois century, Adeline Daumard could not demonstrate that the middle class was more substantial in 1880 than in 1815.

If the economy was not capitalist, the electorate not middle class, and the middle class not substantially larger, was the political class more bourgeois after 1830? Or, to divide that question in two, was political opposition on the eve of the 1830 Revolution bourgeois, and did that revolution deliver power to a non-noble commercial and professional elite?[11] Certainly, on the eve of 1830, the public believed that the industrial and commercial middle classes were hostile to the Bourbon regime, a belief that was fueled by the reports that local prefects sent to the central authorities. The Ultras also framed electoral laws on the reverse assumption that rich landowners were likely to be loyal to the regime of Charles X.

Historians have discovered, however, that neither of these beliefs stands up to scrutiny. The membership of the Chamber of Deputies in 1827, for instance, shows very little correlation between landed wealth and political conservatism: the richest members of the Chamber were in fact marginally more likely to be liberal than conservative. It is true that a majority of industrialists were liberal, and during the economic crisis of the late 1820s many businessmen and manufacturers blamed the government's policies, though there was little consensus among them as to what they themselves might prefer. But conversely, as in the Revolution of 1789, some of the most conspicuous liberals were titled—such as the very aristocratic duc de Broglie—and quite a few Ultras were commoners.[12]

The notion that the 1830 Revolution was bourgeois can be traced back in large part to political discourse and political mythology—the fears of Ultra politicians before 1830 converging with the disappointment, after the fact, of republicans and socialists who complained that middle-class politicians robbed them of the Revolution's gains. The July Revolution did introduce dramatic changes in the Chamber of Peers by abolishing the exclusive right of nobles to membership in it, opening its ranks to non-nobles appointed by the king, and rejecting heredity of the peerage. The proportion of deputies in the lower chamber who listed their primary occupation as landowners did decline after 1830, from 31 percent to 23 percent, and the percentage of titled deputies also dropped, though not dramatically, from 40 percent in 1827 to 30 percent in 1840. But the proportion of businessmen among deputies remained low, going from 14 percent in 1829 to 17 percent in 1831 and back down to 13 percent in 1840.[13] In sum, the historical record does not suggest any great difference between the political elites of the Restoration and those of the July Monarchy, certainly no difference that could be attributed to drastic economic change.[14] For all the conspicuousness of Lafitte and Périer, the Orléans monarchy presided over an electorate and chambers that were not substantially different from those of their Bourbon predecessors. In the end, the bourgeois monarchy was defined as such not by its economic or social base but by its political rivalries, ideologies, and rhetoric.

## THE DANGEROUS MIDDLE GROUND

Vincent Starzinger has described the bourgeoisie of early nineteenth-century France as "a class which disbelieved in itself in the midst of a society which shared that disbelief."[15] The bourgeoisie did have its champions under the July Monarchy, but they failed to endow it with a coherent ideology or identity. On the one hand, the champions of this group resisted identifying it with specific—commercial or industrial—economic interests. On the other hand, they linked the fate of "the middle classes" to what proved to be a problematic and ultimately untenable political position. In the space of a single generation, *juste-milieu* politicians like Guizot managed to give birth rhetorically to the bourgeoisie, and then effectively to kill it off.

The title of a book published in Paris in 1837 suggests that its contents will read like a eulogy of social middlingness. *The New Democracy, or the Manners and Power of the Middle Classes in France* was the work of a writer named Edouard Alletz who explicitly included himself within that class (he referred to its members as "we"), and who opened his book with a blistering critique of the deposed Charles X: "Every part of [the king's] system was marked with his desire to abase the middle classes. He nurtured insurmountable prejudices against them."[16] In 1830, however, the middle classes got the king they needed. One of Alletz's chapters examines the relationship of different groups in society to the July Monarchy. He listed as hostile to the regime the groups one might expect: the clergy, old nobility, large landowners, sections of the intellectual classes, and the working classes. The regime's mainstays were all commercial types, large and small, and middling property owners who stood "heart and soul with the king they gave themselves."[17] Later in the book, however, Alletz went out of his way to argue that France has never been a commercial and industrial nation and never will be: that, he explained, would go against the country's geography, memory, taste, manners, and "genius."[18] With industrial and commercial groups thus shunted aside after so many other groups have been excluded, the author concluded that all of the regime's political energy should be devoted to "middling property, which founded and now preserves the fate of the monarchy."[19] Alletz's candid analysis makes clear just how narrow and precarious was the (perceived) social basis for a regime driven by *politique* rather than ideology.

Where the title of Alletz's volume leads one to expect a triumphalist or at least complacent account, the reader encounters instead expressions of frustration and disorientation as a recurring leitmotif. The Revolution of 1830, he wrote, gave "us" an abundance of rights and freedoms, but little political education or purpose. We have electors, representatives, juries, and local governments, but "[o]ur values are neither those of a monarchical state, nor those of a popular state. There is vacuousness and debility in the application of all the principles established in the Charter of 1830."[20] As soon as the dust settled from the Revolution of 1830, a sense of claustrophobia descended upon the nation. Alletz attributed this variously to the loss of religion by the middle class, or to the effects of commercial and industrial values on the national psyche. The merchants and industrialists who have sat in the Chambers in such numbers "have repressed, through their spirit of temperance and economy, the national impetus towards action and glory." As a result, "France is expiring for want of breath. Ah! it is high time to push back the walls, break through the vaults, show us some sky, give us some air, by which I mean some great actions to carry out."[21]

In the face of what Alletz variously termed *ennui* or *malaise,* the nation must find some suitable object for its energy, whether commercial or martial. Since France was not yet ready, in his estimation, for large-scale, high-risk commerce, only one solution seemed the obvious one: "Our Algerian colony seems to offer all the right conditions, since it provides an outlet for all manner of activity, and through the sentiment of grandeur it awakens and which would sate France's noble appetite for action and glory."[22] Colonialism was offered not as an outlet for capitalism, as in the classic Leninist model, but as a "glorious" and therefore appropriate substitute for it.

Where a triumphant bourgeois ideology should have been, there was a vacuum; and this was the diagnosis of a writer who identified himself as a supporter of the regime. Therein lies one of the great puzzles about this period: while it is easy to find all manner of anti-bourgeois sentiment—open any novel by Balzac or Flaubert—expressions of bourgeois or middle-class pride are few and problematic. One of the best discussions of this problem remains that written nearly forty years ago by Vincent Starzinger. Starzinger's comparison of political ideologies in early nineteenth-century France and Britain concludes that in France an ideology of the social and political middle was both highly "relevant"—a much-needed antidote to dominant political extremisms—and at the same time completely unrealistic.[23] The attempt by Doctrinaire politicians, especially under the July Monarchy, to establish the regime in the political center and to claim the middle classes as their constituency was logical and yet proved ultimately a failure: the celebration of the middle classes and of a middle way in politics never had much currency outside of the narrow political class—Guizot and his associates—which formulated it. Why?

Some of the problems experienced by the liberal party around Guizot were a matter of ineffectiveness and mistakes. Although the Doctrinaires wielded significant power after 1830, and Guizot headed the government from 1840 to 1848, the group never established an effective party or a coherent legislative agenda, and of course they were unable to prevent the revolution which ultimately swept them from power. While they claimed to speak for the *classes moyennes*, their definition of that group had more to do with Platonic ideals ("reason," "justice") than with perceptions of society. Where concrete definitions came into play, they remained wedded to a restrictive definition of the middle classes, which Guizot persisted in identifying narrowly as the couple of hundred thousand men making up the legal electorate, what he called the *pays légal*.[24]

The underlying problem with the regime's middle-class ideology was its lack of content. Guizot and Royer-Collard resisted definitions of the bourgeoisie which linked that class to material functions such as commerce and industry, and their ideology—unlike that of their contemporary Benjamin Constant—was not especially hospitable to notions of the individual.[25] The attempt to formulate a French theory of the middle class without reference to either commercial values or individualist beliefs proved extremely vulnerable, because it was always apparent that it was done for political ends.

The Doctrinaires' "theory of the middle class disguised as an inherent ideal what was in large measure a positional commitment to maintain [the line between left and right]."[26] Even contemporaries outside of the political sphere were aware of this. A self-defined "bourgeois of Paris" and a liberal, doctor Louis Véron noted in his memoirs (published in 1853): "The July Monarchy bore on its brow neither the halo of glory, nor the sanctity of legitimate rights or acquired rights. It was a mere government of circumstance, forced to live off [political] expedients . . . [A]ll was calculation with respect to that day's problems and momentary necessities; all was expedient against partisan maneuvering and the dangers of new situations."[27] Unable to formulate a convincing theory of sovereignty and representation (what was "reason," and why did it belong to so few?) the Doctrinaires never wrested the political and ideological initiative from their opponents on the left and the right. By the 1840s, for all that Guizot was in power, they were standing on very narrow ground.

As Roland Barthes famously argued, ideologies must be naturalized in order to be effective: they must be perceived as emanating directly from the natural world or obvious social experience.[28] The Doctrinaires had managed to naturalize bourgeois political claims under the Restoration by pressing historical narrative into the service of their political ends. But history had accomplished their goals in 1830, and subsequent to that, the historical argument began to backfire: instead of being the class whose time had come, the bourgeoisie began to be viewed as the class whose time had come and gone. Starzinger suggests that the Doctrinaires' belief in the future universal status of the middle class was an attempt to evade the obvious elitism of their position by substituting the promise of history for tangible freedoms in the here and now.[29] But the specific terms of their historical analysis also backfired on them. The question raised by their narratives of bourgeois triumph was, in François Furet's words: "If history is the science of the class struggle, why stop at the bourgeoisie?"[30] Already in his history of the French Revolution, written in the 1820s, Adolphe Thiers had anticipated the self-defeating nature of the Doctrinaires' historical script:

Once satisfied with what they have obtained, the educated classes want to stop but they cannot, and will soon be trampled by those coming in their rear. Those [classes] which stop, be they the penultimate ones, appear to those below as an aristocracy, and in this struggle of classes washing one over the other, the simple bourgeois soon gets called an aristocrat by the laborer and indicted on those grounds.[31]

A short time later, Karl Marx and his followers would provide the technical arguments as to why the proletariat was the group which embodied the end-point of history. In the meantime, the Doctrinaires' claim that the bourgeoisie contained the kernel of a future universal class rang hollow in light of their obvious reluctance to extend the franchise beyond the narrow confines of the *pays légal*.

## ANTIBOURGEOIS UNIVERSALISM

In the face of this ideological hollowness, the left soon regained the initiative that would propel it back into power in 1848. Groups to the left of the dominant liberal establishment redefined *bourgeoisie* in a more negative sense, while recasting the ideology of 1789 so as now to use it against the political and social establishment of the July Monarchy. Opposition to the July Monarchy included a wide variety of groups, ranging from the so-called *gauche dynastique*—the dynastic opposition loyal to the Orleans line—through a series of republican factions to a variety of self-designated "socialists" and "communists." These groups differed considerably from each other on such matters as the sanctity of private property and the desirability of state centralization. There was considerable overlap, however, among many republicans and socialists—latter-day Saint-Simonians, Fourierists, Icarians, Blanquists and Proudhonians—in their diagnosis of society's ills as well as in their ultimate goals. Capitalism and neo-aristocratic "bourgeois egoism" were usually identified as the problem; conversely, various forms of fraternity, harmony, and universal association, often explicitly Christian in inspiration, were promoted as social ideals.[32]

One of the groups responsible for the negative definition of the bourgeoisie in this period was that of Saint-Simon's followers, who took his theories in a more radical direction. Thinkers like Prosper Enfantin and Abel Transon abandoned the count's notion of a bureaucratic and legal intermediate bourgeois class, adopting a purely economic definition of the bourgeois as an idler who lived off the large producer class. The bourgeoisie, made up of idle capitalists and landowners, was by the 1830s identified by the Saint-Simonians as the principal enemy of the people. This was an ideology much different from Marxism, in that it contrasted industrialism as productive work with the exploitative idleness of both bourgeoisie and aristocracy.

While liberals like Guizot and Thierry still saw the rift in the social fabric as that separating the aristocracy from the bourgeoisie-as-nation, the competing and ultimately successful Saint-Simonian view separated noble and bourgeois idlers from the productive bulk of the population. Since no three-stage theory had yet been devised, the bourgeoisie was inevitably portrayed, in an echo of the ideologies of the 1790s, as a form of aristocracy.[33]

The first of two massive rebellions by the silk-workers of Lyon took place in 1831, initially in protest against violations of the fixed minimum wage known as the *tarif,* at a time of sharp economic crisis. At the time of the insurrection, the workers' newspaper, *L'Echo de la Fabrique,* was an important vehicle for Saint-Simonian ideas.[34] The violence of the fighting in Lyon was soon repeated in a Parisian insurrection in June 1832, on the occasion of the funeral of a Republican hero, General Lamarque. As in Lyon, the street fighting claimed dozens of victims on both sides, and further convinced observers that a new and violent social warfare had broken out. The following years saw the increasing politicization of the workers' movement under the banner of the Republican Society of the Rights of Man. That organization, which brought workers together with middle-class Republicans in opposition to the liberal regime, also played an important role in the equally violent revolts that broke out in both Lyon and Paris in 1834 protesting the government's ban on workers' associations.[35]

The influence of both Saint-Simonianism and radical republicanism is apparent in the languages of the workers' newspapers which began to appear in 1830: *L'Artisan, Le Journal des ouvriers, Le Peuple.* The 1830 prospectus of *L'Artisan* echoed the language of the Great Revolution:

> The most numerous and the most useful part of society is, without contradiction, the class of workers. Without it, capital has no value; without it, no machines, no industry, no commerce . . . Certain journalists shut inside their petty bourgeois aristocracy insist on seeing in the working

class nothing but machines producing for their needs alone . . . But we are no longer in a time when the workers were serfs that a master could sell or kill at his ease.[36]

As William Sewell points out, the language in this passage echoes Sieyès, with the working class now taking the place of the Third Estate as the indispensable, universal group whose labor constitutes the nation. The Revolution is further evoked in this passage by the reference to serfdom, but the aristocratic enemy is here identified, in tones dripping with irony, as the "petty bourgeois aristocracy" or "noble bourgeois."[37]

Such views seem to have been common among not only socialist but also republican militants. The papers, seized in 1833, of a coachman named Millon who belonged to the Republican Rights of Man society contain a passage explaining recent history. Before July 1830, Millon wrote, the "active and laboring" portion of the population or "people" were exploited by "the noble and religious aristocracy"; the people had crushed "the head of the aristocracy" in 1830, but their work was still unfinished. Millon called on "citizens . . . to pursue the debris of that same aristocracy that has formed anew under the dominion of the bourgeoisie" and replace the current regime with one more germane to workers' needs, "the government of the Republic."[38] Thus while the *juste-milieu* liberals distanced themselves from Revolution because it was too dangerous a precedent, republican and socialist workers' movements of the early 1830s appropriated the rhetorical legacy of 1789, identifying the working man as *le peuple* and the bourgeois as a stand-in for the aristocracy of old. Workingmen's newspapers throughout the July Monarchy identified "the bourgeoisie" as the new holders of privilege and workers as the sovereign people poised to reclaim their freedom through a new revolution.[39]

Rhetoric adapted from the Great Revolution became central to the struggles of workers under the July Monarchy. The rise of militantism after 1830 had less to do with sudden industrialization than with a combination of economic crises in the early 1830s and later 1840s along with the political mobilization of workers by Saint-Simonians and radical Republicans. The revolutionary discourse of forty years earlier took on new meaning as it adapted to the political and institutional realities of the 1830s. The contrast between selfish aristocracy

on the one hand and revolutionary brotherhood on the other reap-
peared, for instance, as a distinction between working-class solidarity
and prevailing liberal notions of freedom, which the workers denounced as "egoism," "isolation," and "solitude."[40] In the Revolution
of 1789, the basis for the fraternity that was presumed to unite citizens
was purely emotional, a brotherly love cemented by struggles against
internal and external enemies. Forty years later, revolutionary bonding had a much more specific institutional dimension. The Restoration saw the reemergence of workingmen's associations in the form of
mutual aid societies devoted to charitable support and the regulation
of trade, which after 1830 expanded into a movement for the association of workers in different trades.[41] A particularly stringent law passed
in the Chamber of Deputies in April 1834, outlawing all major workers' associations, was the catalyst for that year's massive uprisings in
Lyon and Paris.

In nineteenth-century France, working-class consciousness took
shape around the struggle to expand workers' corporations into larger
inter-trade associations. Like the culture of the Revolution of 1789,
which provided it with a powerful model, the working-class movement
that coalesced by mid-century around the struggle for association was
"universalist and inclusive in moral tone."[42] It revived and adapted the
revolutionary idiom of the undivided people, and spoke the language
of humanity rather than that of class. Although there are specific political reasons why the Doctrinaires failed ultimately to maintain their
power and impose their "middling" beliefs on the nation, these politicians were also undermined, I am suggesting, by the emergence of
compelling ideologies, like those of the left-leaning republican workers, which tapped into a national tradition of universalist idealism.

Equally powerful in fueling the opposition to the July regime was religious sentiment. One of the consequences of the fall of the Bourbons
was the uncoupling of religion from the state. Louis-Philippe may not
have been the sort of Voltairean bourgeois caricatured by Flaubert and
Balzac, but unlike his predecessors, he kept his regime free of embroil-
ment with the Church.

Catholicism, liberated from its association with a reactionary establishment, regained lost ground in society after 1830, and began to
nourish left republican and socialist thinking. It would be hard, indeed, to overestimate the influence of Christianity on oppositional

politics under the July Monarchy. As one historian notes, "Virtually all the prominent thinkers of the republican, socialist, and working-class movements of the July Monarchy echoed the religious sentiments of the leading Romantic writers of the period."[43]

Once again latter-day Saint-Simonianism proved highly influential. After the master's death, Saint-Simon's foremost disciples, Philippe Buchez, Prosper Enfantin, and Saint-Amand Bazard, sounded similar themes though with more clearly mystical overtones, organizing his following as a church and drawing much of their ideology from the count's last work, *Le Nouveau Christianisme* (1825). The Saint-Simonians' diagnosis of the ills of their society will sound very familiar: they deplored the loosening of social bonds, the murderous competition fostered by industrial relations, the pervasive egoism of the times. Typical articles in their periodical, *Doctrine de Saint-Simon,* explained that societies like their own, devoid of transcendent principles and ends, were mere aggregates of isolated and selfish individuals.[44] In response to the social conditions of their age, and in particular the sufferings of the poor, they, like many in the workers' movements, preached universal association, not class conflict: theirs was explicitly a gospel of love, inspired by the message of primitive Christianity. Saint-Simon's disciples took on the role of apostles and teachers dedicated to spreading the message that the highest capacity of humans was their ability to love, a faculty most developed among artists, priests, and poets.[45] The ideal society would be highly structured and centralized, with the economy entirely overseen and directed by a central national bank.[46] The Saint-Simonians also advocated a return to the marriage of state and church: not the Orléans monarchy and the Catholic Church, of course, but their ideals of political and religious power: in an ideal world, social and spiritual authority would emanate from a single enlightened power.[47]

If Saint-Simonians initially took the lead in this religious revival, similar ideas pervaded many other strands of the left. The Lyonnais working-class movements, which coalesced around such newspapers as *L'Atelier* and *Le Populaire,* equated Christianity with democracy, fraternity, and cooperative movements, and described Jesus as "the first communist." The liberal Catholic writer Félicité de Lammenais reached a huge middle-class and working-class readership with works like *Paroles d'un Croyant* (1834) and *Le Livre du Peuple* (1837). Promoting universal suffrage, he argued that true democracy was the only political system compatible with Christianity, stigmatized capitalism as godless, and identified the working man with Christ. The coalition of radical republicans and socialists that eventually toppled the regime in 1848 argued similarly, in organs such as the short-lived newspaper *Le Christ républicain,* that only democratic republicanism could realize in the material world the promise of the Gospels and right the evils born of "capital and credit."[48]

The concerns about society expressed by critics of the July Monarchy are reminiscent in many ways of the literature about luxury so prominent in the closing decades of the Old Regime. The verses of working-class poets and songwriters of the 1840s contain lines such as "Carthage était sans foi, l'Angleterre est de même" ("Carthage was faithless, England is the same") prefacing denunciations of commercial egoism.[49] In both periods writers expressed fears about materialism and the threat of social dissolution; in both cases the yearning was for the reestablishment of some sort of spiritual unity, and for a polity which embodied transcendent values. The Revolution, Empire, and Restoration had carried strong ideological messages, and while these were divisive regimes, even their opponents understood the higher ideals they represented: the people, martial glory, Catholic monarchy. The perceived emptiness at the heart of the Orleanist regime awakened fears and hopes similar to those which had accompanied the "desacralization" of the Old Regime monarchy after 1750. In both cases those perceptions were triggered by the forces of modernity (if not capitalism): the growth of cities, increasing anonymity, changes in material culture, rising commercialism. Before the Revolution those forces had been identified as fiendish luxury; in postrevolutionary France the new label for such threats was the bourgeoisie. In the eighteenth century, the solution proposed to the solvent of egoism was family or *moeurs,* the will to recognize the bonds of common humanity that united all people. After the Revolution, there was widespread recognition that sentiment alone could not unite the French as brothers and sisters: both education and institutions were needed to retrieve the human connections that should be the basis for any just and happy society.

While socialists and Saint-Simonians tried to reimagine the nation around combinations of working, industrial, and intellectual classes, one influential voice advocated a coming-together of the entire nation around its peasant roots. The writer who at this time most strikingly, and perhaps most enduringly, imagined the social reintegration of the French people was Jules Michelet. Michelet was born in 1798 to a working-class couple (his father was a printer), both of them immigrants from the countryside. His parents placed all of their aspirations in their only child, investing their meager resources in his education, and he more than rewarded their hopes, becoming a nationally acclaimed writer, tutor to royalty, and professor at the Collège de France. Throughout his stellar career, Michelet made a point of identifying himself as a son of the people—of the Paris working class, but especially of the rural, provincial world his parents hailed from. He viewed himself not as an avatar of upward mobility, but as a writer who encompassed all classes and could therefore mediate among them.[50]

A man of the left who resisted any specific affiliation, Michelet could perhaps best be described as a mystical Republican. While he read and admired socialist thinkers like Louis Blanc, he rejected their view that the class struggle was inevitable because inscribed in the nature of society. Michelet was distinctive in his insistence that no segment of the French people should be considered the enemy. In his meditation on French society published in 1846, *Le Peuple,* celebrating above all France's small peasant proprietors, Michelet treated the bourgeoisie as an intrinsic part of the people, albeit one which had endangered itself by separating from society's essentially agrarian center. "Bourgeoisie," he wrote, "is not a social class but a position within society—in the countryside, a man may be considered a laborer in one place but called 'bourgeois' in another because he owns some property. The result, God be thanked, is that one cannot categorically oppose bourgeoisie and people, as some are wont to do, which would result in creating two nations. Small rural proprietors, whether or not they are called *bourgeois,* are the very heart of the people."[51]

The crisis besetting the bourgeoisie was one of identity and self-perception. Unlike most of his contemporaries who took the bourgeoisie's existence for granted, Michelet remarked that "it is not easy to define exactly the limits of this class, where it begins and ends. It is not entirely made up of the well-to-do; there are many poor bourgeois."[52] Those who denounced the bourgeoisie were equally misguided in supposing it a class of mercenary entrepreneurs: the "industrial class" at the vanguard of the July Revolution now seemed paralyzed by its brief success. As for the bourgeoisie as a whole, "It is wrong either to blame or to honor the bulk of the bourgeoisie by assuming it so active in pursuit of material interests. These people are very selfish, it is true, but routine-bound and inert."[53] No materialistically driven group was likely to emerge for long, Michelet explained, because, except during some brief "English moments" in its history such the early eighteenth-century Regency and the July Monarchy, "France does not have a merchant soul."[54]

Such bourgeoisie as formed in France had enjoyed a moment of great hope from 1789 to 1830, but its aspirations had come to nothing. The French bourgeoisie, Michelet argued, had tried to become a separate class, a new aristocracy, and failed, because in reneging its true essence as a part of *le peuple* it jettisoned its sense of purpose and source of vitality. This denial of its own past and of the people from whence it came left the bourgeoisie fearful, inert, empty of purpose and of ideals: "Do you know what danger lies in this isolation, this careful closing down of oneself? That of enclosing only emptiness . . . The door is locked, all right; but nobody is home . . . Poor rich man, if you are nothing, what have you to guard?"[55] Echoing countless Old Regime critics of the bourgeoisie, Michelet identified the problem as stemming in part from the hybrid status of a social specimen he identified as "a mongrel creature which nature seems to have arrested in its development, a mixed being, graceless in aspect, neither high nor low, neither walking nor flying."[56] Authenticity, and therefore creativity, belonged to France's traditional aristocratic elites, and even more so to its vital, popular heart. What could one expect, on the other hand, from "those mixed, half-breed, half-cultivated minds"? Commenting on the upward mobility of the age—though apparently not his own!—Michelet declared that originality and invention will never be found in those "mongrel middle grounds where native character loses all vigor." Look at the mule, he wrote: it is sterile.[57]

Michelet in *Le Peuple* rearticulates fears and ideals we have encountered in different forms going back to the prerevolutionary period: the nightmare of social atomization and the dream of fusion into a moral and spiritual community. In a chapter entitled "On Association," Michelet describes a practice that serves as both metaphor and example of his ideals of social solidarity: the fishermen's cooperatives on the coasts of Normandy in which everyone, including young boys and girls, owns a segment of the vast net. The boys fish, the girls make and mend the nets, weaving the dowry that will come from a good catch and bring income to the young fishermen who will marry them. How different is this social net from the stark calculations of other types of rural associations, such as the cheese co-operatives in the Jura mountains, to which you bring your milk and from which you collect your profits: this system, "hospitable to egoism, can coexist with all the barrenness of individualism."[58]

Echoing the sentimental eighteenth-century advocates of *patrie* and *moeurs*, Michelet offered "sociability," "love," and also *patrie* as remedies against corrupting individualism. In the nineteenth century, conceptions of *patrie* drew upon history rather than family models. To Michelet the ideal image of the unified French people was, significantly, the 1790 Fête de la Fédération, the one image from the Great Revolution that involved no division or violence.[59]

Espousing a romantic traditionalism that would earn him an enduring place in the French republican pantheon, Michelet glorified the property-owning small peasantry, resisted economic categories, and denied the primacy of the cash nexus; he refused to accept class struggle as the legacy of the Revolution, or class division as the essence of modern society.[60]

Michelet's ultimate ideal of association is similar to the political goals of the July Monarchy workers' movements in which, according to Sewell, concepts of association trumped notions of class struggle, and workers preached universalism more than confrontation.[61] Michelet shared with left Republicans and Socialists the assumption that because France had never been and would never be hospitable to commercial and individualistic values, the bourgeois ascendancy of the years after 1830 was a short-lived anomaly, already receding into the past by the 1840s. Those accustomed to the notion that the nineteenth century witnessed the inevitable and unstoppable rise of the bourgeoisie may be surprised at how many contemporaries appeared to believe that by mid-century the bourgeoisie was on its way out. No doubt many people were inclined *after* 1848 to assume that the bourgeoisie had met the same historical fate as the aristocracy sixty years earlier: writing during the Second Empire, Gustave Flaubert gloomily commented that 1789 had destroyed the aristocracy, 1848 the bourgeoisie, and

1851 the people.[62] Looking back on the July Monarchy from mid-century, it appeared to many that the bourgeoisie had fallen, the victim of its own hubris and of what had begun to look like an iron law of social change.

The socialist theorist Albert Maurin published in 1851 a multivolume chronicle of post-Napoleonic France entitled *History of the Fall of the Bourbons: Grandeur and Decadence of the Bourgeoisie, 1815–1830–1840*. The lesson of the last quarter century, he concluded, was that the unstoppable course of history pushes new classes upward; regimes topple when they try to stop this irresistible process, when they refuse to accept their normal historical script:

> The normal course of the Restoration was to bring about, through slow and necessary political reform, through institutions and moral norms, through the concurrent development of both public and private life, the rule of the middle classes. Its abnormal impulse was to hold the nation in the thrall of a decrepit aristocracy, to wrap in a shroud the living interests of the age. Three days were then enough to bring the nation to the end it should have attained over the logical and natural course of fifteen years, and the divine-right monarch was replaced by the king of the bourgeoisie.[63]

The bourgeois winners of 1830 subsequently tried to halt the very movement that had carried them to power, and in doing so brought about their own doom. Maybe a rise-and-fall pattern made sense in 1850, but thirteen years earlier Honoré de Balzac had published a novel about bourgeois hubris and downfall whose title interestingly anticipates Maurin's: *History of the Grandeur and Decadence of César Birotteau* (1837). And Michelet, writing two years before the Revolution of 1848, anticipated exactly this same scenario: "In a mere half century [the bourgeoisie] emerged from amidst the people, was carried upwards by its own activity and energy and suddenly, in the very midst of its triumph, collapsed. There is no previous instance of so rapid a decline."[64]

The *juste-milieu* political ideology of Guizot and his fellow Doctrinaires suffered not just because of its own weaknesses, but also because of the presence in the ideological landscape of the July Monarchy of far more compelling oppositional ideas and beliefs—those of republican workers, liberal Catholics, Saint-Simonians, and others who saw the advent of the Orleanist bourgeoisie as a brief anomaly in a national destiny that led elsewhere. Notwithstanding the temporary bourgeois victory, wrote Albert Maurin, the Revolution of 1830 had opened up for France a whole new vista: "At the end one would find the complete abolition of castes, the fusion of all members of a single family in that liberty devoid of hypocrisy which does not merely say to the citizen: *If you can,* but which levels all obstacles before him."[65] The vision of writers like Maurin, Michelet, Buchez, and so many others was not of working-class triumph, for that would still be too partial, too self-interested; it was of the fusion of an entire nation into something greater than the sum of its parts: a universal association, a classless, mystical *patrie.* Was there any social group which could hope to provide a framework or model for this utopian vision?

## BALZAC'S WORLD: BUREAUCRACY, BOHEMIA, AND THE FICTIONAL BOURGEOIS

Historians are nowadays reluctant to describe the events of 1830 and the advent of Louis-Philippe as a "social revolution," because the transition from Bourbon to Orléans involved no drastic change in the social identities of electors and deputies, nor in the broader socioeconomic structures of the nation. After 1830 France remained a predominantly agrarian nation governed by, and in the interests of, a slightly larger segment of the same elite of landed *notables.* There was one segment of society for whom things did change radically in 1830, however, and that was the state bureaucracy: the July Revolution was followed by a more drastic purge and replacement of civil servants than any the nation had seen since 1789.

As soon as Louis Philippe had been installed on the throne, his government carried out what has been called a veritable revolution in administrative personnel, dismissing most of the administrators who had served the Bourbons (many of them resigned on their own) and installing its own men throughout the civil service. The most distinguished American historian of the period concludes that "[This] change of men was probably the most revolutionary aspect of the revolution."[66] The transformation was most spectacular at the prefectoral level, as Guizot began his term as the regime's first Interior Minister by replacing 83 percent of the prefectoral corps, and 88 percent of all

sub-prefects. Only seven (out of ninety) of the prefects who had served
the Bourbons remained, most of them appointed during the Restoration's less reactionary phases. A similar overhaul affected the army,
whose high command was entirely replaced, and the judicial branch
was also purged, with a majority of the Bourbon-picked prosecutors
and judges forced into retirement.[67]

If there was any perception that the July Monarchy was changing
France's social landscape, it must have been prompted by this wholesale replacement of the realm's administration. And yet this
reshuffling was more of a restoration than a revolution, inasmuch as
most of Louis Philippe's new civil servants had been in office before, as
administrators under Napoleon or the more moderate Restoration
governments. Fifty-three of the eighty-three new prefects had previous
experience; most were older men whose careers had begun under Napoleon. Many of them, furthermore, came from families which had
served the state for several generations, clans of distinguished professionals with roots going back into the Old Regime.[68] If there is any
sense in which 1830 was a bourgeois revolution, it was in the sudden
reestablishment or promotion of men from middle- and upper-middle-class backgrounds into government positions.

What are the implications of this development for social values and
beliefs? Although no one has written a detailed study of the culture
and political leanings of this group, David Pinkney does argue that
inasmuch as most of them owed the beginnings of their successful
careers to Napoleon, they must have harbored strong Bonapartist
sympathies. Louis-Napoleon's advent in 1851 was no fluke given that
Bonapartism had numerous and vocal supporters throughout the July
Monarchy, and this may have been especially the case in the state bureaucracy. It was certainly true of Napoleon's military high command,
who returned to France in 1830 after cooling their heels abroad in the
years since Waterloo.[69] More generally, the reshuffling of administrators in 1830 brought back *fonctionnaires* with ties to previous regimes,
and in doing so reinforced the continuity and homogeneity of the civil
service. The July Monarchy bureaucracy was a world unto itself, governed by elaborate hierarchies and rules of precedence and by a rigid
code of honor. (Critics of the patronage system that governed this universe denounced it as "feudal," "barbaric," and "aristocratic," and compared it to the hermetic corporations that governed trade under the

Old Regime.) Its denizens expressed considerable nostalgia for the time under Napoleon when the bureaucratic system was imagined to have been at its apex, and the emperor rewarded brilliant administrators on the spot with the ribbon of the *Légion d'honneur*.[70] In short, the higher civil service of the July Monarchy, a partial revival of its revolutionary and imperial predecessors, seems to have fostered a sense of the glory and honor inherent in state service, sentiments that may well have fed into the contempt directed at those who served only Mammon.

A more obvious source of prolific antibourgeois sentiment under the July Monarchy was the world of writers and artists. Even those who know little about this period are aware of the scathing portrayals of bourgeois types and denunciations of bourgeois philistinism in the works of authors like Balzac and Flaubert or caricaturists like Daumier. Contempt for the bourgeois appears to have been a source of cohesion to the denizens of literary coteries known as *cénacles,* and in the mid-1840s a series of newspaper articles gave the modern literary world one of its most powerful founding myths: Bohemia. Published in 1846 under the title *Scènes de la vie de Bohème,* these pieces were the work of an otherwise obscure writer named Henry Murger, the first to use the metaphor of gypsy or "bohemian" life to characterize the subculture of writers and artists (the work was very successful in Murger's own short lifetime, and later served as the principal source for Puccini's famous opera).[71] In the early nineteenth century as in our own time, literary bohemians cultivated traits that identified them as the opposite of dominant respectability: they were youthful, improvident, generous, unconventional in their appearance and their personal lives, erratic in their work habits, and excessive in their recreations. Given the enduring vagueness and fluidity of the term "bourgeois," the very existence of the myth and reality of Bohemia probably served, as Jerrold Seigel has suggested, as a means of fixing the meaning of bourgeoisie by acting out its social opposite.[72]

Antibourgeois writings have a long pedigree in French literary history, but the prominence and virulence of such themes in post-Napoleonic France begs some sort of explanation, especially now that capitalism can no longer be identified as the likely culprit. The most convincing answer involves more specific developments in social and economic history, namely, the growth and commercialization of publishing and the social situation of writers. Historians of literary bohemia have argued that the emergence of antibourgeois bohemianism must be related to the collapse of patronage and the increasing dependence and artists and writers on more impersonal and less secure sources of income. Before the nineteenth century, writers and artists, unless independently wealthy, were generally supported by rulers or private patrons. In France the Revolution mostly put an end to this practice, although it survived in limited form after 1800: Napoleon and the Bourbon kings, and even Louis-Napoleon after 1852 were eager to have a few writers and artists on their payroll. Under the July Monarchy, however, state patronage dropped to a very low level, at the same time that the demand for books and newspapers increased steadily.[73]

The market for books grew enormously after 1814, especially under the Restoration. The number of yearly published titles tripled between 1814 and 1825, while the number of daily newspapers went from 11 in 1811 to 26 in 1846.[74] During the July Monarchy, newspaper publishing grew faster than the book trade, though the success of the first mass market dailies such as *La Presse* and *Le Constitutionnel* was driven in large part by the serialization of novels penned by the likes of Alexandre Dumas and Eugène Sue.[75] The publishing business as a whole became more strategically profit-oriented, with new forms of advertising and recourse to subscriptions and rebates, while famous authors like Balzac and George Sand were repeatedly embroiled in conflicts over the payment of royalties.[76] The production of books remained artisanal in nature, still dominated by hand-operated presses in small workshops, but the book trade became increasingly competitive and commercial. As César Graña suggested, the hostility of writers to "the bourgeoisie" can be plausibly viewed as the expression of their situation in the social world after 1814: there was greater demand for the written word than ever before, but also increasing insecurity for writers who found themselves at the mercy of the tastes and whims of publishers and readers.[77]

As novels such as Balzac's *Lost Illusions* amply demonstrate, writers both craved and despised the rewards of the market; they resented their lack of autonomy and their dependency on an anonymous reader.[78] Literature had encountered modernity in the form of greatly increased commercialism, and denounced it in the person of the powerful but ignorant bourgeois.

The figure of the despised bourgeois served to define by contrast this society's implicit ideals: transcendence of the material world (and specifically the world of commerce) through service to Art or to the State. A concluding analysis of one of the period's greatest novels will provide a specific fictional illustration of this thesis.[79]

Balzac's *La Cousine Bette,* the last novel he wrote, was published in 1846, the same year as Murger's tales of literary bohemia and Michelet's *Le Peuple.* Its plot revolves around the near destruction of an upper-class family, the Hulots, because of the sexual obsessions of its patriarch, Hector, and the vindictive rage of a cousin, the eponymous spinster Bette Fisher. The novel is in large part the story of how Bette plots and carries out her revenge against the women of the Hulot family: the beautiful Adeline Hulot, who is Bette's first cousin and escaped the poverty of their origins through her fairytale marriage to a baron, Hector Hulot; and Adeline's daughter Hortense, who stole and married the only man Bette ever cared for. Hector Hulot is in his fifties, a senior civil servant and former military man whose family was ennobled by Napoleon. Despite his wife's beauty and virtue, Hector is compulsively unfaithful, and it is his obsessive pursuit of seductive young women that Bette will exploit for her revenge.

Bette steers Hector towards her neighbor, Valérie Marneffe, a young middle-class housewife of great beauty and even greater mercenary appetites. Valérie proceeds to make Hector her slave, ruining him financially while carrying on affairs with several other men. Desperate to keep up with her financial demands, Hector uses his position as a senior military administrator to pressure a subordinate to commit a major embezzlement against the state. When the fraud is uncovered, the subordinate commits suicide and Hector himself is shamefully dismissed from his government position. After hiding in the slums of Paris with a child-mistress, Hector is eventually brought back to the family by his all-forgiving wife. Bette has died of tuberculosis in the meantime, but Hector ultimately proves incorrigible: his wife dies of shock when she discovers him making love to their kitchen maid, whom he eventually marries and follows into rural Normandy.

An important secondary character is Célestin Crevel, the novel's bourgeois anti-hero. Crevel is a very rich man, a former perfume-seller who made a fortune in real estate and financial speculation. He is related to the Hulots through the marriage of his only child, Célestine, to the Hulots' son, Victorin. Crevel, a widower, is a social climber who both emulates and competes with the aristocratic Hulots: although his real passion is for money rather than sex, he tries to get the better of Hector in sexual matters, first by stealing his mistress, the actress Josépha, then by trying to seduce Hulot's wife, and finally by sleeping with and eventually marrying the object of Hector's passion, Valérie. Crevel is the first character introduced to the reader at the beginning of the novel: he is described in the opening scene as "a fat man of average height wearing the uniform of the National Guard."[80] Exuding the smugness of commercial success and flaunting the ribbon of the *Légion d'honneur,* Crevel is on his way to visit Adeline Hulot and attempt to seduce her. Adeline turns him down indignantly, and then complains that the family's financial distress is making it difficult to find a suitor for her daughter. Crevel shoots back that if she were to become his mistress, marrying off Hortense would be no problem: "You'd find the dowry in my wallet."[81]

The vain and self-satisfied Célestin Crevel is one avatar of the numerous bourgeois characters who populate *La Comédie humaine.* As such, he understands the world in narrowly material and commercial terms, as a place ruled by money and driven by greed, competition, and revenge, and he is baffled by any higher motivation. Balzac's bourgeois characters are by no means all identical, and Crevel is a rather worse specimen than some of his predecessors, such as the draper Guillaume in *La Maison du Chat-qui-pelote* (1830), or Balzac's most famous shopkeeper-hero, César Birotteau (1837).[82] Guillaume and Birotteau have none of Crevel's political ambitions, nor do they share his sexual profligacy. They are faithful husbands and good family men, economically active but culturally limited. Crevel is Balzac's most extreme portrayal of bourgeois hubris.

Despite his enormous fortune, Crevel is systematically defined in the novel by what he does *not* have, by his lack of identity. He holds public office, but his fatuousness comically underscores the limited, local nature of the power he wields. He wears two uniforms in the novel, that of battalion commander in the National Guard, and that of mayor of a Parisian district, the garb of ceremonial functions lacking any real substance. In these clothes, however, he fancies himself a martial hero: his attempt to seduce Hulot's wife involves repeatedly striking a pose borrowed from the late emperor, "crossing his arms Napoleon style, turning his head sideways, and casting his gaze into the distance as his portrait painter had told him to do."[83]

Suffering from a cultural deficit, Crevel is constantly appropriating the trappings of other periods, especially the materialistic eighteenth century. He emulates the style of an aristocratic rake, and invokes the libertine tradition of the previous century in a torrent of clichés: "It's Regency, it's Louis XV, it's *oeil de boeuf!*" "Regency, blue frock-coat, Pompadour, extremely maréchal de Richelieu, and dare I say it, *Dangerous Liaisons.*"[84] His cultivation of aristocratic rakishness remains unconvincing, however, since he never loses sight of the bottom line. As he explains to Adeline, whose own husband's passions are ruining her family, he himself is "a *grand seigneur* with a method": you can spend your profits on seduction, but going into your capital would be madness.[85] As Crevel's former mistress Josépha puts it, Crevel is one of those men who "freeze before big spending like a donkey in front of a river."[86]

The problem embodied by a bourgeois character like Crevel is not that he enjoys an unfair surplus of wealth, but that he is unable to perform the alchemy whereby money is redeemed in the service of higher ideals such as passion or art. The bourgeois's money merely reproduces itself endlessly, stuck in the realm of matter. Crevel's dwellings, as described by Balzac, are temples to mechanical reproduction. His decorator Grindot had "once again, for the thousandth time, produced his white and gold salon with red-damask-covered walls." The resulting interior, a riot of faux rococo furniture and mass-produced marble decorations amounts to "a café-style luxury which would surely have made any real artist shrug his shoulders."[87] As César Graña justly observed, the bourgeoisie was assumed to be devoid of culture and values "because the content of its life lacked definition, self-containment, and therefore intrinsic worth." Bourgeois culture, the reflection of commercial exchange, was expansive and extensible, a correlate to its essential lack of depth and definition: "Bourgeois life was condemned to reproduce itself in a qualitative vacuum."[88]

Crevel's female counterpart in the novel is the housewife-turned-courtesan Valérie Marneffe, who is referred to throughout the text as a bourgeoise. When we meet Valérie she is indeed technically a bourgeoise, a wife and mother of modest means whose husband is a lowly employee in the War Ministry headed by Hulot. Valérie's true circumstances are in reality a savage caricature of bourgeois domesticity: a nasty apartment ill furnished with fake luxury, a neglected only child and sullen maidservant, a husband who, degenerate and diseased, encourages his wife's infidelities for the money.[89] In time Hulot installs her in a splendid apartment on the Rue Vaneau, where in the nominal company of her husband she keeps up the appearance of a decent married woman. The author tags her "a Madame de Merteuil bourgeoise"—a libertine schemer with a solid sense of market values.[90] Where Hulot just hands over his money for her to spend, Crevel teaches her about the stock market where she soon excels, building up a large pool of savings. It is no accident that Valérie chooses Crevel over the various artists and noblemen who pursue her: they are sociologically destined for each other.

The Crevel-Valérie couple, a pairing whose logic only becomes obvious by the end of the novel, embodies the familiar link between bourgeoisie and prostitution in the nineteenth-century social imaginary. The usual explanation for this coupling involves commodification: the bourgeois and the prostitute belong together because both are quintessential denizens of the market economy.[91] There is no doubt a lot of truth to this reading, but I would suggest a different emphasis: the bourgeois and the prostitute are both objects of scandal because, or inasmuch as, they transgress the division between private and public realms. The prostitute does this most obviously, by making an intimate function, sex, into a publicly acknowledged marker of her identity. But the bourgeois also acts transgressively whenever he lays claim to the true public realm, for in Balzac's view the defining characteristic of the bourgeoisie is privacy: not intimacy, but dedication to one's private interests.

From this perspective, Hector Hulot stands in contrast to Crevel not because he embodies higher personal qualities (there is little to admire in this vain and self-destructive monomaniac), but because of where he fits in the social taxonomy: with the state, the army, the common good. Balzac makes it immediately clear that the Hulot family is not of ancient lineage, having been ennobled for service in the Napoleonic army, but he clearly views the nobility deriving from state and military service as one of the pinnacles (along with artistic creation) of the social ideal. The baron is one of several male figures in the novel whose identities are shaped by their martial and imperial pasts. Above Adeline's bed hangs "the portrait of Hulot painted by Robert Lefebvre in 1810, depicting him in the uniform of the commissariat officer to the Imperial Guard."[92] Hulot is one of those Napoleonic administrators who was forced onto the sidelines in 1815, brought back by the Bourbons out of necessity in 1823, then promoted to the high position of director of the War Ministry under Louis-Philippe: he embodies that class of civil servants who connected the July Monarchy to the glories of the revolutionary and imperial wars. Everything about Hulot evokes his past in the service of Napoleon: "Baron Hector Hulot appeared in both parliamentary and Napoleonic garb, for it is easy to identify imperials, men formerly attached to the Empire, by their military bearing, their blue suits with gold buttons buttoned up to the neck, their black taffeta neckties, the imperious manner in which they walk."[93]

Baron Hulot is not the only character in the novel to embody the lingering ideals of the imperial past: he answers to other men who share his background but not his moral shortcomings. There is his brother Marshal Hulot, count of Forzheim, an authentic military hero noted for his legendary exploits and personal integrity. And above the Hulot brothers is the Minister of War, the Marshal-Prince of Wissembourg, the "rival of Bernadotte" with his "Napoleonic blue eyes" and his forehead "which one could imagine as a battlefield."[94] Below Hulot are the Fisher brothers, Adeline's father and uncle, simple men imbued with the habit of blind obedience: even in the 1840s Pierre Fisher sees in the much-compromised Hector Hulot "an emanation of the Napoleonic sun."[95]

In postimperial France the state has replaced, for these men, their beloved emperor as the source of all honor and recognition. This is why, when Hulot defrauds the state to subsidize his personal passions, the moral gravity of the crime could not be greater. "You robbed the state," Wissembourg thunders at Hulot during one of several stormy confrontations. "You have shamefully compromised our higher administration, which until now was the purest in all of Europe! . . . And all of it, sir, for two hundred thousand francs and for a slut!"[96] The older Hulot brother experiences the crisis as the most serious kind of collective trauma, one which involves, beyond money and position, the loss of honor: "He dishonored us all, made my own name hateful to me," moans the Marshal, who is described at the beginning of the novel as a man *plein d'honneur*.[97] The honor which inheres naturally in great servants of the state like Wissembourg and Marshal Hulot is contrasted implicitly to honor in its reified form, the ribbon of the *Légion d'honneur* which Crevel wears proudly and Valérie's decrepit husband (another bourgeois) longs for. The bourgeois characters do not realize that the possession of real honor of the sort that makes a man fit for higher state service is incommensurate with the self-serving impulses they embody. Hulot's problem is that he has sunk to their bourgeois level in heeding his selfish compulsions: "You ought to have left the Administration," Wissembourg rages at him, "once it was clear that you were no longer a man but a temperament."[98]

The positive social norm embodied by Wissembourg and Marshal Hulot is martial and fraternal: honor is clearly connected to masculinity. Balzac acknowledges female honor as well, but stresses its fragility by having Adeline offer herself pathetically to Crevel in exchange for the money to save her husband's reputation and her uncle's life. (Crevel turns her down and compounds her humiliation by offering to introduce her to a provincial bourgeois, a rich retired grocer named Beauvisage who would eagerly come up with the money for such a classy mistress.)[99] Even an honorable woman can be expected to rejoin the ranks of the bourgeois and the prostitute when strong personal interests are at stake. These aspects of Balzac's novel illuminate the gendered nature of bourgeois identity. Dedicated to private life and private interests, the bourgeois is a feminized creature. That is why the only aspects of the category "bourgeois" to escape criticism in French culture are related to domesticity (a bourgeois wine, bourgeois cooking, a bourgeois household), and why the figure of the bourgeois is acceptable only inasmuch as he or she remains confined to the private sphere. As Graña suggests, the bourgeois does work that is womanly because reproductive, routinized, and spiritually inert; his labor is implicitly contrasted with masculine activity, which is heroic, spiritual, and unique.[100] In Balzac's social taxonomy, ideal activities are those connected to art or to high state service, and the figure of the bourgeois, with his self-interested outlook and reproductive activities, serves to define those ideals by way of contrast.

The standard view of Honoré de Balzac's social and political stance identifies him as a reactionary monarchist who loathed the bourgeoisie out of nostalgia for some version of the Old Regime. This assumption has been popular with left-wing scholars ranging from Georg Lukács to Fredric Jameson: it is assumed that from a position of right-wing marginality Balzac did the ideological work of the left, exposing the ugliness of a society driven by the predatory values and spiritual emptiness of the bourgeoisie.[101] This traditional view is inaccurate and misleading. By family origin and early training Balzac was rooted in the traditions of the left—Enlightenment liberalism, republicanism, and Bonapartism. Under the Restoration he aligned himself with the liberal end of the political spectrum, though he clearly leaned toward the more pessimistic and authoritarian strains of the revolutionary tradition associated with Rousseau, Robespierre, and especially Bonaparte. Though the labels changed and Balzac did espouse conservative monarchism early in the July Monarchy, his political beliefs were consistent throughout his life: he favored authoritarian regimes and worshiped Napoleon; he despised self-serving materialism; and he was opposed to any form of popular activism.[102]

In sum, the social landscape Balzac presents in *La Cousine Bette,* with its idealized caste of martial heroes and civil servants, corresponds to his deepest sociopolitical inclinations which had little, in the end, to do with reactionary monarchism. Far from an eccentric right-wing point of view, Balzac's disgust with the bourgeois as embodied by Crevel was a standard attitude in a culture which glorified universalism and transcendence by creating as a foil the image of the self-serving, materialistic bourgeois. Balzac's scathing portrayals of moneyed interests and bourgeois spiritual deficiency in *La Comédie humaine* shares its identification of the enemy with utopian socialists and a romantic Republican like Michelet. While Balzac's elitism separated him from socialists and democratic republicans, they would all have converged in their reverence for the state as transcendent collectivity and their contempt for the spiritual vacuousness conveyed by the term "bourgeois."

The standard narratives of modern French history, whether or not they explicitly espouse a Marxian framework, are based on the assumption that a ruling class, the bourgeoisie, was dominant from at least 1830 on: with the brief exceptions of the Second Republic (1848–

1852) and the Paris Commune (1871), the Second Empire and the republics that followed it were dominated by a non-noble economic and intellectual elite. The problem with this view, as with similar interpretations of earlier periods, is not that it is actually wrong, but that it lacks analytical depth and specificity. Certainly the aristocracy's heyday was over, and France was governed by, and in the interests of, a wealthy and educated nontitled upper class.[103] But for periods in which capitalism is still undeveloped, or in approaches that are not explicitly Marxian, the analytical relevance of the category "bourgeois" is vastly unclear. And for French history specifically, hackneyed assumptions about bourgeois hegemony get in the way of some of the most interesting questions in cultural and political history, such as: why did widespread condemnation of the bourgeoisie precede the development of capitalism? And why did France's one attempt at a liberal, middle-class English-style regime prove such a failure?

There were of course many contingent reasons for the unpopularity and eventual demise of the July Monarchy: Louis-Philippe did not exactly suffer from a surfeit of charisma, and his eldest son, the only member of the family to be extremely popular, died accidentally in 1842. As a recent article has suggested, the idea of a bourgeois monarchy may have been too much of an oxymoron in France to function well in the realm of representations: the July Monarchy had a hard time balancing the dynastic *and* meritocratic principles on which it was based, and the king's image evolved (especially after the brutal repressions of 1834) from avaricious and flabby to violent and oppressive.[104]

The answer proposed here to the question of the regime's unpopularity draws on enduring features of French political culture such as the power of the idea of an undivided people, and the importance of the spiritual dimension in understandings of the polity. The historical narratives and political ideologies of Restoration liberals were successful because they construed the bourgeoisie as a whole nation, a reincarnation of the Third Estate under another name. When the Doctrinaires found themselves in power, however, their need to walk the middle ground between right and left exposed their discourse as mere politics rather than ideology: it was strictly positional and disappointingly devoid of substance, a perception much strengthened by Guizot's refusal to enlarge the electorate in any significant way. As Furet suggested, the regime's decision to label itself bourgeois amounted to painting a bull's-eye on it.[105] In response to what was perceived as the regime's favoring of a materialistic and cynical elite, the oppositional ideologies that flourished between 1830 and 1848 appealed to universalistic dreams or spiritual principles: they included utopian and Christian socialism, idealized republicanism, the elitism of literary and artistic creators, and allegiance to a transcendent state by an increasingly autonomous caste of civil servants.

In reaction against the throne-and-altar policies of the Restoration, the July Monarchy kept a careful distance from the Church, leaving itself open to accusations of materialism. Opposition to the regime was as a result strongly tinged with Christian elements, whether explicitly or not. As Bernhardt Groethuysen long ago pointed out, the Gospels acknowledge only two forms of greatness: that of power and that of poverty. The great enjoyed God-like glory, the poor embodied Christ-like penury and suffering. No intermediate state could confer moral stature, and the bourgeoisie, neither powerful nor poor, was therefore abandoned to a spiritual wasteland.[106] What was true of society could also be applied to regimes: they were legitimate inasmuch as their central principle was either power and glory (which even a lesser Bourbon or Bonaparte could embody) or the work and suffering of the people (the basis of republicanism and every ideology to its left). To put it another way, following Pierre Rosanvallon, attempts at liberal constitutional monarchy failed in this period because of widespread resistance, within the tradition of French political culture, to the idea of "neutral power." The Revolution of 1789 did not so much limit sovereignty as transfer it, while retaining its sacred essence.[107] In the broadest of terms, middle-class constitutional governments failed after 1815 because sovereignty could no more be imagined as empty or neutral than social ideals could be conceived as residing in groups whose dominant attribute was a middling location.

In the French context, "bourgeois monarchy" was even more of an oxymoron than the expression at first suggests. The ideal monarchy was a state that embodied the essence of glorious, heroic altruism on behalf of the national community; the adjective "bourgeois" accompanied a group imagined as the incarnation of privacy, selfishness, and spiritual deficiency. In the context of French history and culture, a semantic coupling no doubt imagined as the best possible compromise between the past and the present became instead a disastrously self-defeating idea.

# The Bourgeois, the Jew, and the American

All history, someone once said, is really autobiography, and this is probably true, although the connection between one's topic and one's life may only emerge belatedly, if at all. For most of the time I was working on this book, I believed I was tackling a purely intellectual puzzle. Only at the very end did I come to recognize the ways in which my preoccupation with French attitudes toward an imaginary bourgeoisie grew out of the somewhat unusual circumstances of my upbringing.

I grew up in France, the child of an American-Jewish expatriate family. My French childhood and adolescence spanned the 1960s, a high-water mark of French anti-Americanism, and a time when, in spite of official tolerance, muted antisemitism was still widespread. Like most children I fervently desired to fit in, and I realized early on that my American and Jewish identities posed difficulties that seemed enormous to someone between the ages of six and sixteen. I soon discovered that mastering the language and doing well in school went a long way toward erasing the taint of American-ness. I managed both to some extent, and was applauded as if I had overcome some terrible handicap: "She's American but she's intelligent" was a comment I heard more than once from teachers and peers.

Jewishness was another matter. While I never encountered the crudest and most open forms of hostility, even as a young child I picked up on enough "polite" antisemitism to conclude that *juif* or *juive* was something one did not want to be. Since my surname was not a give-away, I lied by omission, explaining sadly to my friends at age eleven that I would not be participating like them in the rituals of a Catholic confirmation—the white dress, gifts, and elaborate feast—because my family was *pas catholique*. I hoped that they would conclude from this ambiguous "not Catholic" that my family espoused some acceptable form of belief such as Protestantism or atheism. With a child's radar for cultural norms I sensed what was shameful about my two identities, a problem which can be expressed bluntly as too much money, not enough culture.

All of this came back to me as I began to think about the larger historical pattern of French resistance to what can broadly be termed materialism. The French, if such generalizations are permissible, are no more averse to material pleasures and possessions than anyone else. Their interest in food, wine, and eroticism is real, not just the stuff of tired cliché, and to the outsider French enthusiasm for medicine and physical therapy (what is known as *bien-être*) is striking: the density of France's network of pharmacies rivals that of Ireland's pubs. In a society where community life and organizations have historically been weak, property, especially in land and real estate, has served a crucial purpose in securing not just the status of families but also the sort of financial protection beyond the basics that neither the state nor the job market can guarantee. This investment in the material world neither contradicts nor undermines the central aspect of French culture explored in this book: the construction of individual and collective identities through the rejection of material values. The normative French hostility against the abstraction called bourgeoisie is, I have argued, a longstanding and complex aspect of this propensity, which is also reflected in parallel constructions, at different historical times, of "the Jew" and "the American."

In the eighteenth and early nineteenth centuries bourgeoisie was, as we have seen, a complex and multifaceted concept, laden with mostly negative implications. In the Old Regime bourgeoisie was a legally defined social category which granted the nontitled elites of many towns privileges similar to those of the aristocracy. Although many a bourgeois of Paris, Lyon, or Chartres no doubt wore the title with pride, a centuries-old tradition lampooned the bourgeois as graceless and acquisitive. Antibourgeois prejudice originally grew out of the nature of the group's function as a slippery boundary zone between the aristocracy and the plebs. In an ordered society organized around the principle—if not the reality—of strict social ranking, the neither-fish-nor-fowl quality of the bourgeois made them a target for hostility and ridicule. From the Old Regime the French inherited the idea that the bourgeoisie was a lesser, defective form of nobility: it was therefore doubly cursed, suspected both of aristocratic privilege and power, and of the sins of the social climber.

Only once in French history was a concerted effort made to establish the bourgeoisie as a socially and historically central group and the bearers of positive cultural norms: this happened between the 1820s and the 1840s, when Restoration liberals penned histories which cast the bourgeois as anti-aristocratic heroes, and later affixed the label "bourgeois" to the monarchy of Louis-Philippe. This experiment can be described as either a short-lived success or a failure. France's post-revolutionary monarchies were blatantly elitist, restricting the franchise to a minuscule proportion of the population. Liberal rhetoric which equated the bourgeoisie with the Third Estate or the French people rang hollow so long as only one Frenchman in a hundred could cast a ballot.

Eventually, the traditional negative connotations of the concept "bourgeois"—unearned privilege and cultural deficiency—merged with newer marks of infamy. For romantic Republicans like Michelet, for countless artists and writers, and finally for Socialists and Communists, the bourgeois came to stand for all that was frightening about emerging modernity: rootless urban living, the tyranny of the market, the first signs of industrialism. In addition to the burden of social incompetence, Monsieur Jourdain was soon to bear the stigma attached to capitalist exploitation. To this day, when the French talk about *la bourgeoisie* in a certain context, what they have in mind is clearly an upper class. Such a group certainly exists today, as described in Béatrix Le Wita's witty anthropology of a world easily recognized and widely disparaged: the matrons in Hermès scarves and Burberry raincoats, the broods of children enrolled in private Catholic schools, the Paris apartments furnished with inherited antiques, the large country mansions where summers are spent. A few generations of significant financial and cultural capital produce families in which young girls have coming-out dances and children say *vous* to their parents. They, like everyone else, resist the label "bourgeois." But whatever it is, this bourgeoisie is not a middle class.[1]

Indeed, the concept of middle class, while far less fraught with negative connotations than bourgeoisie, never flourished in France either, in the way that it has in the Anglo-American world. Although at various points in history French leaders have invoked an ideal of social middlingness—Guizot's rhetoric about *classes moyennes* in the 1820s, for instance, or Léon Gambetta's invocation of the *nouvelles couches sociales* in the 1880s—such notions have failed to resonate and endure. The absence of a middle-class norm in society can be related to the failure of the Doctrinaires' program of *juste-milieu* politics. Whether applied to politics or to society, the notion of a middle ground seems, in the French context, to have offered nothing of inherent value: as we saw in the last chapter, political life under the July Monarchy was widely described as vacuous, even by the regime's supporters. To the generations following the French Revolution, politics was about ideology, not building coalitions, and it was therefore difficult to justify a political program whose value lay in its position rather than its actual content.[2] Promoting a "middle" implies a vision of society and the state that rests upon quantification. Such a move implicitly reduces the social and the political to realms of mere matter, robbing the public world of transcendent meaning.

Where was transcendence to be located once it became clear, as it rapidly did, that reruns of the Old Regime monarchy were not going to reinfuse the social order with sacred meaning? The problem and its solution are best understood in the terms proposed by one of the French Revolution's near-contemporaries, Friedrich Hegel. Writing in the early years of the nineteenth century, Hegel did not associate bourgeoisie with patterns of capitalist development, which had yet to emerge in Germany and in France. Rather, he wrote of the *Bürger* as one term in the polarity dividing social man's soul; the opposite of the burgher was not the aristocrat or the worker, but the citizen.[3]

The bourgeois/citizen duality reflected a fundamental split, in the wake of the French Revolution, between civil and political life: how was modern man to overcome the tension between selfish, private interests, and public political identity? Hegel's answer, of course, was that the state should serve as agent of reintegration, healing the wound caused by this split in the modern soul: only the state could give men freedom by making them one again. This is why those who serve the state, the class of civil servants, make up society's normative group, a class that is both universal and sacred. This last point was stressed in the mode of sarcasm by Hegel's most famous and brilliant critic, Karl Marx: "The bureaucratic mind," he wrote in a gloss on Hegel, "is through and through a Jesuitical, theological mind. The bureaucrats are the Jesuits and theologians of the state. The bureaucracy is *la république prêtre*."[4]

I have proposed in this book that we might profitably think of the civil service as modern France's universal class and dominant social norm. A powerful ideal of service to the state had roots going deep into the Old Regime, when it was embodied above all by members of the nobility: those who served in the king's ministries, sat in royal courts of law, excelled academically, or won laurels on the battlefield. This ideal—which the Revolution made far more widely accessible— endured as the answer to the threats and temptations of commerce, comfort, and private life, and perhaps also as a source of continuity in the bewildering succession of regimes that followed the Revolution. It is from the perspective of the idealized civil servant, whose honor springs from devotion to the state, that the bourgeois became the quintessential other. The imagined bourgeois, in other words, was much less an avatar of capitalism than the embodiment of selfish urges which threatened the polity, just as the aristocrat had embodied in the 1790s every danger to revolutionary consensus. (It is tempting, if highly speculative, to suggest that the bourgeois represented the lure of self-serving materialism in the heart of every person who denounced him.)

Many aspects of French culture become clearer once the bourgeois is displaced from the center to the periphery. I would propose, for instance, that the cult of honor flourished in the postrevolutionary decades not because, as Robert Nye has argued, the bourgeois embraced this atavistic concept to legitimate their culture, but because ideals of state service and intellectual or martial prowess carried over almost unchanged from the Old Regime, and honor was intimately bound up with such pursuits.[5] (My analysis of Balzac's *La Cousine Bette* is intended to make this point.) A linked concept which historians have uncovered of late is that of emulation. Thomas Crow describes it as central to the language of the Revolution's premier artistic circle, the brilliant coterie made up of Jacques-Louis David and his pupils.[6] Carol Harrison, working on middle-class male sociability in provincial towns in nineteenth-century eastern France, found many Emulation Societies and florid odes and essays composed by locals in praise of emulation.[7]

The principle of emulation, which I am inclined to regard as central to the culture of the modern French elites, differs significantly from the stereotypical competitiveness and self-interest often assumed to govern bourgeois culture. Where competition can be imagined horizontally as the pursuit of victory by equals, emulation works vertically, with participants striving against one another to reach an imagined pinnacle.[8] Competition focuses on substance, emulation on form: the one aims at securing the spoils of victory, the other at achieving virtue and distinction: whereas excellence is merely a side effect of competition, it is the whole point of emulation. Most importantly, the concept of emulation implies a valorizing gaze: if one competes primarily to achieve victory and esteem in one's own eyes, one emulates for the sake of approval by a higher power: a teacher, a monarch, or the state. As Carol Harrison describes it, the ethos of emulation practiced in local societies in nineteenth-century France was conjunctive rather than agonistic: members avoided articulating or acting upon any form of economic self-interest, and the societies shunned potentially divisive political debate, focusing instead on outdoing one another in scientific and intellectual pursuits or charitable projects.[9] Emulation has endured as a governing principle in the training and selection of the French elites.

The emphasis on social cohesion embedded in the idea of emulation, as well as the presence of a higher judging power it implies, bring us back to the religious or spiritual dimension in French understandings of polity and society. Bernhardt Groethuysen pointed out that the Catholic Church recognized only two bases for power, greatness modeled on God or poverty as embodied by Christ.[10] Translated into the realm of postrevolutionary politics, these two models generated initially the competing claims to sacredness of divinely sanctioned monarchy on the one hand, and democratic republicanism on the other. In the nineteenth-century search for a *via media* between these two traditions, the option that failed was that based precisely on seeking the middle ground, the Orleanist or *juste-milieu* compromise: the middle way offered no transcendence, it was as earth-bound as the portly Louis-Philippe himself. The compromise that worked, Bonapartism, was one that managed to combine these two forms of greatness instead of negating them. After 1848, one might argue, the real alternation in French politics was not that between right and left as defined in 1789, but that between left-republicanism and variations of Bonapartism. In very different ways and to different degrees, Napoleon III, Philippe Pétain, and Charles de Gaulle based their regimes on Napoleon's successful mixture of ideological ambiguity, military prestige, and populism; they offered, as an alternative to democratic republicanism, governments claiming a grandeur reminiscent of religious monarchy, but which at the very least paid lip service to the sacred status of *le peuple* as well.

The endurance of this spiritual dimension in French politics—and in visions of society connected to understandings of the polity—explains why the bourgeois has remained for so long the quintessential scapegoat or other in the Gallic social imaginary, the embodiment of centrifugal materialism and self-interest. But he has not been the only figure cast in this role, for the Jew (in the nineteenth century especially) and the American (in the twentieth) have come to join him in this capacity. It is worth noting that one of the earliest texts of modern French antisemitism,[11] Alphonse Toussenel's *Les Juifs rois de l'époque* (*The Jews, Kings of Our Age*) was published in 1845, at a time when antibourgeois sentiment and writings were widespread. Toussenel was a follower of the Utopian Socialist Charles Fourier, and may have been the first writer on the left in France to sound the theme of the Jew as capitalist villain. Only part of his book concerns Jews, as its overall thrust was a Balzacian denunciation of the reign of money under Louis-Philippe; its themes, interestingly, echo the antiluxury diatribes of the later eighteenth century, in that a Jew is anyone driven by the commercial profit motive: for that reason, the English, the Dutch, and the Genevans were Jews as well. As Toussenel triumphantly (if confusingly) concluded: "Whoever says Jew, says Protestant."[12]

The strategy adopted by many Jewish families in nineteenth-century France to escape allegations of greedy materialism is telling. As one of the leading historians of French Jewry, Pierre Birnbaum, has shown, French Jews of this era were unique in Europe in that they both could and did enter the service of the state, many becoming high civil servants and army officers. (Maybe the most remarkable thing about Captain Alfred Dreyfus, Birnbaum has observed, was the extent of his pre-scandal social assimilation and professional success, which would have been impossible anywhere else in Europe.) Those French Jews who could escaped the taint of money by making the transition, as Birnbaum has memorably put it, from *juifs de cour,* scorned but indispensable money brokers, to *juifs d'état,* state Jews who in their public lives fully embraced the culture and ideals of the French Republic.[13] The cruel irony is that under the Third and Fourth Republics notable Jews became the victims of the very strategy that was supposed to bring them unimpeachable honor: it was precisely because of their success in capturing high government positions that they turned into choice targets for the barrage of right-wing antisemitism that crystallized with the publication of Edouard Drumont's *La France juive* in 1886. Instead of proving that Jews could embrace the highest French values, their success demonstrated instead to antisemites that the Third and Fourth Republics, in the persons of an Alfred Dreyfus, a Léon Blum, or a Pierre Mendès-France, had become *les républiques juives.*[14] The Jewish Republic, like the Bourgeois Monarchy a century or so earlier, saw its supporters transformed into scapegoats.

In the waves of antisemitism that began in the late nineteenth century and lasted well into the mid-twentieth, Jews clearly embodied what was most feared about economic and social modernity. As Michel Winock proposes, what the Jew represented can be most clearly grasped if it is contrasted with the meanings attached to the figure of Joan of Arc: the Maid of Orléans became in this period a national icon embraced most fervently, though not exclusively, by the Catholic and antisemitic right. Where Joan represented the French soil and healthy, productive agrarian work, the Jew stood for rootless urban living, economic parasitism, and disease; the Anglophobic and virginal Maid embodied spiritual nationalism in contrast to the cosmopolitan, materialistic whorish Jew, and so on.[15] Granted, the image of the Jew fared differently than that of the bourgeois in many respects. French intellectuals who saw in the bourgeois no redemptive intellectual or artistic qualities often acknowledged the spiritual or intellectual dimensions of Jewish culture: thus Balzac created brilliant Jewish actress-courtesans like Esther or Josépha redeemed by Art or Love alongside the vile usurer Gobseck, and Marcel Proust balanced the vulgar social climber

Bloch with the aesthete Swann. And, to state the obvious, no bourgeois was ever persecuted the way Jews were. It is striking, however, how much the themes of antisemitic literature in the 1890s and later seem to echo the anti-luxury writings of the 1770s and 1780s and the antibourgeois literature of the 1830s and 1840s.

Virulent antisemitism, though influential, had been marginal; Vichy and the Holocaust ultimately made it unacceptable, though of course it still flourishes in some quarters. After World War II anti-American-ism became far more conspicuous, reaching a climax in the 1960s with the convergence of Gaullist and left-wing (mainly Communist) hostil-ity to what was sometimes known as "the American cancer." There are many differences, of course, between French antisemitism and anti-Americanism. The latter, for one, appeared much later; only around 1930 did systematic hostility to American culture and politics replace indifference, breezy contempt, or curiosity about the New World.[16] And the nature of the threats embodied by each of these was rather different: where Judaism was imagined as a liminal danger which had always existed at the interstices of society, America was a dystopia, the negative model of what a whole social world might come to resemble. Unlike such historical others as the Jew, the Englishman, or the Ger-man, the American was what a French person might well become in the future, a figure "not radically different from us."[17] While individual Jews threatened Frenchness from the inside, America represented a different kind of menace, a siren song from the future. And some of the accusations leveled at American culture differed significantly from the stereotyping of either bourgeoisie or Jewishness. In addition to materialism and lack of culture, Americans were often stigmatized for their alleged puritanism, racism, and violence.[18]

Nonetheless, French discourse about America in the twentieth cen-tury contains intriguing parallels to earlier language about luxury, bourgeoisie, and Jewishness in that all of these were ways of talking about the danger of materialism. Antipathy against the United States correlated strongly, of course, with aversion to capitalism and Anglo-American liberal principles. In the 1930s, for instance, a prominent source of anti-American sentiment was the movement known as "personalism," which coalesced around the Catholic journal *Esprit* and its founder Emmanuel Mounier. Historians argue over whether Mounier and his journal belong to a left- or right-wing tradition, but there is no doubt about this group's hostility to capitalism, individualism, and materialism. In his articles Mounier frequently used the word "bourgeois" to describe what was rotten about North American culture: the narrow, soul-shrinking pursuit of comfort, security, and material possessions. America was a bourgeois paradise, and if this dream came to be realized in France, it would rob the nation of what made this ancient Catholic culture historically great: the ability to embrace sacrifice and effort, mystery, suffering, and joy.[19]

The most distinctive feature of anti-Americanism was its use as a vehicle for resistance not just to capitalism and industrialism, but to their specifically twentieth-century features: technocracy, mass production, and mass culture. These were frightening aspects of twentieth-century modernity, but the fears echo those articulated in the nineteenth century via the figure of the Jew. In fact the Jew and the American were sometimes jointly denounced, for instance in Georges Bernanos's *La France contre les robots (France against the Robots)* written in the 1940s. Was it an accident, the Catholic writer queried, that New York, the de facto capital of the "baby-brained giant," was a city of three million Jews?[20] In the 1930s and 1940s the United States represented for intellectuals something similar to what the bourgeoisie meant to Balzac: an environment in which mechanical reproduction would obliterate true creation, in which surface and extension would take the place of depth.

The threat to the position of intellectuals was also analogous: just as writers in the 1830s and 1840s projected onto the bourgeois their resistance to the commercialization of the literary sphere, their descendants a century later used anti-Americanism to express their fear of being displaced by the seductions of mass culture.[21] Like antibourgeois sentiment and like antisemitism, hostility to the United States came from both the right and the left of the political spectrum. It originated in the 1930s with writers like Robert Aron and Arnaud Dandrieu, later founders of the right-wing movement Ordre Nouveau, calling for a "spiritual revolution" against the American threat.[22] The Vichy regime picked up on this strain of Americanophobia, and General de Gaulle's hostility to the United States is well known. By the time the Cold War was at its zenith, however, the loudest voices came from the left to indict the United States on anticapitalist and anti-imperialist grounds.[23] Significant differences notwithstanding, one can still posit generally that in all of these instances—the denunciation of bourgeois, Jews, and Americans—Catholic conservatism and latter-day Jacobinism merged in the construction of a common enemy. While we certainly need to know more about widespread popular opinion in all of these cases, it makes sense to view all three instances as important steps in the construction of individual and collective identities based on the rejection of materialism and modernity.

For the period beyond the scope of this book, my argument is only tentative. The development of industrial capitalism in the later nineteenth century and the emergence at that time of a national organized labor movement along with forms of working-class consciousness may well have crystallized, finally, bourgeois or middle-class consciousness. But this remains to my mind an open question, as does the broader issue of determining to what extent any form of classic class analysis applies to the French case. France gave Karl Marx some of his most explosive historical ammunition, the very experience of the French Revolution and the histories of that event written by the members of Guizot's generation. Ironically, Marxian categories may be less relevant to France than to other countries in and outside of Europe. It is interesting that the two most influential French social theorists of the later twentieth century, Michel Foucault and Pierre Bourdieu, devised analyses of social power which bypassed conventional economic determinism to stress instead such things as knowledge, intellectual discipline, culture, taste, and education. Nobody would argue that money is irrelevant to power in France, but the fact that leading French politicians are eager to publicize their expert knowledge of art and architecture and to flaunt their mastery of Maupassant or Proust is of more than trivial importance.

How particular to France are the patterns of belief described in this book? Research on cultural understandings of the social in other countries might show interesting parallels elsewhere in continental Europe. Germany, for instance, offers a striking contrast to France. On the one hand, the historical autonomy and commercial orientation of German city states made for a strong association between bourgeoisie and citizenship: the term *Bürgerlichkeit* means civil society. On the other hand, German culture in the eighteenth and nineteenth centuries shared notable similarities with its French counterpart where social attitudes are concerned. Germany was, like France, a relative latecomer to industrialization and a country with a numerous, prestigious, powerful state bureaucracy, and one finds in German culture of the age traits strikingly parallel to the Gallic model: a strong Christian ethos (albeit Lutheran rather than Catholic) hostile to moneymaking; influential aristocratic suspicion of capitalism and entrepreneurship; a corresponding high regard for the learned professions, the military, and especially the civil service; a reverence for *Bildung* and *Kultur* as pronounced, no doubt, as in France.[24] Looked at another way, however, the German case can seem like a mirror image of the French: if the French between 1789 and 1850 developed liberal political institutions in the absence of bourgeois social norms, nineteenth-century Germany, some have argued, produced a strong bourgeois civic culture and economy in the absence of a modern polity.[25] It is high time, in any case, to stop projecting the Anglo-American model, with its inevitable linking of capitalism, liberal democracy, and middle-class individualism, onto continental societies. And it may be time to start wondering whether that Anglo-American model does not constitute the exception rather than the norm in the development of Western culture.

I began this project with two objects in mind. The first was to question some of the unexamined ways in which historians describe French society in this period, and in particular the assumption that a group called the bourgeoisie established enduring dominance starting sometime in the eighteenth century. While it would be foolish to deny that wealthy and mostly non-noble groups held power in nineteenth-century France, I hope that by exploding the myth of the bourgeoisie we may be able to arrive at more specific and more interesting ways of describing the identity and culture of the French elites and the ways in which they were perceived by others. More generally, I hope to draw attention to the ways in which the social is constructed, and to the importance of politics in the creation of social identities. Nearly forty years ago, the late Alfred Cobban, a deeply learned and iconoclastic historian of France, remarked that "The supposed social categories of our histories—bourgeois, aristocrats, *sans-culottes*—are all in fact political ones."[26] Only now are historians beginning to pay attention to the implications of such insights. Social identities are fashioned from within, by intimate experiences of family, sexuality, and the material world; they are also imposed from without, by the labels, dreams, and derision offered to us by those—from politicians to advertisers to artists—who want our allegiance. Who we are as social beings is shaped by the constant messages we receive about whom to desire and whom to despise.

NOTES

INDEX

# NOTES

## INTRODUCTION

1. Salient examples of this problem are: Elinor Barber, *The Bourgeoisie in Eighteenth-Century France* (Princeton: Princeton University Press, 1955); Régine Pernoud, *Histoire de la bourgeoisie en France* (Paris: Le Seuil, 1960–1962); Adeline Daumard, *Les Bourgeois et la bourgeoisie en France* (Paris: Aubier, 1987). The same syndrome affects the chapters on bourgeoisie in otherwise excellent textbooks on the history of society: see for instance Pierre Goubert, *The Ancien Régime: French Society, 1600–1750,* trans. Steve Cox (New York: Harper and Row, 1973), pp. 239–252. My characterization of these attempts at synthesis should not be construed as criticism of the many works in French history which describe specific segments of the nontitled urban elites, most of which are very fine pieces of scholarship. They include studies of single families, like Robert Forster, *Merchants, Landlords, Magistrates: The Depont Family in Eighteenth-Century France* (Baltimore: Johns Hopkins University Press, 1980); of local elites like Jean-Pierre Chaline, *Les Bourgeois de Rouen: une élite urbaine au XIXe siècle* (Paris: Presses de la Fondation Nationale de Sciences Politiques, 1982); urban social histories such as Maurice Garden, *Lyon et les Lyonnais au XVIIIe siècle* (Paris: Belles Lettres, 1970); monographs about different professions such as on lawyers, Lenard Berlanstein, *The Barristers of Toulouse in the Eighteenth Century* (Baltimore: Johns Hopkins University Press, 1975) and David Bell, *Lawyers and Citizens: The Making of a Political Elite in Old Regime France* (New York: Oxford University Press, 1994); and on the medical professions, Matthew Ramsey, *Professional and Popular Medicine in France,*

*1770–1830: The Social World of Medical Practice* (Cambridge: Cambridge University Press, 1988) and Laurence Brockliss and Colin Jones, *The Medical World of Early Modern France* (Oxford: Clarendon Press, 1997). Many more examples could be added to these. In the years since I began this project, three important and impressive social histories of the middle classes have appeared, one a family history and the others local histories with broader implications: Christine Adams, *A Taste for Comfort and Status: A Bourgeois Family in Eighteenth-Century France* (University Park: Pennsylvania State University Press, 2000); David Garrioch, *The Formation of the Parisian Bourgeoisie, 1690–1830* (Cambridge, Mass.: Harvard University Press, 1996); and Carol Harrison, *The Bourgeois Citizen in Nineteenth-Century France: Gender, Sociability, and the Uses of Emulation* (Oxford: Oxford University Press, 1999).

2. Adeline Daumard, *La Bourgeoisie parisienne de 1815 à 1848* (Paris: S.E.V.P.E.N, 1963), pp. 216–217. A quarter of a century later, the same classification is reiterated in Daumard's more synthetic work, *Les Bourgeois et la bourgeoisie en France*, pp. 117–119, along with some expressions of doubt about the meaning of it all: "In view of such sharp contrasts, is the extensive way in which the word bourgeois is understood really justified?"

3. A salient exception is Peter Gay's encyclopedic cultural history of the later nineteenth-century European bourgeoisie, *The Bourgeois Experience: Victoria to Freud,* 5 vols. (New York: Oxford University Press, 1984–1998). Although Gay does a magnificent job of undermining many clichés about bourgeois culture, his work on the whole takes for granted the group's social identity and therefore does not effect much of a breakthrough in terms of the definition and location of the bourgeoisie.

4. See Benjamin DeMott, *The Imperial Middle: Why Americans Can't Think Straight about Class* (New York: Morrow, 1990).

5. See the discussions developed in chapters 2 and 6. For useful syntheses on various aspects of this development in historical interpretation, see William Doyle, *Origins of the French Revolution* (Oxford: Oxford University Press, 1980); Colin Heywood, *The Development of the French Economy, 1750–1914* (Cambridge: Cambridge University Press, 1992); Peter McPhee, *A Social History of France, 1780–1880* (London: Routledge, 1992).

6. Alfred Cobban, "The 'Middle-Class' in France, 1815–1848," *French Historical Studies* 5 (1967): 41–52. Cobban precociously argued that the rhetoric about *classes moyennes* and "bourgeois monarchy" was mostly a matter of political propaganda: see p. 49.

7. Richard Klein, *Cigarettes Are Sublime* (Durham: Duke University Press, 1993), p. 18.

8. My views are similar to those of Joan Scott, who states that "Class and class consciousness are the same thing—they are political articulations that provide an analysis of, a coherent pattern to impose upon, the events and activities of daily life." *Gender and the Politics of History* (New York, Columbia University Press, 1988), p. 56. My adherence to this view is informed less by abstract theory than by reading social historians interested in questions of language and culture, such as, in addition to Joan Scott, William H. Sewell, Jr., *Work and Revolution in France: The Language of Labor from the Old Regime to 1848* (Cambridge: Cambridge University Press, 1980); Lynn Hunt, *Politics, Culture and Class in the French Revolution* (Berkeley: University of California Press, 1984); Gareth Stedman-Jones, *Languages of Class: Studies in English Working-Class History* (Cambridge: Cambridge University Press, 1983). For an excellent overview of both classic and recent theoretical discussions of class, see Patrick Joyce, ed., *Class* (Oxford: Oxford University Press, 1995).

9. The most notable example in this field is Patrice Higonnet, *Class, Ideology and the Rights of Nobles during the French Revolution* (Oxford: Clarendon Press, 1981). For a more general discussion see Terry Eagleton, *Ideology: An Introduction* (London: Verso, 1991), ch. 2.

10. The founding text for this tradition is the philosopher J. L. Austin's *How to Do Things with Words* (Cambridge, Mass.: Harvard University Press, 1962). For an overview, see Terry Eagleton, *Literary Theory: An Introduction* (Minneapolis: University of Minnesota Press, 1983), ch. 3, especially pp. 118–119. The most influential current theorist of the performative is Judith Butler: see her *Gender Trouble* (London: Routledge, 1991) and *Bodies That Matter* (London: Routledge, 1993). For a stimulating application of theories of narrative performativity to a historical setting, see Judith Walkowitz, *City of Dreadful Delight: Narratives of Sexual Danger in Late Victorian London* (Chicago: University of Chicago Press, 1992).

11. I am bringing to the realm of the social an approach which Lynn Hunt and François Furet adopted to decipher patterns of political culture in the French Revolution. See Hunt, *Politics, Culture and Class,* ch. 1, and François Furet, *Interpreting the French Revolution,* trans. Elborg Forster (Cambridge: Cambridge University Press, 1981).

12. Some of the first and most important contributions to these lines of inquiry by historians are: on gender, Joan Scott, "Gender: A Useful Category of Historical Analysis" in *Gender and the Politics of History;* on race,

Barbara Fields, "Ideology and Race in American History," in J. Morgan Kousser and James McPherson, eds., *Region, Race and Reconstruction* (New York: Oxford University Press, 1982); on (homo)sexuality, Martin Duberman, Martha Vicinus, and George Chauncey, eds., *Hidden from History: Reclaiming the Gay and Lesbian Past* (New York: New American Library, 1989). In the fifteen or twenty years since these discourses on method first appeared, the historical literature on all of these topics has grown so voluminous that it would be impossible to list even the most important contributions in a reasonable space.

13. Pierre Nora, ed., *Les Lieux de mémoire*, 3 vols. (Paris: Gallimard, 1984–1992). In the English-speaking world the most widely cited general work on the cultural construction of the nation remains Benedict Anderson, *Imagined Communities: Reflections on the Origin and Spread of Nationalism*, rev. ed. (London: Verso, 1991). The works which in French history defined the cultural approach to the political are Furet, *Interpreting the French Revolution*, Hunt, *Politics, Culture and Class*, and Mona Ozouf, *La Fête révolutionnaire, 1789–1799* (Paris: Gallimard, 1976).

14. Two excellent recent collections, however, show a move in this direction on the part of labor historians and sociologists: Lenard Berlanstein, ed., *Rethinking Labor History: Essays on Class and Discourse Analysis* (Urbana: University of Illinois Press, 1993) and John R. Hall, ed., *Reworking Class* (Ithaca: Cornell University Press, 1997).

15. Sewell, *Work and Revolution in France;* Jacques Rancière, *The Nights of Labor: The Worker's Dream in Nineteenth-Century France,* trans. John Drury (Philadelphia: Temple University Press, 1989); Donald Reid, *Paris Sewers and Sewermen: Realities and Representation* (Cambridge, Mass.: Harvard University Press, 1991).

16. In a much quoted sentence, E. P. Thompson declared: "I do not see class as a 'structure', nor even as a 'category' but as something which in fact happens (and can be shown to have happened) in human relationships," *The Making of the English Working Class* (London: Penguin, 1968), p. 9. His approach to class as a relationship defined by culture is perhaps more clearly illustrated in the essays in Thompson's *Customs in Common: Studies in Traditional Popular Culture* (New York: The New Press, 1993).

17. Stedman-Jones, *Languages of Class;* Patrick Joyce, *Visions of the People: Industrial England and the Question of Class, 1840–1914* (Cambridge: Cambridge University Press, 1991) and *Democratic Subjects: The Self and the Social in Nineteenth-Century England* (Cambridge: Cambridge University Press, 1994); Dror Wahrman, *Imagining the Middle Class: The Political Representation of Class in Britain, c. 1780–1840* (Cambridge: Cambridge

University Press, 1995); David Cannadine, *The Rise and Fall of Class in Britain* (New York: Columbia University Press, 1995). More classic approaches to the social history of this class can also be found in British history. Leonore Davidoff and Catherine Hall's *Family Fortunes: Men and Women of the English Middle Class* (Chicago: University of Chicago Press, 1987), an impressive reconstruction of middle-class worlds, does not engage the sorts of questions about social terminologies addressed by Wahrman and others.

18. Wahrman, *Imagining the Middle Class*, pp. 6–9, quote p. 14.
19. The only attempt at a general statement that I know of is Bronislaw Baczko, *Les Imaginaires sociaux* (Paris: Payot, 1984).
20. I used police records and legal records in two previous works which deal with representations of social groups: Sarah Maza, *Servants and Masters in Eighteenth-Century France: The Uses of Loyalty* (Princeton: Princeton University Press, 1983), and *Private Lives and Public Affairs: The Causes Célèbres of Prerevolutionary France* (Berkeley: University of California Press, 1993).
21. For a fascinating, if controversial, attempt to do this, see Robert Darnton, *The Great Cat Massacre and Other Episodes in French Cultural History* (New York: Basic Books, 1984), chs. 1 and 2.
22. Roland Barthes, *Mythologies* (Paris: Éditions du Seuil, 1957), pp. 193–224.

## 1. THE SOCIAL IMAGINARY IN PREREVOLUTIONARY FRANCE

1. Dror Wahrman, *Imagining the Middle-Class: The Political Representation of Class in Britain, c. 1780–1840* (Cambridge: Cambridge University Press, 1995), ch. 1.
2. Georges Dumézil, *Mythe et épopée: l'idéologie des trois fonctions dans les épopées des peuples indo-européens* (Paris: Gallimard, 1968).
3. Georges Duby, *The Three Orders: Feudal Society Imagined,* trans. Arthur Goldhammer (Chicago: University of Chicago Press, 1980), pp. 1–9.
4. See Arthur Lovejoy, *The Great Chain of Being: A Study of the History of an Idea* (Cambridge, Mass.: Harvard University Press, 1936).
5. Marie-France Piguet, *Classe: Histoire du mot et genèse du concept* (Lyon: Presses Universitaires de Lyon, 1996), pp. 20–21, quote p. 21.
6. Duby, *The Three Orders,* pp. 2, 73–75.
7. Jacques Peuchet, ed., *Mémoires tirés des archives de la police de Paris,* 4 vols. (Paris, 1838), I: 197–217.
8. Ibid., I: 204–206.
9. Ibid., I: 206

10. Ibid., I: 207–208.

11. Roland Mousnier, *Les Hiérarchies sociales de 1450 à nos jours* (Paris: Presses Universitaires de France, 1969), p. 63.

12. Ibid., pp. 64–65.

13. Robert Darnton, *The Great Cat Massacre and Other Episodes in French Cultural History* (New York: Basic Books, 1984), pp. 116, 120.

14. Joseph Berthélé, ed., *Montpellier en 1768 et 1836, d'après deux manuscrits inédits* (Montpellier, 1909), pp. 11–110.

15. Ibid., pp. 67–69.

16. Darnton, *Great Cat Massacre*, pp. 24–126, 140.

17. Philippe Auguste de Sainte-Foy, chevalier d'Arcq, *La Noblesse militaire ou le patriote françois* (Paris, 1758), p. 16.

18. Élie Carcassonne, *Montesquieu et le problème de la constitution française au XVIIIe siècle* (Paris, 1927), p. 236; Harvey Chisick, *The Limits of Reform: Attitudes Towards the Education of the Lower Classes in Eighteenth-Century France* (Princeton: Princeton University Press, 1981), p. 65.

19. Michael Bush, ed., *Social Orders and Social Classes in Europe since 1500: Studies in Social Stratification* (London: Longman, 1992), p. 6.

20. Chisick, *Limits of Reform*, pp. 122–123.

21. Carcassonne, *Montesquieu*, p. 248.

22. Antoine Polier de Saint-Germain, *Du Gouvernement des moeurs* (Paris, 1984), pp. 17–23.

23. D'Arcq, *Noblesse militaire*, pp. 16–18; Carcassonne, *Montesquieu*, ch. 5.

24. Régine Pernoud, *Histoire de la bourgeoisie en France*, 2 vols. (Paris: Le Seuil, 1960–62), I: chs. 1–3; Adhémar de Cardevaque, "Essai sur la bourgeoisie d'Arras avant la Révolution de 1789," *Mémoire de l'académie des sciences, lettres et arts d'Arras* IIe série (1888): 195–225; Joseph di Corcia, "*Bourg, Bourgeois, Bourgeois de Paris* from the Eleventh to the Eighteenth Century," *Journal of Modern History* 50 (June 1978): 207–331.

25. Pernoud, *Histoire de la bourgeoisie*, I: chs. 2,3; di Corcia, "*Bourg, Bourgeois*," pp. 213–219; Emile Ducéré, "La Bourgeoisie Bayonnaise sous l'ancien régime (moeurs, usages, costumes)," *Bulletin de la Société des Arts Lettres et Sciences de Pau* 18 (1888–1889): 87–225.

26. Di Corcia, "*Bourg, Bourgeois*," pp. 224–231.

27. Michel Vovelle and Daniel Roche, "Bourgeois, rentiers, propriétaires: éléments pour la définition d'une catégorie sociale à la fin du XVIIIe siècle," *Actes du 77e Congrès des Sociétés Savantes* 84 (1959): 419–452.

28. *Dictionnaire de l'Académie françoise*, 2 vols. (Paris, 1694), article *Bourgeois, Bourgeoise*.

29. *Dictionnaire universel françois et latin* (Trévoux, 1704), article *Bourgeois*.

30. Gauthier, *Dictionnaire de la constitution et du gouvernement français,* article *Citoyen,* reprinted in appendix to Sonia Branca-Rosoff, "Les Mots de parti-pris: *Citoyen, Aristocrate,* et *Insurrection* dans quelques dictionnaires (1762–1798), in *Dictionnaire des usages socio-politiques (1770–1815),* 3 vols. (Paris: Klincksieck, 1988), p. 71.

31. Articles *Bourgeois* in the *Dictionnaire de l'Académie française,* 1694 and 1798 eds.; *Dictionnaire universel,* 1704 ed.; Antoine Furetière, *Dictionnaire universel,* 3 vols. (Paris, 1690); Pierre Richelet, *Dictionnaire françois,* 2 vols. (Geneva, 1680).

32. Articles *Bourgeois* in *Académie française* (1694), Richelet (1680), and Furetière (1690).

33. Article *Bourgeois* in *Académie française* (1798).

34. Pierre Carlet de Marivaux, *Journaux et oeuvres diverses* (Paris: Garnier, 1969), p. 14.

35. Jean Alter, *Les Origines de la satire antibourgeoise en France,* 2 vols. (Geneva: Droz, 1970).

36. Ibid., II: 89.

37. Sarah Maza, *Servants and Masters in Eighteenth-Century France: The Uses of Loyalty* (Princeton: Princeton University Press, 1983), chs. 3 and 5.

38. Article *Bourgeois* in the 1762, 1798, 1802, and 1835 editions of the *Dictionnaire de l'Académie française.* For the 1762 and 1802 editions see the appendix to Michel Perronet, "Bourgeois, Bourgeoisie: Les définitions du dictionnaire de l'Académie (1762–1802)," *Il Pensiero Politico* 19 (1986): 111–112.

39. Darnton, *Cat Massacre,* pp. 137, 140.

40. For descriptions of Coyer's pamphlet and the ensuing debate see Carcassonne, *Montesquieu,* pp. 223–232; J. Q. C. Mackrell, *The Attack on "Feudalism" in Eighteenth-Century France* (London: Routledge & Kegan Paul, 1973), ch. 4; John Shovlin, "Towards a Reinterpretation of Revolutionary Antinobilism: The Political Economy of Honor in the Old Regime," *Journal of Modern History* 72 (March 2000): 35–66. The most illuminating recent discussion of the debate is Jay Smith, "Social Categories, the Language of Patriotism, and the Origins of the French Revolution: The Debate over *Noblesse commerçante," Journal of Modern History* 72 (June 2000): 339–374.

41. Abbé Gabriel Coyer, *La Noblesse commerçante* (Paris, 1758).

42. Mackrell, *Attack on "Feudalism,"* pp. 87–98.

43. Octavie Guichard, dame Belot, *Observations sur la noblesse et le tiers-état* (Amsterdam, 1758), pp. 80–81.

44. Pierre Antoine de Sainte-Foix, chevalier d'Arcq, *La Noblesse militaire ou le patriote françois* (Paris, 1758), pp. 10–13.

45. *Lettre de M. D\*\*\* à M. D\*\**, quoted in Carcassonne, *Montesquieu*, p. 226.
46. D'Arcq, *Noblesse militaire*, p. 16.
47. Guichard, *Observations*, pp. 13, 104–105.
48. D'Arcq, *Noblesse militaire*, p. 48.
49. In his many works on the sociology of the eighteenth-century world of letters, Robert Darnton has emphasized its aristocratic component, in opposition to a longstanding tradition of viewing it as a "bourgeois" ideology. See, most notably, "The High Enlightenment and the Low-Life of Literature" in *The Literary Underground of the Old Regime* (Cambridge, Mass.: Harvard University Press, 1982), pp. 1–40. See also his "The Facts of Literary Life in Eighteenth-Century France" in Keith Baker, ed., *The Political Culture of the Old Regime* (Oxford: Pergamon Press, 1987), pp. 261–291. On the aristocratic presence in local intellectual societies see Daniel Roche, *Le Siècle des lumières en province: académies et académiciens provinciaux, 1680–1789*, 2 vols. (Paris: Mouton, 1978). On the prominence of nobles in the opposition to the monarchy see Carcassonne, *Montesquieu*, and Franklin Ford, *Robe and Sword: The Regrouping of the French Aristocracy after Louis XIV* (New York: Harper Torchbooks, 1953).
50. Guy Chaussinand-Nogaret, *La Noblesse au XVIIIe siècle: de la Féodalité aux Lumières* (Brussels: Editions Complexe, 1984), pp. 53–64.
51. Jay Smith, *The Culture of Merit: Nobility, Royal Service, and the Making of Absolute Monarchy in France, 1600–1789* (Ann Arbor: The University of Michigan Press, 1996).
52. Ibid., ch. 4, quote p. 163.
53. Ibid., ch. 5.
54. Pierre Augustin Caron de Beaumarchais, *The Marriage of Figaro*, Act 5.
55. Mackrell, *Attack on "Feudalism,"* ch. 3; Hilton Root, *Peasants and King in Burgundy: Agrarian Foundations of French Absolutism* (Berkeley: University of California Press, 1987), ch. 5.
56. Mackrell, *Attack on "Feudalism,"* ch. 6.
57. Ibid., ch. 5.
58. For discussions of this literature see Mackrell, *Attack on "Feudalism,"* ch. 2; Piguet, *Classe*, pp. 22–30; Carcassonne, *Montesquieu*, ch. 4; Jean-Marie Goulemot, *Le Règne de l'histoire: Discours historiques et révolutions, XVIIe–XVIIIe siècle* (Paris: Albin Michel, 1996), chs. 9 and 10.
59. Quoted in Piguet, *Classe*, p. 24.
60. Johnson Kent Wright, *A Classical Republican in Eighteenth-Century France: The Political Thought of Mably* (Stanford: Stanford University Press, 1997), esp. ch. 6.
61. Gabriel Bonnot de Mably, *Observations sur l'histoire de France*, 2 vols.

(Geneva, 1765). See Keith Baker, *Inventing the French Revolution: Essays on French Political Culture in the Eighteenth Century* (Cambridge: Cambridge University Press, 1990), pp. 48–49.

62. Ibid., I: 77–78.
63. Mackrell, *Attack on "Feudalism,"* pp. 35–38.
64. Shovlin, "Revolutionary Antinobilism," 57.
65. The classic work on the Physiocrats is Georges Weulersse, *Le Mouvement physiocratique en France de 1756 à 1770,* 2 vols. (Paris: F. Alcan, 1910). See also Elizabeth Fox-Genovese, *The Origins of Physiocracy: Economic Revolution and Social Order in Eighteenth-Century France* (Ithaca: Cornell University Press, 1976), and most recently Jean-Claude Perrot, *Une Histoire intellectuelle de l'économie politique, XVIIe–XVIIIe siècles* (Paris: Éditions de l'École des Hautes Études en Sciences Sociales, 1992).
66. Piguet, *Classe,* pp. 42–43.
67. Ibid., pp. 53–59.
68. See Jean Ehrard, *L'Idée de nature en France à l'aube des Lumières* (Paris: Flammarion, 1970).
69. Piguet, *Classe,* pp. 49–50, 57.
70. Ibid., pp. 55–58.
71. Victor de Riquetti, marquis de Mirabeau, *L'Ami de hommes, ou traité de la population,* 4 vols. (Avignon, 1756), I: 142.
72. Smith, "Social Categories and the Language of Patriotism."
73. Keith Baker, *Condorcet: From Natural Philosophy to Social Mathematics* (Chicago: University of Chicago Press, 1975), pp. 203–204.

## 2. COMMERCE, LUXURY, AND FAMILY LOVE

1. Joseph Berthélé, ed., *Montpellier en 1768 et 1836, d'après deux documents inédits* (Montpellier, 1909), p. 68.
2. Ibid.
3. Ibid., pp. 57–58.
4. Ibid., pp. 68–69.
5. Ibid., p. 148.
6. Ibid., p. 149.
7. Ibid., pp. 148–49.
8. Robert Darnton, *The Great Cat Massacre and Other Episodes in French Cultural History* (New York: Basic Books, 1984), pp. 114–115.
9. Berthélé, *Montpellier,* pp. 98–99.
10. The most concise yet nuanced expression of this view remains Georges Lefebvre's *Quatre-vingt-neuf* (1939), published in English just prior to

the onslaught of "revisionism" as *The Coming of the French Revolution* (Princeton: Princeton University Press, 1967).

11. See the initial attack by Alfred Cobban, *The Social Interpretation of the French Revolution* (Cambridge: Cambridge University Press, 1964), esp. chs. 6–8. The most important work of that generation to challenge the economic underpinnings of the Marxian interpretation was George Taylor's "Types of Capitalism in Eighteenth-Century France," *English Historical Review* 79 (1964): 478–497, and "Noncapitalist Wealth and the Origins of the French Revolution," *American Historical Review* 72 (1967): 469–496.

12. Early and important contributions to this argument were Jan Marczewski, "The Take-Off and French Experience" in Walt Rostow, ed., *The Economics of Take-Off into Sustained Growth* (New York: St. Martin's Press, 1963), and François Crouzet, "Angleterre et France au XVIIIe siècle: Essai d'analyse comparée de deux croissances économiques," in *Annales: économies, sociétés, civilisations* 21 (1966): 254–291. In the 1970s and 1980s a new generation of economic historians built the evidence of France's eighteenth-century growth into a full-blown revisionist argument. The most substantial statement of the argument is Patrick O'Brien and Caglar Keydar, *Economic Growth in Britain and France, 1780–1914: Two Paths to the Twentieth Century* (London: Allen and Unwin, 1978). See also Richard Roehl, "French Industrialization: A Reconsideration," *Explorations in Economic History* 13 (1978): 233–281; Don Leet and John Shaw, "French Economic Stagnation, 1700–1960: Old Economic History Revisited," *Journal of Interdisciplinary History* 8 (1978): 531–544; Rondo Cameron and Charles E. Freedman, "French Economic Growth: A Radical Revision," *Social Science History* 7 (1983): 3–30; Nicholas Crafts, "Economic Growth in France and Britain, 1830–1910: A Review of the Evidence," *Journal of Economic History* 44 (March 1984): 49–67; Robert Aldrich, "Late Comer or Early Starter? New Views on French Economic History," *Journal of European Economic History* 16 (1987): 89–100.

13. Leet and Shaw, "French Economic Stagnation," 536–537; Cameron and Freedman, "French Economic Growth," 16–17; François Crouzet, *De la Supériorité de l'Angleterre sur la France: l'économique et l'imaginaire, XVIIe et XVIIIe siècles* (Paris: Perrin, 1985), 55–57.

14. Roehl, "French Industrialization," esp. pp. 246–249. For an illuminating discussion of the term and the debate around it, see Tessie Liu, *The Weaver's Knot: The Contradictions of Class Struggle and Family Solidarity in Western France, 1750–1914* (Ithaca: Cornell University Press, 1994), pp. 23–32.

15. William H. Sewell, Jr., *Work and Revolution in France: The Language of Labor from the Old Regime to 1848* (Cambridge: Cambridge University Press, 1980), p. 153.

16. Georges Duby et al., *Histoire de la France urbaine,* 4 vols. (Paris: Le Seuil, 1981), III: 295–298; Daniel Roche, *La France des Lumières* (Paris: Fayard, 1993), pp. 160–163; Roche, *Histoire des choses banales: Naissance de la consommation, XVIIe–XVIIIe siècles* (Paris: Fayard, 1997), pp. 45–48.

17. Roche, *Histoire des choses banales,* pp. 55–58; Roche, *The People of Paris: An Essay on Popular Culture in the Eighteenth Century,* trans. Marie Evans and Gwynne Lewis (Berkeley: University of California Press, 1987), pp. 19–24; Sarah Maza, *Servants and Masters in Eighteenth-Century France: The Uses of Loyalty* (Princeton: Princeton University Press, 1983), chs. 1 and 3.

18. Roche, *The People of Paris;* Roche, *The Culture of Clothing: Dress and Fashion in the Ancien Régime,* trans. Jean Birrell (Cambridge: Cambridge University Press, 1994); Cissie Fairchilds, "The Production and Marketing of Populuxe Goods in Eighteenth-Century Paris," in John Brewer and Roy Porter, eds., *Consumption and the World of Goods* (London: Routledge, 1993), pp. 228–248; and especially Annick Pardailhé-Galabrun, *La Naissance de l'intime: 3000 foyers parisiens, XVIIe–XVIIIe siècles* (Paris: Presses Universitaires de France, 1988). The breakdown of households in Pardailhé-Galabrun's massive study ranges from at the top 2.5% nobles, 2% royal officers, 4.5% financial officers, 5% lawyers, and 1% doctors, to at the bottom 7% domestics (though some of them were actually quite rich). Journeymen and other workers account for 15.5% of the total, and the two largest categories are master artisans (27%) and merchants and bourgeois (22.5%). See her ch. 3. While all these historians draw fine distinctions within the group thus captured, it can safely be said that these inventories document for the most part the environment of the comfortably-off but not the strikingly wealthy.

19. Roche, *Histoire des choses banales,* pp. 111–114.

20. Ibid., pp. 255–259; Roche, *People of Paris,* pp. 119–120.

21. Pardailhé-Galabrun, *Naissance de l'intime,* p. 239.

22. Ibid., pp. 216, 250–261.

23. Ibid., pp. 251–252.

24. Ibid., pp. 287–291; Roche, *People of Paris,* pp. 132–137; Roche, *Histoire des choses banales,* pp. 140–145.

25. Pardailhé-Galabrun, *Naissance de l'intime,* pp. 275–282; Roche, *People of Paris,* pp. 130–132.

26. Pardailhé-Galabrun, *Naissance de l'intime,* pp. 319–324; Roche, *People of Paris,* pp. 147–149.

27. Pardailhé-Galabrun, *Naissance de l'intime,* pp. 368–370, 398–400; Roche, *People of Paris,* 150–152.

28. Pardailhé-Galabrun, *Naissance de l'intime,* chapter 10.

29. Ibid., pp. 305–308; Roche, *People of Paris,* pp. 141–143.

30. Fairchilds, "Populuxe Goods," passim.

31. François Yves Besnard, *Souvenirs d'un nonagénaire,* 2 vols. (Paris, 1880), I: 28–31.

32. Roche, *Culture of Clothing,* pp. 106–107.

33. Maza, *Servants and Masters,* pp. 119–123.

34. Jennifer Jones, "The Taste for Fashion and Frivolity: Gender, Clothing and the Commercial Culture of the Old Regime" (Ph.D.diss., Princeton University, 1991), chs. 1 and 2.

35. Roche, *Culture of Clothing,* ch. 5.

36. Ibid., pp. 121–125, 141–142.

37. Ibid., pp. 142–143.

38. Jennifer Jones, "Repackaging Rousseau: Femininity and Fashion in Old Regime France," *French Historical Studies* 18 (1994): 939–968.

39. Jean-Claude Perrot, *Genèse d'une ville moderne: Caen au XVIIIe siècle,* 2 vols. (Paris: Mouton, 1975).

40. Jonathan Dewald, *Pont-Saint-Pierre, 1398–1789: Lordship, Community, and Capitalism in Early Modern France* (Berkeley: University of California Press, 1987).

41. Colin Jones, "The Great Chain of Buying: Medical Advertisement, the Bourgeois Public Sphere, and the Origins of the French Revolution," *American Historical Review* 101 (February 1996): 13–40.

42. Ibid., p. 34

43. Ibid., passim, quote p. 25.

44. For the more general argument, see Colin Jones, "Bourgeois Revolution Revivified: 1789 and Social Change," in Colin Lucas, ed., *Rewriting the French Revolution* (Oxford: Clarendon Press, 1991), pp. 69–118.

45. Ibid., pp. 96–109.

46. Ibid., p. 114.

47. Keith Michael Baker, *Condorcet: From Natural Philosophy to Social Mathematics* (Chicago: The University of Chicago Press, 1975), p. 19.

48. John Sekora, *Luxury: The Concept in Western Thought, Eden to Smolett* (Baltimore: The Johns Hopkins University Press, 1977), pp. 1–47.

49. Ibid., p. 74.

50. The following overview is based on Ellen Ross, "The Debate on Luxury in Eighteenth-Century France: A Study in the Language of Oppo-

sition to Change," Ph.D. diss., University of Chicago, 1975, and Renato Galliani, *Rousseau, le luxe, et l'idéologie nobiliaire* (Oxford: The Voltaire Foundation, 1989). For shorter surveys see Harvey Chisick, *The Limits of Reform: Attitudes towards the Education of the Lower Classes in Eighteenth-Century France* (Princeton: Princeton University Press, 1981, ch. 4, Roche, *La France des lumières*, ch. 17, and Pierre Rétat, "Luxe," *Dix-Huitième Siècle* 26 (1994): 79–88.

51. Jean-Baptiste Beauvais, cited in Ross, "Debate on Luxury," p. 37.

52. Ibid.

53. Paul Henri Thiry, baron d'Holbach, *Éthocratie ou le gouvernement fondé sur la morale* (Amsterdam, 1776), p. 132.

54. See for instance François Béliard, *Lettres critiques sur le luxe et les moeurs de ce siècle* (Amsterdam, 1771), pp. 25–30.

55. Chisick, *Limits of Reform*, pp. 197–205; Ross, "Debate on Luxury," pp. 59–65.

56. René Girard, *Violence and the Sacred*, trans. Patrick Gregory (Baltimore: Johns Hopkins University Press, 1972); see Lynn Hunt's use of this argument for a slightly later period in *The Family Romance of the French Revolution* (Berkeley: University of California Press, 1992), pp. 114–118.

57. Similar themes were ubiquitous in political pamphleteering, particularly in the illicit literature that blamed the failures of the last two monarchs on the anomalous influence of Louis XV's mistresses and Louis XVI's wife. See Sarah Maza, *Private Lives and Public Affairs: The Causes Célèbres of Prerevolutionary France* (Berkeley: University of California Press, 1993), ch. 4.

58. Jean Egret, *Louis XV et l'opposition parlementaire* (Paris: Armand Colin, 1970); Dale Van Kley, *The Jansenists and the Expulsion of the Jesuits from France, 1757–1765* (New Haven: Yale University Press, 1975) and *The Damiens Affair and the Unraveling of the Ancien Régime* (Princeton: Princeton University Press, 1984); Jeffrey Merrick, *The Desacralization of the French Monarchy in the Eighteenth Century* (Baton Rouge: LSU Press, 1990).

59. Anne-Robert Turgot, "Mémoire sur les municipalités" (1775) in Gustave Schelle, ed., *Oeuvres de Turgot et documents le concernant*, 5 vols. (Paris: Félix Alcan, 1913–1923), IV: 576.

60. Josephine Greider, *Anglomania in France, 1740–1789: Fact, Fiction and Political Discourse* (Geneva: Droz, 1985); Frances Acomb, *Anglophobia in France, 1763–1789: An Essay in the History of Constitutionalism and Nationalism* (Durham, N.C.: Duke University Press, 1950).

61. Keith Baker, "Politics and Public Opinion under the Old Regime" in

Jack Censer and Jeremy Popkin, eds., *Press and Politics in Prerevolutionary France* (Berkeley: University of California Press, 1987), pp. 208–213.

62. Octavie Guichard, *Observations sur la noblesse et le tiers-état* (Amsterdam, 1758), pp. 86–87.

63. Perrot, *Genèse,* I: 298–299.

64. Paul Henri Thiry, baron d'Holbach, *Système social ou principes naturels de la morale et de la politique,* 3 vols. (London, 1773) II: 67–70.

65. Ibid., II: 72–74.

66. Antoine Polier de Saint-Germain, *Du Gouvernement des moeurs* (Lausanne, 1784), p. 58.

67. *Moeurs* is usually translated as either "morals" or "manners," since it can mean either customs in a neutral sense or moral rectitude. In his widely read translation of Rousseau's "Letter to d'Alembert," Allan Bloom opted for the awkward solution of translating the French term as "morals [manners]" (Jean-Jacques Rousseau, *Politics and the Arts: Letter to M. d'Alembert on the Theater,* trans. Allan Bloom [Ithaca: Cornell University Press, 1960]). Some translators use either English term depending on the context, but to my mind this betrays the French meaning, which lies precisely in the overlapping of inner and outer norms of behavior. I have therefore chosen to leave the term in French.

68. For an example of the analysis of such imagery see Maza, *Private Lives,* ch. 2.

69. Gabriel Bonnot de Mably, *Entretiens de Phocion sure le rapport de la morale avec la politique* (Amsterdam, 1763), p. 45.

70. d'Holbach, *Système social,* p. 137.

71. Chisick, *Limits of Reform,* pp. 225–236.

72. D'Holbach, *Système social,* p. 156, and *Éthocratie,* pp. 7, 12–13.

73. Chisick, *Limits of Reform,* pp. 215–225.

74. James Rutlidge, *Essai sur le caractère et les moeurs des françois comparés à celles des anglois* (London, 1776), pp. 182–184. This work was originally published in English as *An Account of the Character and Manners of the French* (London, 1770).

75. David Bell, *The Cult of the Nation in France: Inventing Nationalism, 1680–1800* (Cambridge, Mass.: Harvard University Press, 2001), ch. 2.

76. Polier, *Gouvernement des moeurs,* p. 26, writes that in a society governed by *moeurs,* "Chacun s'y tiendroit naturellement à sa place." See also [Abbé] Jaubert, *Éloge de la roture dédié aux roturiers* (London, 1766), p. 45. Compare with d'Holbach *Éthocratie,* pp. 117–120, and Claude Adrien Helvétius, *De l'Esprit et de l'Homme,* ed. Albert Keim (Paris, 1909), pp. 235–243.

77. The classic statements of this argument are Lawrence Stone, *The Fam-*

*ily, Sex and Marriage in England, 1500–1800* (New York: Harper and Row, 1977), especially Part 4, and Randolph Trumbach, *The Rise of the Egalitarian Family: Aristocratic Kinship and Domestic Relations in Eighteenth-Century England* (New York: Academic Press, 1978). Although no comparably broad-ranging studies exist for France, see Jean-Louis Flandrin, *Familles: parenté, maison, sexualité dans l'ancienne société* (Paris: Hachette, 1976), ch. 3.

78. The classic study of the *drame,* and still the most exhaustive in its documentation is Félix Gaiffe, *Le Drame en France au XVIIIe siècle* (Paris: Armand Colin, 1910). Long ignored as an inferior genre, somewhat embarrassing on account of its sentimental excesses, this type of literature has recently regained popularity among scholars who have examined these plays and more broadly the sentimental style as an important cultural phenomenon. Some of the notable works on the subject include Julie Candler Hayes, *Identity and Ideology: Diderot, Sade and the Serious Genre* (Amsterdam: John Benjamins, 1991); Scott Bryson, *The Chastised Stage: Bourgeois Drama and the Exercise of Power* (Stanford: Anima Libri, 1991); David Denby, *Sentimental Narrative and the Social Order in France* (Cambridge: Cambridge University Press, 1994); William Reddy, "Sentimentalism and Its Erasure: The Role of Emotions in the Era of the French Revolution," *Journal of Modern History* 72 (March 2000): 109–152. For England see especially G. J. Barker-Benfield, *The Culture of Sensibility: Sex and Society in Eighteenth-Century Britain* (Chicago: The University of Chicago Press, 1992).

79. Denis Diderot, *Paradoxe sur le comédien précédé des Entretiens sur le Fils naturel* (Paris: Garnier-Flammarion, 1967). See the discussion of "conditions," pp. 96–97.

80. Mark Ledbury, "Intimate Dramas: Genre Painting and New Theater in Eighteenth-Century France" in Richard Rand, ed., *Intimate Encounters: Love and Domesticity in Eighteenth-Century France* (Princeton: Princeton University Press, 1997), pp. 60–62.

81. Michel Sedaine, "Le Philosophe sans le savoir" in Casimir Zdanowicz, ed., *Four French Comedies of the Eighteenth Century* (New York: Scribner's, 1933), p. 279.

82. Sébastien Mercier, *Théâtre complet,* 4 vols. (Amsterdam, 1778–1784), III: 87.

83. Ibid., III: 114.

84. Pierre Augustin Caron de Beaumarchais, *Théâtre* (Paris: Garnier-Flammarion, 1964), p. 441.

85. Suzanne Pucci, "The Nature of Domestic Intimacy and Sibling Incest in Diderot's *Fils Naturel,*" *Eighteenth-Century Studies* 30 (1997): 279.

86. Denby, *Sentimental Narrative,* pp. 21–47.

87. Diderot, *Paradoxe*, p. 47.
88. Bell, *The Cult of the Nation.*

### 3. REVOLUTIONARY BROTHERHOOD

1. Alfred Cobban, *Aspects of the French Revolution* (New York: George Braziller, 1968), ch. 5; Michael Fitzsimmons, *The Parisian Order of Barristers and the French Revolution* (Cambridge, Mass.: Harvard University Press, 1987); Timothy Tackett, *Becoming a Revolutionary: The Deputies of the French National Assembly and the Emergence of a Revolutionary Culture (1789–1790)* (Princeton: Princeton University Press, 1996) ch. 1.

2. The most important group presiding over the articulation of ideas and publication of pamphlets in support of the political interests of the *tiers état* was the so-called Society of Thirty, a group of liberals which included members of the Paris Parlement, liberal nobles like Lafayette, Condorcet, and Mirabeau, and some prominent commoners such as the lawyer Jean-Baptiste Target. See Daniel Wick, *A Conspiracy of Well-Intentioned Men: The Society of Thirty and the French Revolution* (New York: Garland Press, 1987) and Kenneth Margerison, *Pamphlets and Public Opinion: The Campaign for a Union of Orders in the Early French Revolution* (West Lafayette: Purdue University Press, 1998), esp. ch. 3.

3. This is the case even for recent studies, most notably William H. Sewell, Jr., *A Rhetoric of Bourgeois Revolution: The Abbé Sieyès and "What Is the Third Estate?"* (Durham, N.C.: Duke University Press, 1994).

4. Pierre-Laurent Bérenger, *Les Quatre États de la France* (n.p., 1789), pp. 3–8; Jean Paul Rabaut Saint-Étienne, *Considérations sur les intérêts du Tiers-État adressées au peuple des provinces* (Paris, 1788), pp. 32–33.

5. *Mémoire du tiers-état à présenter au roi* (n.p., 1788), p. 6; *Le Réveil du tiers-état, c'est-à-dire de la Nation* (Paris, 1789), p. 14.

6. Emmanuel Sieyès, *Qu'est-ce que le Tiers-état?* Ed. Roberto Zapperi (Geneva: Droz, 1970), p. 144.

7. Charles de Beauvau, *Avis au Tiers-État* (London, 1788), pp. 19–20; *Lettre des bourgeois aux gens de la campagne* (Angers, 1789), pp. 16–17; *Petit Prosne aux roturiers* (n.p., 1788), pp. 17–21.

8. Jean-Sylvain Bailly, *Mémoires*, 3 vols. (Paris, 1820) I: 11–12.

9. Charles Élie, marquis de Ferrières, *Correspondance inédite* (Paris: Armand Colin, 1932), p. 43.

10. Claude Fauchet, *De la Religion nationale* (Paris, 1789), p. 258.

11. Lynn Hunt, *The Family Romance of the French Revolution* (Berkeley: University of California Press, 1992). On the exclusion of women see also Joan Landes, *Women and the Public Sphere in the Age of the French Revolu-*

*tion* (Ithaca: Cornell University Press, 1988), and Carole Pateman, *The Sexual Contract* (Stanford: Stanford University Press, 1989).

12. Sieyès, *Tiers-état,* pp. 119–122.

13. Rabaut, *Considérations,* pp. 29–30.

14. *Le Dernier Mot du tiers-état à la noblesse de France* (n.p., n.d.), pp. 8–9.

15. Jean-Paul Marat, *Offrande à la patrie ou discours au tiers-état de France* (Paris, 1789), p. 14.

16. Christopher Hodson, "'In Praise of the Third Estate': Religious and Social Imagery in the Early French Revolution," *Eighteenth-Century Studies* 34 (Spring 2001): 337–362.

17. *French Caricature and the French Revolution, 1789–1799* (Los Angeles: University of California Press, 1988). See prints in catalog numbers 27, 28, 30, 31, 33, 34, 36, 40, 41, 42, 43.

18. Beauvau, *Lettre des bourgeois,* pp. 7–8.

19. See ch. 1, n35.

20. Keith Michael Baker, *Inventing the French Revolution: Essays on French Political Culture in the Eighteenth Century* (Cambridge: Cambridge University Press, 1990), ch. 4.

21. Margerison, *Pamphlets and Public Opinion,* p. 46.

22. Ibid., ch. 3.

23. Sewell, *Rhetoric,* chs. 2 and 6.

24. Emmanuel Sieyès, *Essai sur les privilèges,* in *Oeuvres complètes* (Paris: EDHIS, 1989), p. 17.

25. Sieyès, *Tiers-état,* p. 125.

26. Ibid., pp. 127–129.

27. Ibid., pp. 139–140.

28. Sieyès, *Privilèges,* pp. 23–24.

29. Jean Michel Servan, *Avis salutaire au tiers-état* (n.p., 1789), pp. 57–58.

30. Adrien Duquesnoy, *Journal d'Adrien Duquesnoy, député de Bar-le-Duc,* 2 vols. (Paris, 1994), I: 133.

31. Bailly, *Mémoires,* p. 46.

32. Duquesnoy, *Journal,* I: 38, 114–115.

33. Bailly, *Mémoires,* p. 329.

34. Ibid., pp. 328, 371.

35. Adrien-Joseph Colson, *Lettres d'un bourgeois de Paris à un ami de province, 1788–1793* (Saint-Cyr-sur-Loire: Christian Pirot, 1993), pp. 54–59.

36. Duquesnoy, *Journal,* I: 208–209.

37. Ferrières, *Correspondance,* pp. 96–97.

38. Colin Lucas, "The Crowd and Politics," in Colin Lucas, ed., *The Political Culture of the French Revolution* (Oxford: Pergamon Press, 19  ), p. 274.

39. Duquesnoy, *Journal,* I: 217–218.

40. Lucas, "The Crowd," p. 280.

41. Duquesnoy, *Journal,* I: 400–422.

42. Tackett, *Becoming a Revolutionary,* pp. 195–206.

43. Duquesnoy, *Journal,* I: 400–422.

44. Ibid., I: 451.

45. *Réflexions d'un membre du tiers-état à ses confrères* (n.p., January 1789). Evidence internal to the pamphlet suggests that the author may well have been a member of one of the first two estates. On privilege as a form of property, see William H. Sewell, Jr., *Work and Revolution in France: The Language of Labor from the Old Regime to 1848* (Cambridge: Cambridge University Press, 1980), ch. 6.

46. Philippe Buchez and Prosper Roux, *Histoire parlementaire de la révolution française,* 40 vols. (Paris: Paulin, 1834–38), II: 200–204, quote p. 201.

47. William Doyle, *The Oxford History of the French Revolution* (Oxford: Oxford University Press, 1989), pp. 124, 155; William H. Sewell, Jr., "Le Citoyen/La Citoyenne: Activity, Passivity, and the Revolutionary Concept of Citizenship" in Lucas, *Political Culture,* pp. 105–123; Sewell, *A Rhetoric of Bourgeois Revolution,* ch. 5.

48. Jack Censer, *Prelude to Power: The Parisian Radical Press, 1789–1791* (Baltimore: The Johns Hopkins University Press, 1976), pp. 61–64; Buchez and Roux, *Histoire parlementaire,* III: 431.

49. *Archives parlementaires,* VII: 320–321, 323.

50. Duquesnoy, *Journal,* I: 468.

51. *Archives parlementaires,* VII: 323.

52. Ibid., VII: 324.

53. For a discussion of the distinction between privilege as property and Enlightenment notions of property see Sewell, *Work and Revolution,* pp. 120–142.

54. Bailly, *Mémoires,* I: 389–390.

55. Ibid., I: 390.

56. Hans-Jürgen Lüsebrink and Rolf Reichardt, *The Bastille: A History of a Symbol of Despotism and Freedom* (Durham, N.C.: Duke University Press, 1997), p. 51.

57. Louis Gottschalk and Margaret Maddox, *Lafayette in the French Revolution: Through the October Days* (Chicago: University of Chicago Press, 1969), pp. 171–175.

58. The decree of June 12, 1790, limited membership in the Guard to "active citizens," those paying three days' labor in taxes. The final law of 29 September/14 October 1791, the object of a heated debate, reiter-

ated the citizenship criterion and added a residence requirement. See Georges Carrot, *Une Institution de la Nation: la Garde Nationale (1789–1871)* (Sens: CIAPN, 1979), pp. 67–69.

59. Dale Clifford, "The National Guard and the Parisian Community, 1789–1790," *French Historical Studies* 16 (1990): 864–877.

60. Duquesnoy, *Journal*, I: 229.

61. Ferrières, *Correspondance*, p. 120.

62. Clifford, "The National Guard," p. 850.

63. Bailly, *Mémoires*, II: 242.

64. George Rudé, *The Crowd in the French Revolution* (Oxford: Oxford University Press, 1959), p. 65.

65. Dale Clifford, "Can the Uniform Make the Citizen? Paris, 1789–1791," *Eighteenth-Century Studies* 34 (Spring 2001): 363–382.

66. Bailly, *Mémoires*, I: 389–390.

67. Carrot, *Garde Nationale*, vii–ix; Jean-Paul Donnadieu, "'Bourgeois, bourgeoisie': emploi des mots autour des cahiers de doléances des sénéchaussées de Béziers et de Montpellier," in Michel Vovelle, ed., *Bourgeoisies de province et révolution* (Grenoble: Presses Universitaires de Grenoble, 1987), pp. 30–31.

68. Ferrières, *Correspondance*, pp. 87–88.

69. Gabriel Bonnot de Mably, *Observations sur l'histoire de France*, 2 vols. (Geneva, 1765), II: 98–100.

70. Carrot, *Institution*, pp. 2–4; Donnadieu, "'Bourgeois,'" p. 35.

71. Ferrières, *Correspondance*, p. 103.

72. Louis Gottschalk and Margaret Maddox, *Lafayette in the French Revolution: From the October Days Through the Federation* (Chicago: University of Chicago Press, 1973), ch. 18; Marcel David, *Fraternité et Révolution française, 1789–1799* (Paris: Aubier, 1987); Simon Schama, *Citizens: A Chronicle of the French Revolution* (New York: Knopf, 1989), pp. 500–503.

73. Marcel David, *Fraternité*, p. 53.

74. Sewell, *Work and Revolution*, chs. 2 and 3. For discussions of the oath in the culture of the French Revolution, see Emmet Kennedy, *A Cultural History of the French Revolution* (New Haven: Yale University Press, 1989), pp. 314–315, and Jean Starobinski, *1789: Les Emblèmes de la raison* (Paris: Flammarion, 1979), pp. 65–81.

75. Gottschalk and Maddox, *From the October Days*, p. 435.

76. Mona Ozouf, *La Fête révolutionnaire, 1789–1799* (Paris: Gallimard, 1976), p. 65.

77. Ibid., pp. 67–68.

78. Benedict Anderson, *Imagined Communities: Reflections on the Origin and Spread of Nationalism* (London: Verso, 1991), p. 36.

79. Ozouf, *La Fête*, pp. 72–72.

80. Ibid., p. 74.

81. David Andress, "The Denial of Social Conflict in the French Revolution: Discourses around the Champ de Mars Massacre, 17 July 1791," *French Historical Studies* 22 (Spring 1999): 196–199. For a fuller account see David Andress, *Massacre at the Champ de Mars: Popular Dissent and Political Culture in the French Revolution* (Rochester, N.Y.: Boydell Press, 2001).

82. Andress., "The Denial of Social Conflict," pp. 203–209, quote p. 209.

83. Sophie Wahnich, *L'Impossible Citoyen: l'étranger dans le discours de la Révolution française* (Paris: Albin Michel, 1997), p. 64.

84. Duquesnoy, *Journal*, I: 38.

85. Ferrières, *Correspondance*, p. 335.

86. Buchez and Roux, *Histoire parlementaire*, VI: 280–298; *Archives parlementaires*, 16: 374–378.

87. Buchez and Roux, *Histoire parlementaire*, VI: 289.

88. Ferrières, *Correspondance*, p. 211.

89. Ibid., p. 223.

90. Gaston Maugras, ed., *Journal d'un étudiant pendant la révolution (Edmond Géraud, 1789–1793)* (Paris: Plon, 1910), p. 61.

91. Censer, *Prelude to Power*, pp. 48–58; Jacques Guilhaumou, "Aristocrate(s)/Aristocratie, 1789–1793," in Institut National de la Langue Française, *Dictionnaire des usages socio-politiques*, 5 vols. (Paris: Klincksieck, 1985–1991), I: 9–26. For a more general overview of anti-noble sentiment see Henri Carré, *La Noblesse de France et l'opinion publique au XVIIIe siècle* (Paris: Champion, 1920).

92. Carré, *La Noblesse*, p. 443; Maugras, *Journal*, p. 61.

93. Schama, *Citizens*, pp. 492–493.

94. Cited in Guilhaumou, "Aristocrate(s)/Aristocratie," p. 14.

95. Cited in Buchez and Roux, XIII: 177.

96. Françoise Dorigny, "'Honnêtes gens': L'expression dans la presse Girondine, juin-septembre 1792," in *Dictionnaire des usages socio-politiques*, I: 79–87, quote p. 83.

97. Walter Markov and Albert Soboul, eds., *Die Sansculotten von Paris: Dokumente zur Geschichte der Volksbewegung, 1793–1794* (Berlin: Akademie Verlag, 1957), pp. 52, 248.

98. Albert Soboul, *Les Sans-culottes parisiens en l'an II: Mouvement populaire et gouvernment révolutionnaire, 2 juin 1793–9 thermidor an II* (Paris: Clavreuil, 1958), ch. 1.

99. Ibid., pp. 420–421.

100. Markov and Soboul, *Die Sansculotten*, p. 222.

101. See for instance Maximilien de Robespierre, *Oeuvres*, 3 vols. (ed. Laponneraye; New York: Burke Franklin, 1970), I: 230–240, 283, 326–327, 426–427; II: 23, 138, 303.

102. On England see Dror Wahrman, *Inventing the Middle Class: The Political Representation of Class in Britain, c. 1780–1840* (Cambridge: Cambridge University Press, 1995), esp. chs. 9 and 10.

103. François Furet, *Penser la Révolution française* (Paris: Gallimard, 1978), pp. 75–76.

## 4. THE SOCIAL WORLD AFTER THERMIDOR

1. Alfred Cobban, *The Social Interpretation of the French Revolution* (Cambridge: Cambridge University Press, 1964). Cobban's initial challenge actually predates the publication of this book, since he first questioned the orthodox paradigm in a lecture, "The Myth of the French Revolution," delivered in 1955, and later reprinted in his *Aspects of the French Revolution* (New York: George Braziller, 1970), pp. 90–111.

2. George Taylor, "Noncapitalist Wealth and the Origins of the French Revolution," *American Historical Review* 52 (January 1967): 491. For a good overview of the contributions of the "first wave" of British and American revisionism, including the work of scholars like Taylor, Colin Lucas, William Doyle, Elizabeth Eisenstein, Betty Behrens, Robert Darnton, and David Bien, see William Doyle, *Origins of the French Revolution*, 2nd ed. (Oxford: Oxford University Press, 1988), pp. 7–40.

3. The most notable British and French versions of this argument are presented in Colin Lucas, "Nobles, Bourgeois, and the Origins of the French Revolution," *Past and Present* 60 (August 1973): 84–126, and Guy Chaussinand-Nogaret, *La Noblesse au XVIIIe siècle: de la féodalité aux lumières* (Paris: Hachette, 1976).

4. Lucas, "Nobles, Bourgeois, and the Origins of the French Revolution."

5. Ibid., p. 126.

6. For fuller discussions of the turn to political culture see Jack Censer, "The Coming of a New Interpretation of the French Revolution," *Journal of Social History* 21 (1987): 295–309, and "Social Twists and Linguistic Turns: Revolutionary Historiography a Decade After the Bicentennial," *French Historical Studies* 22 (1999): 139–167; Sarah Maza, "Politics, Culture, and the Origins of the French Revolution," *Journal of Modern History* 61 (1989): 703–723. Notable works in the "political culture" vein besides those of Furet and Hunt discussed below include Keith Baker, François Furet, and Colin Lucas, eds., *The French Revolution and the Creation of Modern Political Culture*, 4 vols. (Oxford:

Pergamon Press, 1987–1994) and Keith Baker, *Inventing the French Revolution: Essays on French Political Culture in the Eighteenth Century* (Cambridge: Cambridge University Press, 1990). In France, the trend was manifest in the works of colleagues and disciples of Furet's such as Ran Halévi and Patrice Gueniffey. For a sampling of the French work in this vein see François Furet and Mona Ozouf, eds., *A Critical Dictionary of the French Revolution,* trans. Arthur Goldhammer (Cambridge: Harvard University Press, 1989).

7. François Furet, *Penser la Révolution française* (Paris: Gallimard, 1978), p. 41.

8. Lynn Hunt, *Politics, Culture and Class in the French Revolution* (Berkeley: University of California Press, 1984).

9. Gary Kates characterizes these historians as Neo-Liberal, a label I find problematic because Furet and his followers in France were known as *libéraux* owing to their interest in Anglo-American ideas and suspicion of French statism. Kates avoids the term Neo-Marxist because it evokes the more conventional leftism of latter-day Marxists like George Comninel and Eric Hobsbawm. Perhaps a better term for the likes of Colin Jones and William Sewell would be "New Left." See Gary Kates, ed., *The French Revolution: Recent Debates and New Controversies* (London and New York: Routledge, 1998), pp. 11–12.

10. Colin Jones, "Bourgeois Revolution Revivified: 1789 and Social Change," in Colin Lucas, ed., *Rewriting the French Revolution* (Oxford: Clarendon Press, 1991), pp. 69–118; and "The Great Chain of Buying: Medical Advertisement, the Bourgeois Public Sphere, and the Origins of the French Revolution," *American Historical Review* 101 (February 1996): 13–40.

11. William H. Sewell, Jr. *A Rhetoric of Bourgeois Revolution: The Abbé Sieyès and What Is the Third Estate?* (Durham, N.C.: Duke University Press, 1994), p. 39.

12. Ibid., p. 186.

13. Timothy Tackett, *Becoming a Revolutionary: The Deputies of the French National Assembly and the Emergence of a Revolutionary Culture (1789–1790)* (Princeton: Princeton University Press, 1996).

14. Ibid., p. 311.

15. Peter McPhee, *A Social History of France, 1780–1880* (London: Routledge, 1992), ch. 5. Richard Roehl, "French Industrialization: A Reconsideration," *Explorations in Economic History* 13 (1976): 244; Don Leet and John Shaw, "French Economic Stagnation, 1700–1960: Old Economic History Revisited," *Journal of Interdisciplinary History* 8 (1978): 538–539.

16. Hunt, *Politics, Culture and Class*, ch. 5. For a more detailed account see Isser Woloch, *The New Regime: Transformations of the French Civic Order, 1789–1820s* (New York: W. W. Norton, 1994), chs. 1–5.

17. David Garrioch, *The Formation of the Parisian Bourgeoisie, 1690–1830* (Cambridge, Mass.: Harvard University Press, 1996), p. 288.

18. Hunt, *Politics, Culture and Class*, pp. 176–178.

19. Such is the title of the volume on this period in one of the most popular multivolume histories of France: Denis Woronoff, *La République bourgeoise: de Thermidor à Brumaire, 1794–1799* (Paris: Éditions du Seuil, 1972).

20. Lynn Hunt, David Lansky, and Paul Hanson, "The Failure of the Liberal Republic in France, 1795–1799: The Road to Brumaire," *Journal of Modern History* 51 (December 1979): 742–743.

21. Quoted in William Doyle, *The Oxford History of the French Revolution* (Oxford: Clarendon Press, 1989), p. 318.

22. *Le Tribun du Peuple*, 26/1–19 (Nivôse year III), in Maurice Dommanget, ed., *Pages choisies de Babeuf* (Paris: Armand Colin, 1935), p. 192.

23. Dommanget, *Pages choisies*, p. 172.

24. Patrice Higonnet, *Class, Ideology and the Rights of Nobles During the French Revolution* (Oxford: Clarendon Press, 1981), p. 168.

25. Dommanget, *Pages choisies*, p. 236.

26. The following discussion draws on Bronislaw Baczko's illuminating work on the theme of vandalism in his *Comment sortir de la terreur: Thermidor et la révolution* (Paris: Gallimard, 1989), and his article "Vandalism" in Furet and Ozouf, eds., *Critical Dictionary*, pp. 860–868.

27. Baczko, "Vandalism," p. 861.

28. Baczko, *Comment sortir*, p. 293.

29. Ibid., pp. 266–270.

30. Ibid., p. 300.

31. Ibid., p. 303.

32. Higonnet, *Class, Ideology*, pp. 234–238.

33. Ibid., pp. 239–242, quote p. 242.

34. Ibid., p. 241.

35. Ibid., pp. 234–235.

36. Baczko, *Comment sortir*, p. 159–160.

37. Ibid., p. 159.

38. The most explicit discussion of bourgeois universalism is the one running through Higonnet, *Class, Ideology*. In Higonnet's view, the revolutionary bourgeois leaders found themselves caught in a contradiction between their individualistic pursuit of property and their

commitment to the universalist language of classical humanism; their persecution of nobles, which was illogical given how many objective interests the two groups shared, was a by-product of the need for the revolutionary leadership to advertise their commitment to the common good embodied by "the people." The assumption that the revolutionary leaders were pursuing their class interests without explicitly saying so permeates in less explicit fashion a great deal of the literature on the French Revolution. For a useful overview of the origins and implications of the concept of universalism, see Terry Eagleton, *Ideology* (London: Verso, 1991), ch. 2. For a discussion of the Marxian origins of this view of the Revolution see François Furet, *Marx et la Révolution française* (Paris: Flammarion 1986), pp. 48–53.

39. Hunt, *Politics, Culture and Class,* pp. 21–24.

40. Hunt, Hanson, and Lansky, "The Failure of the Liberal Republic," makes this point with respect to competing political parties, but given the overlap between the social and the political it is also true, I think, of social interests.

41. Giddens defines class awareness as "a common awareness and acceptance of similar attitudes and beliefs, linked to a common style of life." Class awareness, he continues, "does *not* involve a recognition that these attitudes and beliefs signify a particular class affiliation or the recognition that there exist other classes characterized by different attitudes, beliefs, and styles of life; 'class consciousness' by contrast . . . does imply both of these." Anthony Giddens, *The Class Structure of the Advanced Societies* (London: Hutchinson, 1980), p. 111.

42. Suzanne Desan, "Reconstituting the Social After the Terror: Family, Property and the Law in Popular Politics," *Past and Present* 164 (August 1999): 81–121.

43. Ibid., p. 111.

44. Ibid., p. 120.

45. Emanuel Chill, ed., *Power, Property and History: Barnave's Introduction to the French Revolution and Other Writings* (New York: Harper and Row, 1971), pp. 4–16.

46. Antoine Barnave, *De la révolution et de la constitution,* ed. Patrice Gueniffey (Grenoble: Presses Universitaires de Grenoble, 1988), p. 52.

47. Ibid., p. 61.

48. Ibid., p. 52.

49. Ibid., p. 72.

50. Ibid., pp. 71–72.

51. On Staël and the Revolution, see G. E. Gwynne, *Madame de Staël et la révolution française* (Paris: Nizet, 1969); For biographical details see J.

Christopher Herold, *Mistress to an Age: A Life of Madame de Staël* (Indianapolis: Bobbs-Merrill, 1958); Wayne Andrews, *Germaine: A Portrait of Madame de Staël* (New York: Atheneum, 1963); Madelyn Gutwirth, *Madame de Staël, Novelist: The Emergence of the Artist as Woman* (Urbana:University of Illinois Press, 1978); Ghislain de Diesbach, *Madame de Staël* (Paris: Perrin, 1983).

52. Marcel Gauchet, "Staël," in Furet and Ozouf, eds., *Critical Dictionary*, pp. 1003–1010.

53. Germaine de Staël, *Des circonstances actuelles qui peuvent terminer la révolution et des principes qui doivent fonder la république en France*, ed. Lucia Omacini (Geneva: Droz, 1979), p. 19.

54. Ibid., pp. 22–23.

55. Marcel Gauchet, "Constant," in Furet and Ozouf, eds., *Critical Dictionary*, p. 97. See Staël, *Circonstances actuelles*, p. 927.

56. Staël, *Circonstances actuelles*, pp. 183, 10.

57. Ibid., p. 166.

58. Ibid., pp. 188–189.

59. See for instance Benjamin Constant, *De la liberté chez les modernes* (Paris: Livre de Poche, 1980), pp. 315–319.

60. For an argument along these lines which stresses the attachment of figures like Staël and Constant to principles of aristocracy, see George Kelly, "Liberalism and Aristocracy in the French Restoration," *Journal of the History of Ideas* 26 (1965): 509–530.

61. The classic argument for the rule of the *grands notables* is André-Jean Tudesq, *Les Grands Notables en France (1840–1849): Étude historique d'une psychologie sociale*, 2 vols. (Paris: Presses Universitaires de France, 1964). Although Tudesq initially applied the concept only to the later years of the July Monarchy, it was extended to designate the ruling classes of the entire 1815–1848 period, as reflected in the titles of two volumes authored by Tudesq and André Jardin in a popular multivolume history of France: *La France des notables*, 2 vols. (Paris: Le Seuil, 1973).

62. Madame de Staël, *Considérations sur la Révolution française*, ed. Jacques Godechot (Paris: Tallandier, 1983), p. 63.

63. Ibid., pp. 83, 132, 192.

64. See, for instance, her description of the mob that invaded the Tuileries Palace on June 20, 1793, ibid., p. 273: "Their physiognomies were marked by the sort of physical and moral crudeness which causes unbearable disgust, however much of a philanthropist one might be . . . their terrible curses mixed with shouts, their menacing gestures and murderous weapons offered the most terrifying spectacle . . ." For

other instances see pp. 162 and 211 on July 14, 1789, and the 1789 October Days.

65. Staël, *Circonstances actuelles,* p. 36. She refers to this group, however, to condemn it because it "armed against the nobles the lowest ranks of society," thereby unleashing hideously vindictive violence (p. 37).

66. Emmet Kennedy, *A Philosophe in the Age of Revolution: Destutt de Tracy and the Origins of Ideology* (Philadelphia: American Philosophical Society, 1978).

67. [Antoine Destutt de Tracy], *A Commentary and Review of Montesquieu's Spirit of the Laws* (Philadelphia, 1811), p. 12. Destutt's text was originally published in English, in this edition.

68. Kennedy, *Destutt,* ch. 5.

69. [Destutt], *Commentary,* p. 18.

70. Marc Régaldo, "Lumières, élite, démocratie: La difficile position des idéologues," *Dix-huitième siècle* 6 (1974): 201–204, quote p. 203.

71. Staël, *Circonstances actuelles,* p. 184.

72. Régaldo, "Lumières, élite," pp. 203–204.

73. Clive Church, *Revolution and Red Tape: The French Ministerial Bureaucracy, 1770–1850* (Oxford: Clarendon Press, 1981), chs. 1 and 2.

74. Ibid., chs. 3–4.

75. Alexis de Tocqueville, *The Old Regime and the French Revolution,* trans Stuart Gilbert (New York: Doubleday, 1955), p. 209.

76. J. F. Bosher, *French Finances, 1770–1795: From Business to Bureaucracy* (Cambridge: Cambridge University Press, 1970).

77. Ibid., p. 311.

78. Ibid., p. 313.

79. Church, *Revolution and Red Tape,* ch. 8.

80. Rafe Blaufarb, "The *Ancien Régime* Origins of Napoleonic Social Reconstruction," *French History* 14 (2000): 408–423.

81. Ibid., pp. 415–416.

82. Ibid., pp. 418–419.

83. Ibid., pp. 420–422.

84. See David Bien, "La Réaction aristocratique avant 1789: l'exemple de l'armée," *Annales: économies, sociétés, civilisations* 29 (1974): 23–48, 505–534, and Jay Smith, *The Culture of Merit: Nobility, Royal Service, and the Making of Absolute Monarchy in France, 1600–1789* (Ann Arbor: University of Michigan Press, 1996).

85. Charles Taylor, *Hegel* (Cambridge: Cambridge University Press, 1975), pp. 185–188, 403–410. Karl Marx, *Critique of Hegel's Philosophy of Right,* Annette Johns and Joseph O'Malley, eds. (Cambridge: Cambridge

University Press, 1970); Shlomo Avineri, *Hegel's Theory of the Modern State* (Cambridge: Cambridge University Press, 1972), chs. 5 and 8.

## 5. THE POLITICAL BIRTH OF THE BOURGEOISIE

1. Peter McPhee, *A Social History of France, 1780–1880* (London: Routledge, 1993), pp. 131–133; William H. Sewell, Jr., *Work and Revolution in France: The Language of Labor from the Old Regime to 1848* (Cambridge: Cambridge University Press, 1980), pp. 146–153.
2. Dror Wahrman, *Imagining the Middle Class: The Political Representation of Class in Britain, c. 1780–1840* (Cambridge: Cambridge University Press, 1995), pp. 6–7.
3. The liveliest account of Saint-Simon's life, including a good account of his thought, remains Frank Manuel, *The New World of Henri Saint-Simon* (Cambridge, Mass: Harvard University Press, 1956).
4. Ibid., pp. 246–248.
5. Claude Henri de Saint-Simon, *L'Organisateur,* in *Oeuvres,* 6 vols. (Paris: Anthropos, 1966), II: 79–86.
6. Ibid., II: 86–87.
7. Ibid., II: 88.
8. Ibid., II: 82.
9. Ibid., II: 131.
10. Ibid., II: 20, 148, 149, 208, 209.
11. Ibid., II:20–21.
12. Saint-Simon, *L'Industrie* in *Oeuvres* II: 120–123, 161–164. Shirley Gruner, "The Revolution of July 1830 and the Expression 'Bourgeoisie,'" *The Historical Journal* 11 (1968): 463–464; Manuel, *Saint-Simon,* pp. 266–270.
13. Marie-France Piguet, *Classe: Histoire du mot et genèse du concept* (Lyon: Presses Universitaires de Lyon, 1996), pp. 134–136.
14. Manuel, *Saint-Simon,* chap. 22.
15. Ibid., p. 192.
16. Gruner, "The Revolution of July," 465.
17. The standard account of this period, still lively and informative, is Guillaume de Bertier de Sauvigny, *The Bourbon Restoration,* trans. Lynn M. Case (Philadephia: University of Pennsylvania Press, 1966). For a more concise up-to-date analytical treatment, see François Furet, *Revolutionary France, 1770–1880,* trans. Antonia Nevill (London: Blackwell, 1993), ch. 6. For a stimulating recent account of the political culture of the regime see Sheryl Kroen, *Politics and Theater: The Crisis of Legiti-*

*macy in Restoration France, 1815–1830* (Berkeley: University of California Press, 2000).

18. *Archives parlementaires de 1787 à 1860,* 127 vols. (Paris: P. Dupont, 1862–1913), 17: 721, 711.

19. Ibid., 18: 61–62.

20. Ibid., 18: 699–700.

21. Ibid., 18: 14–15. These arguments were voiced by a conservative deputy named Richard.

22. See, for instance, ibid., 17: 700, 721–723.

23. Ibid., 18: 14.

24. Ibid., 18: 9, 21.

25. Ibid., 17: 698, 703.

26. Ibid., 18: 21.

27. Furet, *Revolutionary France,* p. 294.

28. Bertier de Sauvigny, *Bourbon Restoration,* pp. 170–171.

29. Alan Spitzer, "Restoration Political Theory and the Debate over the Law of the Double Vote," *Journal of Modern History* (March 1983): 54–70.

30. *Archives parlementaires,* 27: 665.

31. Ibid., 28: 119–120.

32. Ibid., 27: 666.

33. Prosper de Barante, *La Vie Politique de M. Royer-Collard, ses discours et ses écrits,* 2 vols. (Paris: Didier, 1863), I: 290.

34. Ibid., I: 456.

35. Ibid., II: 30. See also *Archives parlementaires,* 27: 658.

36. Barante, *Royer-Collard,* II: 17, 30–31.

37. Ibid., II: 19–20.

38. Ibid., II: 17.

39. Ibid., II: 16–17.

40. *Archives parlementaires,* 27: 745.

41. Ibid., 27: 667. The *mainmorte* was a notorious feudal restriction on the property of serfs which made it impossible to bequeath land to any but one coresident dependent.

42. Ibid.

43. Barante, *Royer-Collard,* II: 22–23.

44. Ibid., II: 33.

45. Ibid.

46. Ibid., II: 37.

47. Ibid.

48. Ibid., II: 37–38.

49. For a stimulating comparative study of Guizot's concept of the middle

ground, see Vincent Starzinger, *Middlingness: Juste-Millieu Political Theory in France and England, 1815–1848* (Charlottesville: University Press of Virginia, 1965), ch. 3.

50. François Guizot, *Des Moyens de gouvernment et d'opposition dans l'état actuel de la France* (Paris: Ladvocat, 1821), pp. 216–218.

51. Ibid., p. 218.

52. Ibid., pp. 157, 171.

53. Ibid., p. 175.

54. Ibid., p. 166–168.

55. Ibid., pp. 2, 7, 56, 131.

56. Pierre Rosanvallon, *Le Moment Guizot* (Paris: Gallimard, 1985), chs. 1–5, quote p. 76.

57. Ibid., ch. 5.

58. Beth S. Wright, *Painting and History during the French Restoration: Abandoned by the Past* (Cambridge: Cambridge University Press, 1997), chs. 4 and 5.

59. Martyn Lyons, *Le Triomphe du livre: une histoire sociologique de la lecture dans la France du XIXe siècle* (Paris: Promodis, 1987), chs. 5 and 7. Bertier de Sauvigny, *The Bourbon Restoration*, pp. 338–342. James Allen, *Popular French Romanticism* (Syracuse: Syracuse University Press, 1981), pp. 40–51, 127–150.

60. Piguet, *Classe*, pp. 147–150; Shirley Gruner, "Political Historiography in Restoration France," *History and Theory* 8 (1969): 347–349.

61. Quoted in Piguet, *Classe*, p. 149.

62. Gruner, "Political Historiography," p. 349.

63. Stanley Mellon, *The Political Uses of History: A Study of Historians in the French Restoration* (Stanford: Stanford University Press, 1958), p. 72.

64. Cited in Rulon Nephi Smithson, *Augustin Thierry: Social and Political Consciousness in the Evolution of a Historical Method* (Geneva: Droz, 1972), p. 54.

65. Ibid., pp. 60, 72.

66. Augustin Thierry, *Lettres sur l'histoire de France* (Paris: Furne, 1851), pp. 179–180, 183–184.

67. Ibid., pp. 215–230.

68. Ibid., p. 230.

69. Ibid., p. 13.

70. Ibid., pp. 179–185.

71. Gruner, "Political Historiography," pp. 351–355.

72. François Guizot, *Histoire de la civilisation en France*, 4 vols. (Paris: Didier, 1879), IV: 78.

73. Ibid., IV: 78–79.

74. François Guizot, *Histoire de la civilisation en Europe depuis la chute de l'empire romain* (Paris: Didier, 1875), pp. 217–218, quote p. 218.

75. Ibid.

76. Gruner, "Political Historiography," p. 361.

77. Guizot, *Civilisation en France,* pp. 89–90.

78. Gruner, "Political Historiography," pp. 359–361. Rosanvallon, *Moment Guizot,* pp. 267–270.

79. Rosanvallon, *Moment Guizot,* p. 185.

80. Piguet, *Classe,* ch. 6.

81. Ibid., p. 159. For a general account see Jacques Barzun, *The French Race* (New York: Columbia University Press, 1932).

82. Ibid., pp. 160–163, 167–171.

83. Guizot, *Civilisation en Europe,* p. 208.

84. Wahrman, *Imagining the Middle Class,* passim.

85. David Garrioch, *The Formation of the Parisian Bourgeoisie, 1690–1830* (Cambridge, Mass.: Harvard University Press, 1996).

86. Ibid., chs. 6 and 9.

87. Ibid., p. 244.

88. Ibid., ch. 10.

89. Ibid., p. 288.

90. M. Baignoux, *Histoire philosophique de la réformation de l'état social en France* (Paris: Fournier, 1829).

91. Charles Comte, *Histoire de la Garde Nationale de Paris* (Paris: Sautelet, 1827), p. 2.

92. Ibid., pp. 158, 219.

93. Ibid., pp. 246–247.

94. Ibid., p. 401.

95. Ibid., p. 520.

96. Furet, *Revolutionary France,* p. 344.

## 6. THE FAILURE OF BOURGEOIS MONARCHY

1. David Pinkney, *The French Revolution of 1830* (Princeton: Princeton University Press, 1972), chs. 3–5; Pamela Pilbeam, *The 1830 Revolution* (New York: St. Martin's Press, 1991), chs. 4–5.

2. François Furet, *Revolutionary France, 1770–1880,* trans. Antonia Nevill (Oxford: Blackwell, 1992), pp. 333–334. Peter McPhee, *A Social History of France, 1780–1880* (London: Routledge, 1992), pp. 118–120. Furet does note that while national elections remained socially restrictive, voting rights were more substantial on the municipal and departmental levels, where the right to elect members of commune and department councils was extended to around one million male citizens.

3. McPhee, *Social History,* p. 119.

4. In the 1970s, economic historians began to make the case that France's pattern of economic development in the nineteenth century should not be measured by the British yardstick or viewed as a failure. France's slower pace of growth and the enduring dominance of cottage industry and the agrarian sector represented, rather, an appropriate response to geographical and demographic givens. France's transition to economic modernity may in fact have been preferable to Britain's in human terms, since it bypassed some of the social and cultural disruptions that accompany more rapid forms of industrialization. The most comprehensive version of this argument is Patrick O'Brian and Caglar Keydar, *Economic Growth in France and Britain: Two Paths to the Twentieth Century* (London: Allen and Unwin, 1978). See also Richard Roehl, "French Industrialization: A Reconsideration," *Explorations in Economic History* 13 (1976): 233–281; Don Leet and John Shaw, "French Economic Stagnation, 1700–1960: Old Economic History Revised," *Journal of Interdisciplinary History* 8 (1978): 531–544; Rondo Cameron and Charles E. Freedman, "French Economic Growth: A Radical Revision," *Social Science History* 7 (Winter 1983): 3–30; Robert Aldrich, "Late-Comer or Early Starter? New Views on French Economic History," *Journal of European Economic History* 16 (1987): 89–100.

5. Richard Price, *A Social History of Nineteenth-Century France* (London: Holmes and Meier, 1987), pp. 3–44.

6. Christophe Charle, *Histoire sociale de la France au XIXe siècle* (Paris: Le Seuil, 1991), pp. 34–38.

7. Price, *Social History,* pp. 39–40.

8. Ibid., p. 44.

9. Adeline Daumard, *La Bourgeoisie parisienne de 1815 à 1848* (Paris: S.E.V.P.E.N., 1963), pp. 15–21.

10. Adeline Daumard, *Les Bourgeois et la bourgeoisie en France depuis 1815* (Paris: Aubier, 1987), pp. 85–93.

11. Pilbeam, *The 1830 Revolution,* ch. 7.

12. Ibid., pp. 130–131.

13. Ibid., pp. 132–135.

14. Ibid., p. 135.

15. Vincent Starzinger, *Middlingness: Juste-Milieu Political Theory in France and England, 1815–1848* (Charlottesville: University Press of Virginia, 1965), p. 79.

16. Edouard Alletz, *De la démocratie nouvelle ou des moeurs et de la puissance des classes moyennes en France,* 2 vols. (Paris: F. Lequin, 1837), I: vii.

17. Ibid., I: 39–41.

18. Ibid., I: 268–269.

19. Ibid., I: 43.

20. Ibid., I: 5–7, 37–38.

21. Ibid., I: 267–268.

22. Ibid., II: 33.

23. Starzinger, *Middlingness,* pp. 16–17, 144–147.

24. Ibid., pp. 21–24, 70–80, 85–95.

25. On this point see also Pierre Rosanvallon, *Le Moment Guizot* (Paris: Gallimard, 1985), pp. 265–270.

26. Starzinger, *Middlingness,* p. 79.

27. Louis Véron, *Mémoires d'un bourgeois de Paris,* 6 vols. (Paris: Gabriel de Genet, 1853), IV: 42.

28. Roland Barthes, *Mythologies* (Paris: Le Seuil, 1957), see esp. pp. 215–217.

29. Starzinger, *Middlingness,* pp. 101–118.

30. Furet, *Revolutionary France,* p. 343.

31. Cited in Marie-France Piguet, *Classe: Histoire du mot et genèse du concept* (Lyon: Presses Universitaires de Lyon, 1996), p. 169.

32. H.A.C. Collingham, *The July Monarchy: A Political History of France, 1830–1848* (London: Longman, 1988), esp. chs. 9, 11, 26, 27; Christopher H. Johnson, *Utopian Communism in France: Cabet and the Icarians, 1839–1851* (Ithaca: Cornell University Press, 1974); Edward Berenson, *Populist Religion and Leftwing Politics in France, 1830–1852* (Princeton: Princeton University Press, 1984).

33. Shirley Gruner, "The Revolution of July 1830 and the Expression 'Bourgeoisie,'" *The Historical Journal* 11 (1968): 466–471.

34. Ibid., p. 469.

35. McPhee, *Social History,* pp. 137–140.

36. Cited in William H. Sewell, *Work and Revolution in France: The Language of Labor from the Old Regime to 1848* (Cambridge: Cambridge University Press, 1980), p. 198. For the French text and further discussion see William H. Sewell, "La Confraternité des prolétaires: conscience de classe sous la Monarchie de Juillet," *Annales: Économies, sociétés, civilisations* 36 (1981): 650–671.

37. Ibid., pp. 656–657.

38. Johnson, *Utopian Communism,* p. 32.

39. Sewell, *Work and Revolution,* p. 215.

40. Sewell, "La confraternité," pp. 659–660.

41. Sewell, *Work and Revolution,* chs. 8–9.

42. Ibid., chs. 11–12, quote p. 283.

43. Berenson, *Populist Religion,* p. 38.

44. Frank Manuel, *The Prophets of Paris* (Cambridge, Mass.: Harvard University Press, 1962), pp. 158–162. Paul Bénichou, *Le Temps des prophètes: Doctrines de l'âge romantique* (Paris: Gallimard, 1977), pp. 279–281.

45. Manuel, *Prophets of Paris,* pp. 138–193.

46. Ibid., p. 177.

47. Bénichou, *Temps des prophètes,* p. 309.

48. Berenson, *Populist Religion,* chs. 2 and 4.

49. Ibid., p. 53.

50. Lionel Gossman, *Between History and Literature* (Cambridge, Mass.: Harvard University Press, 1990), ch. 5.

51. Jules Michelet, *Le Peuple* (Paris: Flammarion, 1974), p. 132.

52. Ibid.

53. Ibid., pp. 133–134, quote p. 134.

54. Ibid., p. 134.

55. Ibid., p. 137.

56. Ibid., p. 132.

57. Ibid., pp. 163–164.

58. Ibid., pp. 210–211.

59. Gossman, *History and Literature,* pp. 180–181.

60. Ibid., pp. 180–185.

61. Sewell, *Work and Revolution,* p. 283.

62. César Graña, *Bohemian versus Bourgeois: French Society and the French Man of Letters in the Nineteenth Century* (New York: Basic Books, 1964), p. 111.

63. Albert Maurin, *Histoire de la chute des Bourbons,* 6 vols. (Paris, 1849–52), IV: 86.

64. Michelet, *Le Peuple,* p. 133.

65. Maurin, *Histoire de la chute des Bourbons,* IV: 86.

66. David Pinkney, *The French Revolution of 1830* (Princeton: Princeton University Press, 1972), p. 276. See also Charle, *Histoire sociale,* pp. 42–47; Clive Church, *The French Ministerial Bureaucracy, 1770–1850* (Oxford: Clarendon Press, 1981), chs. 9–10.

67. Pilbeam. *The 1830 Revolution,* pp. 135–139.

68. Ibid., pp. 140–141.

69. Pinkney, *French Revolution,* pp. 292–293.

70. Ibid., pp. 291–295. William Reddy, *The Invisible Code: Honor and Sentiment in Postrevolutionary France* (Berkeley: University of California Press, 1997), pp. 172–183.

71. Jerrold Seigel, *Bohemian Paris: Culture, Politics, and the Boundaries of Bourgeois Life, 1830–1930* (New York: Penguin, 1987), chs. 1 and 2. (Henry Murger, spelled this way in French, is often also spelled Henri.)

72. Ibid., p. 6.

73. Ibid., p. 13.

74. Martyn Lyons, *Le Triomphe du livre: une histoire sociologique de la lecture dans la France du XIXe siècle* (Paris: Promodis, 1987), pp. 12–13; James Allen, *Popular French Romanticism* (Syracuse, N.Y.: Syracuse University Press, 1981), p. 127; Graña, *Bohemian versus Bourgeois*, p. 127.

75. Lyons, *Triomphe du livre*, pp. 48–52.

76. Ibid., ch. 2, passim.

77. Graña, *Bohemian versus Bourgeois*, pp. 37–42.

78. Ibid., pp. 35–42.

79. For a fuller version of the argument presented in the next section, see Sarah Maza, "Uniforms: The Social Imaginary in Balzac's *La Cousine Bette*," *French Politics, Culture, and Society* 19 (2001): 21–42.

80. Honoré de Balzac, *La Cousine Bette* (Paris: Gallimard, 1972), p. 31. All translations of the novel's text are my own.

81. Ibid., p. 38.

82. Emmanuel Failletaz, *Balzac et le monde des affaires* (Lausanne: Payot, 1932), ch. 1; Ronnie Butler, *Balzac and the French Revolution* (London: Croom Helm, 1983), chs. 6–9. For a more general guide to Balzac's characters, see Anthony Pugh, *Balzac's Recurring Characters* (Toronto: University of Toronto Press, 1974).

83. Balzac, *Cousine Bette*, p. 38.

84. Ibid., pp. 224–227, 326.

85. Ibid., p. 325.

86. Ibid., p. 366.

87. Ibid., p. 143.

88. Graña, *Bohemian versus Bourgeois*, pp. 104–105.

89. Balzac, *Cousine Bette*, pp. 84–86.

90. Ibid., p. 385.

91. See for instance Peter Brooks, *Reading for the Plot: Design and Intention in Narrative* (New York: Knopf, 1984), ch. 6. The connection between nineteenth-century obsessions with prostitution and the wider rise of commercialism is implicit in two recent treatments of the theme which are more psychoanalytically than sociologically oriented: Charles Bernheimer, *Figures of Ill Repute: Representing Prostitution in Nineteenth-Century France* (1989; rpt. Durham: Duke University Press, 1997), ch. 2, and Jann Matlock, *Scenes of Seduction: Prostitution, Hysteria and Reading Difference in Nineteenth-Century France* (New York: Columbia University Press, 1994), chs. 2, 3, 5.

92. Balzac, *Cousine Bette*, p. 194.

93. Ibid., pp. 74–75.

94. Ibid., p. 346.

95. Ibid., p. 163.

96. Ibid., p. 347.

97. Ibid., pp. 356, 80.

98. Ibid., p. 352.

99. Ibid., ch. 89.

100. Graña, *Bohemian versus Bourgeois,* pp. 164–165.

101. Georg Lukács, *Studies in European Realism: A Sociological Survey of the Writings of Balzac, Stendhal, Zola, Tolstoy, Gorki* (London: Hillway Publishing, 1950), ch. 1. Lukács convincingly diagnoses Balzac's obsessive denunciation of his society's growing materialism and of "the bourgeoisie," but it is a lot more debatable that Balzac "mourns the decline of the French aristocracy" (p. 39). For a corrective to the latter view, see Camille Laparra, "L'Aristocratie dans *La Comédie humaine* de Balzac," *The French Review* 68 (March 1995): 602–614. For a restatement of the conventional view in an otherwise brilliantly insightful article see Fredric Jameson, "*La Cousine Bette* and Allegorical Realism," *Publications of the Modern Language Association of America* 86 (1971): 253.

102. The classic, and most exhaustive study is Bernard Guyon, *La Pensée politique et sociale de Balzac* (Paris: Armand Colin, 1967), which unfortunately takes the writer only into the mid-1830s; see esp. ch. 6. On Balzac's obsession with Napoleon, see Saint-Paulien [Maurice Sicard], *Napoléon, Balzac et l'empire de la Comédie humaine* (Paris: Albin Michel, 1979).

103. Historians sometimes argue, however, that aristocratic social dominance in Europe did not really come to an end until the early twentieth century. See Arno Mayer, *The Persistence of the Old Regime: Europe to the Great War* (New York: Pantheon Books, 1981).

104. Jo Burr Margadant, "Gender, Vice, and the Political Imaginary in Nineteenth-Century France: Reinterpreting the Failure of the July Monarchy, 1830–1848," *American Historical Review* 104 (December 1999): 1461–1496.

105. Furet, *Revolutionary France,* p. 344.

106. Bernhard Groethuysen, *Origines de l'esprit bourgeois en France* (Paris: Gallimard, 1927), 167–177.

107. Pierre Rosanvallon, *La Monarchie impossible: les Chartes de 1814 et 1830* (Paris: Fayard, 1994).

## CONCLUSION

1. Béatrix Le Wita, *French Bourgeois Culture,* trans. J. A. Underwood (Cambridge: Cambridge University Press, 1994).

2. See Vincent Starzinger, *Middlingness: Juste-Milieu Political Theory in France and England, 1815–1848* (Charlottesville: University Press of Virginia, 1965).

3. Charles Taylor, *Hegel* (Cambridge: Cambridge University Press, 1975), chs. 15–16. Karl Marx, *Critique of Hegel's Philosophy of Right*, trans. Annette Jolin and Joseph O'Malley (Cambridge: Cambridge University Press, 1970), pp. xl–xlix.

4. Ibid., p. 46.

5. Robert Nye, *Masculinity and Male Codes of Honor in Postrevolutionary France, 1814–1848* (Oxford: Oxford University Press, 1993).

6. Thomas Crow, *Emulation: Making Artists for Revolutionary France* (New Haven: Yale University Press, 1995).

7. Carol Harrison, *The Bourgeois Citizen in Nineteenth-Century France: Gender, Sociability and the Uses of Emulation* (Oxford: Oxford University Press, 1999).

8. Interestingly, emulation seems to work not just as imitation and rivalry of those above or of peers, but also of competitors coming in one's wake. The painter David responded to the death of the painter Jean-Germain Drouais, his most brilliant pupil, with the lament: "I have lost my emulation." Crow, *Emulation*, p. 1.

9. Harrison, *The Bourgeois Citizen*, pp. 3–5, 56–58.

10. Bernhardt Groethuysen, *Les Origines de l'esprit bourgeois en France* (Paris: Gallimard, 1927), pp. 167–177.

11. By "modern antisemitism" I mean antisemitism based on secular rather than religious arguments.

12. Michel Winock, *Nationalisme, antisémitisme et fascisme en France* (Paris: Éditions du Seuil, 1990), pp. 125–127.

13. Pierre Birnbaum, *The Jews of the Republic: A Political History of State Jews in France from Gambetta to Vichy*, trans. Jane M. Todd (Stanford: Stanford University Press, 1996); Pierre Birnbaum, *Jewish Destinies: Citizenship, State and Community in Modern France*, trans. Arthur Goldhammer (New York: Hill and Wang, 2000).

14. Pierre Birnbaum, *Un Mythe politique: la "république juive" de Léon Blum à Mendès-France* (Paris: Gallimard, 1988).

15. Ibid., pp. 150–156.

16. Richard Kuisel, *Seducing the French: The Dilemma of Americanization* (Berkeley: University of California Press, 1993), pp. 12–13; Seth Armus, "The Eternal Enemy: Emmanuel Mounier's *Esprit* and French Anti-Americanism," *French Historical Studies* 24 (2001): 217–304.

17. Winock, *Nationalisme*, p. 50.

18. Kuisel, *Seducing the French*, p. 3.

19. Armus, "The Eternal Enemy," 280–284; Kuisel, *Seducing the French,* p. 12.

20. Winock, *Nationalisme,* pp. 410–411.

21. Ibid., p. 71. Jean-Philippe Mathy, *Extrême-Occident: French Intellectuals and America* (Chicago: University of Chicago Press, 1993).

22. Armus, "The Eternal Enemy," pp. 277–278.

23. Mathy, *Extrême-Occident,* pp. 141–162.

24. Fritz Stern, *The Failure of Illiberalism: Essays on the Political Culture of Modern Germany* (New York: Knopf, 1972); Jürgen Kocka, *Industrial Culture and Bourgeois Society: Business, Labor and Bureaucracy in Modern Germany* (New York: Bergahn Books, 1999), chs. 4 and 9.

25. David Blackbourn and Geoff Eley, *The Peculiarities of German History: Bourgeois Society and Politics in Nineteenth-Century Germany* (Oxford: Oxford University Press, 1984).

26. Alfred Cobban, *The Social Interpretation of the French Revolution* (Cambridge: Cambridge University Press, 1964), p. 162.

# INDEX